SIMON COOPER is the Wainwright Prize short-listed author of *The Otter's Tale* and *Life of a Ch*... ... of the UK's leading chalkstream conserva... ...rked in the horse-racing industr... ... the stud farms, stables and racet... ...tory, including actually meeting the ...

Praise for *Frankel*:

'Cooper paints a complete picture of Frankel, charting his meteoric rise from the first years of his life through to his glorious send-off when winning the Champion Stakes at Ascot ... transporting the reader with his vivid descriptions ... While he is undoubtedly the star of the show, this book is about so much more than just Frankel ... Thanks to Cooper, and his dedication to colouring the blanks in this famous story, we can now know Frankel a little better too'

Racing Post

'Well-researched and written with an enthusiast's brio. Moreover, it is utterly engrossing ... Frankel's story is an extraordinary one and Cooper tells it in an easy, compelling style ... [He] takes the reader on an equine pilgrimage, all the more thrilling as the object of veneration is still just 12 years old and standing at stud near Newmarket'

The Field

'Simon Cooper does a sterling job ... a wry, amiable guide, Cooper takes intriguing tangents aplenty ... his real skill, though, lies in detailing Frankel's day-to-day life'

i newspaper

Praise for Simon Cooper:

'He summarizes his observations ... with the charm of a Kenneth Grahame but with the scientific rigour of modern behavioural science. It is the best popular account of the lives of otters written so far'   *Times Literary Supplement*

'Offers something new, and ultimately optimistic'   *New Scientist*

'Boldly imaginative and with great skill, conservationist Simon Cooper fictionalises the story of the otter family ... Cooper's knowledge of otter behaviour is profound, but it's his brilliant storytelling that really brings the animals to life'   *Daily Mail*

'I loved the gentle flow of this book and the insight into both a pastime and a wonderful corner of the land'   *BBC Countryfile*

'Cooper's enthusiasm is so infectious'   *Daily Mail*

Simon Cooper

Frankel

*The Greatest Racehorse of All Time
and the Sport That Made Him*

WILLIAM
COLLINS

William Collins
An imprint of HarperCollins*Publishers*
1 London Bridge Street
London SE1 9GF

WilliamCollinsBooks.com

HarperCollins*Publishers*
1st Floor, Watermarque Building, Ringsend Road
Dublin 4, Ireland

First published in Great Britain by William Collins in 2020
This William Collins paperback edition published in 2021

2022 2024 2023
2 4 6 8 10 9 7 5 3

A catalogue record for this book is
available from the British Library

ISBN 978-0-00-830707-3

Typeset in Minion Pro
Printed and bound in the UK using
100% renewable electricity at CPI Group (UK) Ltd

MIX
Paper from
responsible sources
FSC™ C007454

This book is produced from independently certified FSC™ paper
to ensure responsible forest management.

For more information visit: www.harpercollins.co.uk/green

Mum
Sorry I didn't finish in time.

'And Allah took a handful of southerly wind,
blew His breath over it, and created the horse.'

Bedouin legend

Contents

The Newmarket 11

The Frankel File

Prologue

In horse racing, greatness is defined by speed. Being the second fastest counts for little. You have to win. And win. And keep on winning until every challenger of your generation is put to the sword. Such a thing so rarely happens that most people pass through life without the privilege of seeing such an animal. Occasionally a contender will arrive, burning up the turf until the dream of greatness is shattered in defeat; that precious cloak of invincibility torn to shreds by another.

On a rainy Suffolk evening, did our locally trained bay colt have any idea that he was about to embark on that path to the ultimate in racing greatness? To become the one against which all horses of the past, present and future would be judged and likely fall short. Let's face it, he probably didn't.

In truth, despite the remote possibility of such a thing, he had a whisper of a chance; he was bred if not to be great then at least to be fast. But that counts for only so much. Hundreds of thoroughbred racehorses debut each season with bloodlines as good as our horse. But breeding will only take you so far; the rest lies deep within, far beyond human intervention.

If you'd been a casual observer among the thousands gathered at Newmarket races on 13 August 2010, the third race of the night didn't promise very much. In fact, it was a meeting far removed from the highest rank, designed more to draw a big holiday crowd than for quality racing. It was one of those humdrum, unregarded work-aday fixtures which are the bread and butter of horse racing around the globe – excepting one horse.

You probably didn't bother to go to the paddock after the second race to watch the horses parade for the next; few did. What was meant to be a balmy summer evening had turned cold with squally-soon-to-become-heavy rain. Trainers, jockeys, stable hands and officials were all scurrying around truncating the preliminaries to the shortest possible duration. The lawns in front of the stands were pretty well deserted; the crowds were jammed inside. A few hardy types sheltered under umbrellas to be close to the horses, but in truth they were few and far between. After all, this was just a minor race with a dozen horses, eight of which had never raced before and the remaining four had hardly set the world alight, without a win between them.

For our horse, this was to be his racecourse debut; he was one of that eight. But was he the special one? Maybe. There was a buzz about him. He'd lit up the training gallops. Been the gossip of this racing town. He'd been named in honour of one of the greatest train-ers of modern times. Expectations were high. A sick man, his trainer, was being rejuvenated just by his very being. But this was a wretched night; his stable hand had even lost his shoe in the quagmire leading up to the start. If it all went wrong, there were at least excuses to hand.

By the time you'd extracted yourself from the bar, placed a bet and found a vantage point in the stands, the horses would have been long gone, gathered at the start a mile away. Without high-powered binoculars they would have been nothing more than a wet smudge on the otherwise empty horizon of Newmarket Heath that doubles as a racecourse. With binoculars you'd have seen jockeys hating the rain, crouched over their horses, keeping them calm with a circling routine. Had you been at the start, you would have heard the starter's assistant complete the roll call as the handlers stepped forward to lead each horse in turn into the designated compartment of the starting stalls. A moment later, the loading complete, the gates of the stalls would spring open. The race was on.

Did our horse lead from pillar to post, leaving all others struggling in his wake, the rain-sodden crowd gasping in awe at his performance? I'd like to tell you yes, but it wasn't really that way. In a race that lasts less than two minutes – this was just a mile – a quick getaway helps. But our young blood blew it. Months of training counted for nothing as this critical moment vanished in a trice. He was closer to last than first with half the race run. Had you placed a bet on him – he was the favourite, after all – you might have had reason to worry. But really you need not have done. Our horse was a cut above the rest. He knew it. And you, too, would know it soon.

He had been trained to run this way. He was headstrong. A horse who knew his mind but was prone to run too fast, too soon. His trainer, the best of the best, saw this in him so taught him the value of patience. The waiting game. Cruising behind the others until the moment was right. And that is how this race has become a part of horse-racing history.

In the wet gloom, as the track rose towards the finishing line, the jockey eased our horse out from behind the pack to make his run. There was nothing hurried. Really, there was nothing to doubt. He drew level with the leaders, kept time with them for a few strides as if to make some point before pulling away with ease as the winning post flashed by. Whether you were a seasoned racing professional or a once-a-year punter, our horse would have caught the eye. 'Impressive', you'd have said. 'Very impressive.' And you'd have logged the name of our horse in that part of your brain reserved for something out of the ordinary.

One hundred and three seconds on from the start, the horse drawn in stall ten had passed the winning post ahead of the rest. That was to become something of a habit as Frankel was now, despite the apparent inauspiciousness of the occasion, on his way to becoming the greatest racehorse to ever live.

1

Genetic alchemy

Yesterday I met Frankel who crept up on me all of a sudden. One moment I was deep in conversation and the next I sensed a presence behind me. Maybe someone said something along the lines of 'here's the man'. In truth, I don't recall precisely but when I turned around there he was: the greatest racehorse that has ever strode out on God's turf.

As I wended my way across the Cambridge fens, which in turn gave way to the ordered horse paddocks that surround Newmarket, I tried not to elevate this meeting to something of a semi-religious experience. An audience with the Pope. A pilgrimage to a Tibetan mountaintop to meet the Dalai Lama. It seemed the wrong side of sane to equate a horse on such a level.

And indeed that is true. But rarely in life does one ever get to meet the truly great. They are the stuff of legends. Stories passed down through generations. The prism of time only giving us a hint of what the truth may have been. But here was I doing that very thing. A chance to look, see and touch. Make a judgement all of my own. To burn into my memory a horse that will likely never, ever exist again.

You'd barely give Frankel's home a second glance if you drove past. Yes, the sweeping turn to the entrance looks immaculate, but the redbrick walls are low and the signs discreet. Beyond the gates that swing open to acknowledge your arrival, the scene that greets you appears to be anything other than a horse stud farm.

The smooth tarmac gives way to immaculately raked gravel that scrunches under my tyres. In the absence of signs, a kindly gardener points me in the right direction, curving me around the tall copper beech that was hiding the offices. Well, these are not offices in the absolute sense of the word, but rather the most magnificent country house, known as Banstead Manor Stud, that people just happen to work in. It is the European headquarters of the world-famous racing and breeding operation, Juddmonte, owned by His Highness Prince Khalid bin Abdullah bin Abdulrahman Al Saud, known universally across racing as Mr Khalid Abdullah, befitting his privacy and pursuit of excellence. I honestly don't know if Juddmonte's Banstead Manor was designed by the British architect Sir Edwin Lutyens, but it has all the heritage. Long, horizontal, thin red bricks delineated by perfectly trowelled lime mortar. Tall, slender chimneys, artworks in their own right. Narrow windows that mimic the first Elizabethan age. I'm ushered into a rather grand room which is full of Frankel memorabilia; even the mints are wrapped in his racing colours. Among the paintings and prints is a faded handwritten letter from a son to his mother in old-fashioned copperplate script. It seems Frankel is not the only one to achieve world fame to have lived at Banstead Manor; this was the childhood home of Winston Churchill.

I'm met by Shane Horan who is introduced to me with a job title I've never heard spoken of before, but that speaks more to my ignorance in these matters than the title itself: Nominations Manager. He is, it transpires, responsible for which mares are chosen each season (requests to mate with Frankel are significantly oversubscribed). We sit down in what I guess would once have been the drawing room, with furniture as comfortable today as it would have been back when this was a grand home. Reclining on the sofa, I have a glorious view across a York stone terrace, striped lawns, and between the house and yet another copper beech, a statue of a full-sized horse on a Portland stone plinth. I hazard a guess that it might just be Frankel. I am correct.

I pull out my pad and start to ask Shane a few questions, but we both know that really I am being polite. Seeing Frankel is the thing. The answers will come later. We are just playing for time. Soon Shane looks at his watch, stands up, and beckons me to follow. 'We'll just catch him on the way back.' It is shortly before 3 pm but I'm none the wiser as to where Frankel has been or where he is going. I don't like to ask, as the assumption seems to be that I should know.

My other assumption was that I'll need a pair of wellington boots to tramp around, or at least make my way to the stud yard. Shane gives me a quizzical look when I ask whether I should change footwear. I'll take that as a no. The walk to the stables is both short and perfection. Another striped lawn gently slopes away from the house. A small lake gurgles as a pulsing fountain spouts water. The yew hedges are geometrically precise. Gertrude Jekyll, Lutyens' landscape gardener of choice, would most definitely have approved of the splendid herbaceous borders, the flock of colours rising from low at the front to tall at the back. Less than a hundred yards from the house, Shane swings open a small gate and beyond the shiny, black-painted tubular steel of the estate fencing is more striped lawn, specimen trees, soft pale shingle pathways and three turreted stable blocks.

Disabuse yourself that this is any ordinary stable block; if there was a star rating for horse accommodation this would be seven star plus a bit more. The original building, that houses just two horses, repeats the brickwork of the house, with dark-wood stained stable doors at either side adorned with solid brass catches and bolts. In the centre a corbelled arch leads to a white-painted door, slightly knocked and careworn by daily stud life, with the tack and feed store beyond. The slate roof is topped by two jaunty looking turrets, which serve as ventilation shafts, each of which is capped by what you might easily mistake for a black pointed witch's hat. The shafts, a sort of forerunner to air conditioning, were by all accounts originally installed by army engineers who were billeted in the stables during World War II, and the style has been replicated with the three later stable blocks, perfect facsimiles both, with housing for eight stallions in total. This is, and has been for the past six years, Frankel's home.

There is most definitely a sense of theatre leading up to meeting the equine who is often termed, with no sense of anything other than the truth, the wonder horse. In turn, I am shown stallions Bated Breath, Kingman and Oasis Dream who are led out of their respective stalls for my perusal. Privileged though I am to see them, I do feel a bit of a fraud. If you are a keen follower of horse racing, and breeding in particular, those names will leap from the page. For me, just starting my equine genetic education, they are simply the most beautiful specimens in the prime of life, living in the most splendid surroundings. In time I'll piece it all together, but for now, without wishing to diminish them in any way, they are the *amuse-bouche*.

As I turned to see Frankel for the first time, he was most definitely different to the others but perhaps not quite as I imagined. While the first three had variously danced on their toes, squiggled their ears, held heads high, eyes darting to every person and chewing on the brass chain that connects leading rein to head collar, along came Frankel, head bowed down. There was no fuss. No ceremony. I would say he sauntered up to me, but that suggests a levity of demeanour which is not him at all. He moved with considered purpose. Each stride was for a reason, delivering one foot in front of the other with an economy of effort. Pausing at the required spot as if to say, I'm not going to move further unless it is absolutely necessary. But don't mistake this for laziness. Here was a horse who was alert to everything and everybody around him.

He took to my scratching at the white star on his forehead in good part. Just patting him on the neck seemed rather inadequate; too small and fleeting a gesture to connect with this great beast. He kept his head slightly bowed as we went eye-to-eye. I slid my hand down the front of his face, tracing the line of his blaze, the white hairs that narrow then widen again just as the coat gives way to the soft, dark skin of the muzzle. Warm breath gently exhaled from his nostrils, the steady beat of breathing pacing out the comfortable moments between us. There was a slight damp odour in the air, but not unpleasant. Oats and hay maybe? As I jiggled my fingers around his wet mouth, we ended up playing a little game as he twisted his lips as if to capture a stray piece of my hand. Until, quite suddenly, without breaking eye contact, he nudged my hand away. The game was over.

For Rob Bowley, his stallion man, had just produced the most enormous carrot. However potentially tasty my fingers might have been, carrots were clearly a known quantity in Frankel's life. It is fair to say, he was not a tidy eater. As he bit, crunched and chewed his way through this industrial-sized vegetable, a pool of carrot juice and orange-coloured pulp, certainly enough to fulfil one of your five-a-day, gathered at his feet. So intent on eating, he didn't seem to notice the brief arrival of the stud cat George who sidled over to sniff, then reject, a possible windfall. That said, George and Frankel go back a long while, as the cat arrived at Banstead just a month before the horse, though the pedigree of the latter was considerably more certain than that of the former. George just appeared from nowhere, the grey tabby taking up residence without so much as a by-your-leave. Despite much asking around the village nobody ever claimed him so, as the Frankel express has thrilled ever faster, George had been along for the ride, elbowing his way into photo-shoots and among film crews. I'm not sure Frankel liked sharing the limelight, for he studiously ignored George, as all the while I stood at his head he kept me fixed in his gaze, those dark brown eyes giving nothing away.

And that is what I recall most about my first meeting with Frankel. Not his impressive frame. Not his beautiful home. But his eyes. They followed the unknown quantity, in this case me, everywhere. Rob, Shane and all the other Banstead people – Frankel had locked them away deep inside that head of his. But of the new, he was curious. Something to be sized up, evaluated and considered. As Frankel was wheeled away and he gave me one last sidelong glance, it was hard not to come to the conclusion that he had been judging me more than I had been judging him. It was an odd and slightly perplexing sensation. He is, after all, only a horse but I felt I had undergone some sort of benediction.

Once Frankel was gone everyone definitely relaxed – now that is odd – as the conversation turned to his daily regime. The question in my mind was soon answered without me ever having to ask it – Frankel was on the way back from his 3 pm covering. Or to put it in layman's terms, a mating with one of the 150 or so mares that would be visiting with him from mid-February (breeders with some sense of humour commence the season the day after St Valentine's Day) until mid-June. If you are starting to do the maths to conclude that is a lot of covers in not a lot of time, you'd be right. Plus you have to account for some multiple covers of the same mare to ensure success. So, at the moment of my mid-afternoon meeting, Frankel was only just past the halfway point in his day with 7 am, 3 pm and 9 pm appointments in his daily diary. Great genes are in great demand.

Today Frankel is ten and has spent the greater part of his adult life at Banstead Manor Stud in Suffolk. Indeed, this was where he was born, but his story really starts 400 miles due west in another horse county of another horse country. County Tipperary in Ireland.

There is a fine motorway that takes you from Cork in the direction of Dublin. It's very twenty-first century with wide lanes and tolls; maybe it is the latter that discourages traffic because it seemed very empty to me. But the moment you turn off to follow the signs to Fethard, you are in old Ireland. The lanes are narrow. The stone walls in need of repair. Topped with hedges interspersed with ragged barbed-wire fencing. You would never call the rural architecture that plots your journey beautiful. The grey, squat, rectangular bunga-lows are built with practicality rather than beauty in mind, often juxtaposed by the adjacent farmyards that seem to have been forever falling down awaiting a wave of gentrification that may never arrive.

And pretty soon you are in Fethard. The roads are potholed. Shops are boarded up. This seems like a bit of Ireland still awaiting the arrival of the Celtic tiger. But you can't help but smile at the sign on the wall outside the bar: *McCarthy's est. 1840. Publican. Restaurant. Undertaker. One of Ireland's oldest unchanged pubs.* If that doesn't arrest the progress of a hungry traveller nothing will, though the slight carbolic smell that hangs over the town is discon-certing. Here is a place where peat is still burned as the fuel of choice.

On, through and out the other side of Fethard and suddenly twenty-first-century Ireland seems to be back, but with a twist of rural chic. Instead of just driving down a road you appear to be driving down an avenue. The verges are trimmed. The hedges cut box-straight, lined on the field side with gradually maturing trees planted perfectly parallel to the road, and beyond that post and rail fences delineating paddocks. Even the farm gates are a cut above your usual rural offering, with sweeping turn-ins and fancy stone pillars. Helpful signs direct you off the road to such-and-such farm or so-and-so stud. Occasionally, you catch a glimpse of a group of mares and their foals.

If Banstead Manor was the last word in understated stud luxury, then Coolmore Stud is something very different. That is not to say it is not smart; witness the mile-and-a-half 'avenue' approach which has brought me to their door, the entrance more akin to a small European palace than a working stud farm. But it is unashamedly commercial. In the world of breeding, it is rivalled only, at least in numerical terms, by Godolphin, the name that covers the racing and breeding interests of Sheikh Mohammed and the famous all-blue Godolphin racing colours.

The scale and spread of Coolmore is, in every sense of the word, awesome. As I was driven around (covering 7,000 acres, you don't walk) I have to confess to frequently suffering from information overload. It really is quite something to take in, but here are the salient facts of how it has become what it is today. Coolmore is owned by the Magnier family, but its origins lie with Battle of Britain fighter pilot Tim Vigors who, having been demobbed from the Royal Air Force, came to Ireland to work as a bloodstock auctioneer then agent, and inherited Coolmore, which was at the time just 350 acres. It was here he set about establishing the stud in 1968.

At that time, seven miles away across the fields at Ballydoyle, Vincent O'Brien was hitting the prime of his flat training career, along with jockey Lester Piggott, with a string of great horses. Sir Ivor, Nijinsky, Roberto, and The Minstrel come immediately to mind. If those names don't mean much to you, don't worry. It is possibly just enough to know that they were Derby winners all, the most prestigious race on the planet, in a ten-year purple patch that ran from the same year Vigors set up shop. And this success initially came within the partnership of Vigors, O'Brien and football pools magnate (a huge UK national gambling pastime until it was first decimated by the National Lottery and then put out of its misery by the internet), Robert Sangster.

But Coolmore wasn't just a breeder, it was a buyer of bloodstock, in the early years supplementing European bloodlines with North American horses, especially the offspring of Canadian sire Northern Dancer who just happens to be Frankel's great-grandfather. You might now have a clue where this is all going. At the time, Coolmore was not the only one to recognise the value of this particular sire, leading to epic showdowns in the sales ring as it went head-to-head with the Arab buyers in the bloodstock boom of the 1980s. This resulted in the first eight-figure sum ever paid for a horse when a yearling, who was subsequently named Snaafi Dancer, sold in 1983 for $10.2 million ($25.1 million in today's money), bought by Sheikh Mohammed. If you are assuming he went on to do great things, you'll be disappointed. Sent into training in England, this colt was considered too slow to even race, and attempts to harvest the genes of his father failed; in two years at stud, with all sorts of fertility problems, he sired just four offspring, three of which won minor races. It is said that he ended his days eating grass in a Florida paddock.

Not to be outdone, the Coolmore syndicate went higher still two years later, paying $13.1 million ($29.8 million adjusted in real terms) for the son of Nijinsky (who himself was the son of Northern Dancer), making him the most expensive yearling ever sold at public auction. This story had a slightly happier ending as Seattle Dancer, as he was named, without ever being considered a world beater, won some good races for Vincent O'Brien and competed against some of the best. He retired to become a Coolmore stallion standing in the USA, Ireland, Japan and finally Germany until his death in 2007 at twenty-three years of age.

So evolved this powerful triumvirate: Sangster provided the cash, Coolmore the raw material and O'Brien the training expertise. It is a model that many have copied since, admittedly rarely with this scale of success. Three decades on, the essential template persists, though with some subtle changes. John Magnier is now the sole owner of Coolmore. As the son-in-law of Vincent O'Brien, and previously a successful fourth-generation National Hunt breeder at the nearby Castlehyde Stud, Magnier has over time bought the interests of Vigors, O'Brien and Sangster. However, the connection with Ballydoyle remains, where Aidan O'Brien took over in 1996 following the retirement of Vincent in 1994 (the two are not related), training the Coolmore homebreds and purchases.

During the writing of this book, you may not be surprised to learn that I visited all manner of horse farms, studs, stables and training yards across countries and continents. And the one thing I will always take away from them all is an immense feeling of calm. Away from the hustle and bustle of the racecourse, horses lead the most perfectly ordered lives. Everything, wherever possible, is refined down to routine and peacefulness. When you pass through the gates of any horse establishment, the world as most people know it is left behind. Time exists at the pace that suits the horses. The animals come first. People come second. Once the daily chores are over, the horses settled and the stable hands departed for breakfast or a well-deserved afternoon nap, human activity is supplanted by stillness. Horse heads hang over the stable doors quietly, watching very little. If you happen to pass through the yard, you might hear the grating grind from somewhere deep inside a dim-lit stall as a mouthful of hay is chewed as much for its properties as a calming balm as for its food value. Or the slurping sucking of water through tightened lips. Occasionally, a steel-shod hoof scrapes against a concrete floor or bangs against the wooden door, drawing disapproving glances from the neighbours. But that is about it. The biggest excitement might be a flock of doves whistling by or the stable cat on patrol.

Somehow, I think that is what draws people into the horse business and captures their hearts forever. There is a wonderful other-worldliness about caring for these highly-bred thoroughbreds who are, once you strip away the speed and contest of the racing, calm, benign and content.

I say all this because you might expect Coolmore, with its giant scale and financial heft, to be anything other than this. At the height of the breeding season, in addition to the fifteen resident stallions, there will be in the region of 900 resident mares. Just under half will be there with a foal, while the others will be in foal, at some stage from conception to pre-birth, or there being readied for one of the stallions. They are attended by a huge team: nine vets, three farriers – you can imagine how this list goes on. It even includes an acupuncturist. In all, 380 staff work at Coolmore, and that takes no account of the US operation in Kentucky and the Australian stud in the Hunter Valley.

But big really does, in this case at least, mean beautiful. As far as the eye can see, life is dedicated to the horses; railed paddocks and green pastures. In the far distance, the ridged peaks of the Galtees, Ireland's highest inland mountain range, provide shelter from the worst of the weather, ensuring a temperate climate. For Coolmore, along with the myriad of horse studs and farms, from the one-man bands to the truly huge, are all clustered around the Rock of Cashel in Tipperary because of nature not man. We might have named this the Golden Vale, but it was the Ice Age that gave us the right to call it that, leaving behind as it did a land of limestone from which grows the most perfect turf.

You don't need to see it to know it – just walk on it. It might not feel like the soft lawns of Banstead Manor. In fact, it slightly scrunches underfoot as the aroma of wild thyme, basil and marjoram is released by your footfalls. It is said that a square metre of this calcareous grassland contains forty species of native flowering plants, which along with the butterflies, insects, curlews and skylarks, thrive with the chalky soil. And for growing foals and broody mares, what could be better than picking at calcium-rich grass?

Coolmore is not ordered in the sense that the paddocks are in regimented lines. Nor are the connecting roads Roman straight. Each stable yard is not a cookie-cutter creation of the next. I assume this is because Coolmore has evolved over four decades. And for that, it has a certain charm. Humpbacked stone bridges cross little limestone streams. Wiggly lines of mature horse chestnut trees and hawthorn bushes decorate the landscape. Ponds have gathered in low-lying ground. The buildings range from spartan utility to perfectly formed yards in quiet, out-of-the-way corners. As you travel around, I'd be tempted to say everywhere you look there are horses. But that is not altogether true.

For of all the things I didn't expect to see at Coolmore were cattle; there are more white, large-muscled Charolais, black Aberdeen Angus and the white and brown Simmental beef animals than you might imagine, all mixed in with the mares and foals, sharing the same paddocks and grass. That said, there does seem to be a certain demarcation within each enclosure, with a small herd of cattle, maybe six or eight in all, and a similar numbered harras of horses. Without any suggestion of animosity, they appear to be keeping to very separate groups. So you might wonder, as did I, if they don't offer any companionship why they are there at all? For surely it can't be economic; the cattle, even if they run to a few hundred in number across the stud, can't be worth in aggregate more than a single mare or foal. The answer lies in land management. Horses are horribly fussy eaters of pasture. Look at a field grazed by cattle or sheep and it will be lawn-like; evenly cropped. But a horse paddock will be an unsightly patchwork of the tightly eaten, the almost bare, rank looking tall grass and thrusting weeds. Cattle on the other hand eat it all, keeping the grass both healthy and fertile.

After shock of the incongruity, the cattle soon become part of the scenery; it is really the groups of foals and mares that draw the eye. If you thought the idyll Anna Sewell describes in the opening chapter of *Black Beauty* was fantasy, think again: 'While I was young I lived upon my mother's milk, as I could not eat grass. In the daytime I ran by her side, and at night I lay down close by her.' This picture-book tale of contented mothers, in the bloom of maternity, letting long-legged foals suckle, idly wafting tails to disperse the first few flies of spring, actually exists. The groups of six or eight are loosely circled both for companionship and out of some long-inherited knowledge that they are safer when in together. Occasionally, a brave foal wanders to the periphery, but a single look or a low snort will draw it back into the fold. The foals are mostly still young – a few days to a few months – and their coats raggedy, with clumps of hair, in contrast to the smooth sheen of the mothers. In time that will change. For now the world offers the sort of great adventures only a young foal would appreciate within the confines of a paddock: fluttering butterflies, buzzing bees and overly bold crows who strut from one fresh horse hoof divot to the next in search of newly exposed worms.

As with Banstead Manor, my trip to Coolmore is part research, part reveal; that moment when I'm presented with the thing I have come to see. Leaving the paddocks, mares and foals, you cross into what might best be described as the inner sanctum. The holy of holies. The place where this story really begins: at the stable of a horse called Galileo, Frankel's father.

As you approach, the security is discreet but impressive. Twenty-four-hour-a-day guards monitor every arrival and departure. Cameras look upon you. Gates glide open. There is something a little James Bond about it all as the driveway welcomes you, lined with statues of the Coolmore greats. It might seem a little over the top, but behind these gates lie assets. Though they may be in horseflesh form, that is indeed what they are: as valuable as currency, diamonds or works of art, demanding the same level of protection. You think I'm exaggerating? You'll see.

If, as a horse, you ever had the chance to determine your own paternity, you'd likely choose Galileo. He is the supreme stallion of his generation. In recent history, he might only have been bettered by his father Sadler's Wells. In the future, he might be bettered by his son Frankel. But I suspect you, along with most others, would be happy to pick him as your father for now. As part of the Northern Dancer dynasty (you recall he was Sadler's Wells's father) Galileo was born to be great, but as you might also recall from the auction duds, this does not always turn out to be so. But in his particular case, genetics came up trumps. In a short but explosive career, he was the horse that carried nearly all before him. He raced just once as a two-year-old, slaughtering a field of his contemporaries right at the butt end of the season by fourteen lengths. This began a run of six consecutive wins that continued into the following year when he won the Derby, Irish Derby and King George VI & Queen Elizabeth Stakes. In Europe, as a three-year-old, it is difficult to win a trio of races any better than that, but when he tried to make it seven in a row he tasted his first defeat in the Irish Champion Stakes at Leopardstown before heading to the United States for the

Breeders' Cup Classic, the most valuable race of his life. But whether it was the travelling or racing on the dirt surface for the first time, Galileo's racing career closed on its 364th day when he came sixth and was retired to stud. That has turned out to be a very wise decision.

My first meeting with Galileo is altogether more friendly than with his famous son. Maybe that's just a reflection of age; the young buck versus the sage old man. For at just past twenty years of age, Galileo is getting on a bit these days. Perhaps he has mellowed. His groom Noel Stapleton tells me he is incredibly laid back and easy to handle. No quirks. No oddities. Just a particular love of having his teeth and gums rubbed. He arrives in the yard wearing an anonymous green, waterproof horse blanket, with piped red edging. It is early April. The days are still chilly and damp. The trees still bare. Galileo likes to keep dry and warm. It is hardly a big ask for one so valuable.

As Noel goes to strip off the blanket, I feel tempted to say don't bother. Let the old man be. But Galileo seems up for the inspection. Clearly he doesn't know how little I know as he pricks his ears, looks me in the eye and nods his head in my direction as if by way of greeting. I keep silent as this amazing stallion is exposed, because I know I really want to see Galileo in the raw. Measure him in my mind against his son. Or maybe I should be measuring the son against the father?

My immediate thought is that Galileo is a bigger horse than Frankel, even though they both stand a shade over 16 hands high. That is, translated into more normal measurement, 65 inches (a hand is 4 inches, an ancient measure based on the breadth of a male hand) taken from the ground beside front leg to the top of the withers, the ridge between the shoulder blades. But the size thing is a marginal difference, for in many respects they are so much the same, though the son is more muscled than the father, but again like demeanour that might just be as much about age as physique. True, Frankel has four white socks (well, that's what it says on his passport, but really it is three and a half because one is a rather indistinct sock) and his father just the one. Otherwise they are both bays, coats a reddish-brown colour with black mane, tail, insides of the ears and lower legs from just above the knees. Both have those distinctive white stars on their foreheads, though it is Galileo that has the most pronounced, with a more obvious blaze.

As with Frankel, I have the insistent urge to do more than just rub my hand along the horse that had sired not only the greatest race-horse ever but a plethora of other champions. Being petted and handled is almost in the DNA of thoroughbreds; from the very first day of birth it is something they become accustomed to. In fact, they almost expect it. Good horse handlers make a point of it. It becomes a conditioned response for both horse and human. So I take Noel's tip and rub Galileo's gums. It is true, he really does like it. And like many a horse he revels in the attention, though what he thinks of the meaningless babble of words I mutter, I do not know. But he takes it all in good part. It has happened thousands of times before, and will, God willing, happen thousands of times again. But, and we have to be realistic, he is coming towards the end of a truly epic life at stud.

Winning two Derbies is an impressive achievement by any meas-ure, but if we are being truthful Galileo would only just make it into the list of the top one hundred racehorses of all time. His short burst of a racing career, allied with that famous bloodline, would suggest at the outset solid and successful years at stud. But horse genes are a peculiar thing.

We will be back to see Galileo again, but for now let us savour where he stands just past his twentieth birthday. As we all know, Frankel is his most famous son, but even if you took him out of the equation, Galileo would still reign as the supreme stallion. Since he first came to Coolmore in 2001, he has sired 2,743 foals, 2,089 of which reached the racecourse winning 3,868 races all over the world, amassing total prize money of £177,088,490.* And as I stood beside him on that greyish April day, he didn't seem to have any inclination to stop. In the previous season, he had been the leading sire in Great Britain and Ireland, eclipsing his nearest rival (the title is determined by racecourse earnings, in this case £13,663,938) by a factor of three. His roster of great sons and daughters, many of them now successful at stud themselves, would take up more pages than this book has to spare; his stud record (i.e. every significant race his children have won or been placed in) on the Coolmore website runs to fifty-seven pages. Suffice to say, there is barely a major race anywhere on the globe that the Galileo progeny haven't won, in many cases more than once, including three Derby winners, winners of all five of the English Classics and in one year the first three home in continental Europe's premier race, the Prix de l'Arc de Triomphe.

All this, as you might imagine, comes at a price. If you visited that same Coolmore website to see exactly how much you will have to pay, you are going to be disappointed: the stud fee for the current year is marked as private. But the rumour is €600,000. That is to say, over half a million pounds to have your already valuable mare mated with Galileo. And you will not be the only one. Galileo will 'cover', as they like to call it in the business, around 150 mares in the breeding season. Forget your Cristiano Ronaldos, LeBron James, Lionel Messis, Roger Federers and Lewis Hamiltons of this world, for Galileo leaves them puffing in his wake. With an annual income of close to £80 million (some of his progeny have been foal shares), he has been one of the highest earning and most valuable sporting athletes on the planet in recent times. And if you think your cheque

* Foals' figure to 2017. Other figures to 2016.

book will be enough to guarantee visiting rights, think again. Each year over three hundred applications are made for the available places.

But when I see Galileo, do these figures tumble through my mind? Not a bit of it. All I see is a horse completely at ease with himself and with people who love him for what he is. A truly magical creature, the equine incarnation of genetic alchemy, who continues to sow the seeds to an ever-growing dynasty. And who knows, maybe another Frankel?

2

A certain kindness

Another Frankel? What are the chances? Realistically speaking, infinitesimally slim, but maybe even more slim than we might ever imagine, even though the thoroughbred you see striding out on the racecourse is very much the product of man.

As a nation we started riding horses in the seventh century; up to then horses were beasts of burden carrying loads, pulling carts or, in the time of Boudicca, war horses powering chariots. By the early 600s, it was considered a matter of status to appear on horseback, with the riders largely confined to those of the first rank of a society still adjusting itself after the departure of the Romans. Wind forward three centuries and the first mention of racehorses appears, called at the time 'running horses', and were so well regarded that Athelstan, the tenth-century king of England, passed a law prohibiting their export. However, the owners were not blind to the benefits of new bloodlines and started importing stallions from the continent, a process that was inevitably accelerated a century later in the aftermath of the Battle of Hastings and the arrival of William the Conqueror from France.

So the sport of racing evolved, largely under the patronage of royalty, noblemen and the well-to-do. But it wasn't always smooth. Oliver Cromwell banned racing in England, dissolving the Royal Stud at Tutbury, disposing of both Charles I and his 140 horses, though the latter were sold, meeting a better fate than their master. Happily the restoration of the monarchy in 1660 marked the restoration of horse racing, for in the new king Charles II the English had an enthusiast for the sport. He hosted races at his park at Windsor before establishing Newmarket as the place to be devoted to horse racing, running his own horses and putting up prize money with silver trophies. With this royal imprimatur, racing as we know it today was on its way and the emergence of the thoroughbred as a specific breed of horse was just around the corner.

The word thoroughbred is not unique to horses; it is often used to refer to somebody or something of outstanding quality. However, in the context of horses, with the T capitalised, it denotes a very particular hybrid of the breed. The Thoroughbred has a specific genetic make-up, with all the unique characteristics of agility and speed that flow from that. It has been bred for a singular purpose – racing – which sets it apart from other horses, in the same way that say the Shetland pony or the Shire horse have become deft at the tasks for which they have been bred over the centuries. However, while the Shetland is a product of island isolation, the Thoroughbred came about due to a very different set of circumstances, both at the same time deliberate and accidental.

The deliberate was the arrival of three stallions from the Middle East over a period of forty years from the 1690s, imported to breed with the native mares to produce 'bigger, tougher, stouter and faster racehorses' as Binns and Morris, authors of the definitive book *Thoroughbred Breeding*, succinctly put it. The accidental is how Byerley Turk, the first of those three, arrived in England to take up his stud duties. You might imagine that a party was dispatched to the Arabian Desert to track down nomadic Bedouin tribes. In a wind-swept tent, among ever-shifting dunes the adventurers would, over sweetened tea, parlay gold or some such into horseflesh before making the long and arduous journey home with this newly prized stallion. It would be quite the adventure; reminiscent of Indiana Jones. But the truth even out-Hollywoods Hollywood.

The Turk, as he tends to be known for reasons that will become apparent, was foaled in the Balkans in 1679 and, as the story goes, was adopted by a near-penniless groom who saw in him great poten-tial and the chance to escape to make a new life for the both of them. So, having trained this young horse in the art of warfare, the pair made their way to Constantinople (now Istanbul), the capital of the Ottoman Empire, where they joined the Turkish cavalry. By way of the Siege of Vienna, the Turk, along with his groom, ended up in June 1686 as a military charger protecting the Hungarian capital of Buda (now Budapest), a Turkish conquest since the sixteenth century, in yet another siege. The odds against their side, the Turks, winning were slim: they numbered 7,000 soldiers with the massed ranks of the European army, including the British, somewhere close to 100,000. By the end of the summer, Buda had fallen and the Turk along with his groom were captured by a group of English aristo-crats who brought them back to England.

At this point, we don't exactly know how the dark brown colt came into the ownership of Captain Robert Byerley. Some say he purchased him in London; others that he was himself at the Siege of Buda. But regardless, the Turk's fighting days were far from over. Byerley was a professional soldier with a horse to match. The two were in service together, and when the time came he rode his war horse to Ireland in opposition to the Jacobites. But it wasn't all skir-mishes and battles. They stopped along the way to win a contest at

Downpatrick Races, before the pair went to war one last time at the Battle of the Boyne. And it is only at this point that the Byerley Turk truly becomes part of our story, because whether it was out of sentimentality or a recognition that he was something special, Captain Byerley retired his stallion to stud. And over the next eleven years, the Byerley Turk, a horse of decidedly Arabian appearance but otherwise unknown pedigree, stood in northern England to head the bloodstock revolution.

But for all the importance of the Byerley Turk, who was followed to English studs by the Darley Arabian in 1704 and the Godolphin Arabian in 1729, there was no great plan as such. It just so happens that a few of the great and the good of English society took it into their heads that by mixing the Middle Eastern bloodline with the native stock, they would produce a better racehorse. There was no overarching genetic science to suggest it would work – that explanation was some centuries away. It was simply a notion of an idea. But it was an idea of astonishing perceptiveness, for within the space of a few decades they had bred what was termed the 'enhanced English racehorse'; and with a further nod to Middle Eastern heritage, the Middle Eastern word Thoroughbred was adopted to define this new breed of equine that was by the 1750s being exported to North America, Europe and around the globe. The international bloodstock business is older than you might suppose.

So, if you took the trouble to trace back Frankel's family tree for the thirty or forty generations to those pioneering days of the early eighteenth century, you would find in his pedigree at least one of those three Arabian stallions. And Frankel is not alone. For it is a remarkable fact that every single Thoroughbred racehorse you see alive today is a blood relative of at least one of those three foundation sires. It is odd to think had a stray bullet hit the Turk on a distant battlefield, in a time far removed from ours today, all this might never have come to be.

The Port of Holyhead does not look much like a hub of the international bloodstock trade. Arrivals from across the Irish Sea are greeted by a sign that welcomes them to the Isle of Anglesey, with the next prominent landmark the Lidl supermarket. Those departing from this northwest outpost of Wales probably don't feel inclined to shed a tear. It is not a place to linger. Swathes of tarmac. Chain link fencing. Custom sheds. Signs pointing you in every direction. Passport control. All bathed in the halogen orange glow from the array of tall lights that suck yet more life out of an already depressing scene. Huge juggernauts wait in line, their engines humming away as their drivers, experts in long waits, fiddle with their phones or doze. And among the lines of freight are horses. Lots of horses. For this is the primary (and shortest) route along which thousands of racehorses, from valuable stallions in their prime to newly born foals just a few days old, will pass each year between the UK and Ireland.

Sometimes they are easy to spot; the Coolmore transporters are giant billboards. The commercial horse movers have sleek wagons and the livery to announce their trade. There are maybe a dozen or more horses on board each lorry, plus accompanying grooms. But oftentimes the horse boxes are so discreet that you would barely recognise them as such. White lorries, not much bigger than a box van, with little to identify the cargo of two inside. And a Juddmonte lorry, on a bleak February evening awaiting the night ferry, was a six-year-old mare called Kind with her first foal, a bay colt who had been born at Banstead Stud just nineteen days earlier. As the lorry mounted the ramp into the oily aura of the cargo deck, the foal might have felt some trepidation. The swaying of the boat. The shouted instructions. The echoing roar of diesel engines that reverberate in the hugeness of the hold, booming for one last time before falling silent. The banging and clanking is alarming even to those who understand such things, as the stevedores haul chains to lock down the chassis to the steel floor. A winter Irish Sea is rarely calm.

I'd like to think Kind was a good mother to her young foal on that journey, reassuring him as each new day brought new things to learn and experience. Though I can't be sure, I'm fairly confident I'm right.

I've met Kind, who is sweet and kind. The last time I saw her, she was with her newly arrived filly. The pair were in one of the stalls in the American-style barn at Coolmore while Kind underwent acupuncture. The past years have not always been easy for Kind. After five consecutive foals, she had a barren year when she did not conceive, then had another live foal who raced as Proconsul, then slipped (that is to say, aborted), then was barren again, then slipped the next two seasons to finally produce in her seventeenth year the filly foal that I met.

As the stable hand held her head and the acupuncturist did her work, the leggy foal wandered out of the gaze of her mother to join me at the half-opened door, curious at the new arrival. As she nuzzled her head into my chest, I stroked her young hair, which was clumpy rather than smooth, more like soft wool to the touch. Looking over, I saw mother turn her head away from watching the pin woman to check on her foal and check me out. It was kindness exemplified. For in that nanosecond, you could see in those brown eyes concern, care and then contentment all in a flash of maternal assessment. She's definitely a good mother.

You probably know, or at least have gathered, that Kind is Frankel's mother. In many ways, I feel a bit mean not starting out by telling you about Kind first but it seems that, at least in terms of headline grabs and eye-watering valuations, it is the sires that win out. But not everyone feels that way. There are plenty in the bloodstock world who value the female line above the male. In fact, it is no accident that the Arabs sold stallions to the avaricious English. They did then, and do now, hold on to their fillies. The truth is that sires get star billing through sheer weight of numbers. Even the most fecund mare will likely not produce more than a dozen or fourteen foals in her lifetime; as we have seen, for a leading sire the number can run into thousands. Whichever way you cut it, for good or ill, the odds are weighted in favour of the guys, and the sheer familiarity of their names, so frequently repeated in race cards and race reports, reinforces any stallion brand. So, let me tell you about Kind.

She was born in Ireland, bred by Frankel's owner Prince Khalid who still owns her today. Her father was a great stallion called Danehill, also bred by Prince Khalid. Her mother was the daughter of a Derby winner and her great-grandfather was Northern Dancer, that bloodline so coveted by Coolmore. If all these various names become something of a blur, I understand; it is maybe enough to know that Kind, and so in turn Frankel, had great parentage. Her racing career, it is probably fair to say, was successful without being stellar. Like her famous son she raced at two, three and four, notching up a run of five consecutive wins in her middle year and with one further win in her last. She was retired to Banstead Manor that summer to become a broodmare, and it was to be there rather than on the racecourse that her destiny truly lay.

She arrived at her new home at what was to be the perfect time in her life for her new calling. Though as a filly she would have been sexually mature at two, ready to breed in a wild herd, at four coming up to five she was now fully developed. And that is important for there is little point rushing these things – a healthy, well-looked-after mare will be able, accidents and difficulties aside, to produce a foal every year into her early twenties.

Her new life would have been both similar and different to that of being in training. The stables are not so different, laid out in rectangular blocks amid which the daily routine of a horse yard – feeding, grooming and light exercise – ticks on by. But the testosterone-charged young colts are absent. The highs and lows of racing success that inevitably both fire up and disappoint the stable staff are no longer present. In fact, it is noticeable that everyone is generally a generation older. They've done their time in the cauldron of a racing yard or come straight into the stud industry, opting for a life where the results of what you do today will be measured in the years to come rather than in the months or weeks. You sense they know they are the guardians of the future. Doing something that takes a certain care and patience.

For Kind, she has been ridden for the last time; nobody will ever sit on her back again. Nor will a bit part her mouth or a bridle be placed on her head. No saddle girths tightened around her middle. The farrier will remove her shoes; she will remain unshod until the day she dies. Gradually, she will lose the musculature of a fit racehorse as her frame fills out a little. More rounded. More feminine. Gallops are replaced with paddock life. It is, in a beautiful place, with people who care for your every need, about as perfect a life as you might imagine.

Arriving from the racecourse, Ed Murrell, then the Banstead Manor stud groom (now assistant stud manager), describes her as a 'slab of a horse', weighing in at a racing-fit 550 kg. Out of context that figure doesn't mean much, but if you consider that Frankel was not much heavier, you'll understand what a tremendously strong filly she is. It sounds a little unkind when Ed adds that she has a 'massive behind', but it is a statement of what Kind was: a sprinter.

A mare endowed with exceptional acceleration and speed, powered by those 'massive' rear quarters that made her such a potent force in races of under a mile. There is not much subtlety about sprinting. Tactics are not the thing. Break fast from the stalls. Keep out of trouble. Cruise at speed in the middle section and then fire up that equine body for all it is worth once the winning post looms. In the shortest of the sprint races held in the UK and Ireland of five furlongs (five-eighths of a mile), it will all be over in sixty seconds. In understanding Frankel, you need to know how important the speed genes of Kind were. It is vital to the tale.

But all this was a little way off as Kind was let slip to run free in an empty field. For close on four years she had led the life of a prime athlete with training, conditioning and diet all focused on the single aim of making her fast. But now with Quiff, her turn-out companion, also on the way to becoming a broodmare, they explore the tiny paddock, no more than a quarter of an acre, in a remote corner of Banstead's 379 acres. Day and night they have nothing but the skies above. Gone is the life in a stable. The daily gallops. The wind up, or the wind down, from competitive racing.

Free of all the paraphernalia of being a racehorse, bar a single head collar, they roll in the dusty turf of summer. Standing head to tail in the heat of the day, gently flicking flies from around their respective heads. At night they stare at the stars. At dawn they lick the fresh dew from the grass. Sometimes, with a sudden burst of energy, one of them will kick up heels and do a rapid circuit of the field, but for the most part little moves, fast or slow. A few times a day, one of the stud hands comes by to check all is well. They soon understand the rhythm of these visits, anticipating with remarkable precision the ones that include a bucket of feed. Sometimes, the farrier drops by to inspect their feet but it is routine; no more complicated than a pedicure.

Quiff and Kind become inseparable, even as they move to ever-larger paddocks; trusted to cope with ever-widening freedom, they stay by each other's side day and night. If one is led away for any reason, the other stands by the gate until her partner returns. It is, in truth, a relationship deliberately nurtured by the stud as two mares of similar ages, background and breeding evolve from competition to the brink of motherhood. For we sometimes assume that animals know it all. All habits and instinct passed down through the generations by some invisible hand. But that really isn't so. Horses, like people, learn from each other. They observe. They replicate. They take comfort from each other. As herd animals, they need each other.

But it cannot forever be summer, even in the idyll of Banstead Manor. Gradually, the chill of the late September mornings are upon us. As people don their coats for the morning commute so do Quiff and Kind of the horse kind, with light blankets that cover their backs and sides. As autumn morphs into winter, the pair are brought in at night, housed in adjacent stables still connected by way of a grilled partition between the two stalls.

But the changes to Quiff and Kind are not just confined to the daily routine. They are reverting to their natural state. The shorter days and longer nights trigger a change in their reproductive cycle which goes into abeyance. This time, the anoestrus, is a period of sexual inactivity when, in a throwback to their time in the wild, mares are not receptive to mating. If you think about it, it makes perfect sense. The gestation period for a horse is roughly eleven months, so conceiving in winter would result in a winter birth, greatly reducing the likely survival of both foal and mare. Evolution is nothing if not ingenious.

But for Ed, Mother Nature is sometimes something of an impediment to a smooth breeding programme. The difficulty is that the days of February, when the covering season starts, are just as short as November and horses are, in the jargon, long-day breeders, the ovulation cycle triggered by that and the availability of food. Strangely, temperature doesn't have much impact which, as it turns out, is fortunate since in deepest Suffolk, though you can't do much about the weather, you can do something about day length and food. So, without them probably even noticing, the daily routine of Quiff and Kind is subtly altered in January. Gradually, the nutrition of their feed is increased while at the same time the lights in the stable are kept on until 10 pm. Without the use of drugs or any other intervention, January is all of a sudden May.

And so it was that both Quiff and Kind were readied to lose their maidenhood. For Kind it came quickly, one of the early-season breeders, visiting Sadler's Wells at Coolmore Stud in Ireland on 27 February. With almost impeccable promptness, she gave birth eleven months and a day later to that young foal we met on the ferry when he was just shy of three weeks old. It would be reasonable to assume that his part in the story, as simply Kind's first foal, ends here. But racing has all sorts of interconnections and we will see, and hear, a great deal more about this horse who was to be named Bullet Train. Not only is he Frankel's half-brother,* but he was to be involved in six races against his part sibling, including one that had an almost calamitous ending.

Back to that Irish Sea crossing, as the ferry docks in Dublin, the humans rejoin the horses. The horses, who are left alone for all the journey bar the occasional inspection, look more alert than the

---

* In bloodstock terms the two horses are actually three-part brothers: in addition to sharing their mother, Kind, Frankel's grandfather, Sadler's Wells, was Bullet Train's father.

bleary-eyed driver and travelling groom. However often you travel the night ferry, it still manages to sap the soul. The constant dull thud of the diesel engines. The sometimes alarming hollow bang as a big wave hits the side. Travellers in uncomfortable poses stretched out on plastic bench seats. Staff in cheap white shirts and inappropriate black bow ties pushing a cloth across the counter top, trying not to think that the return trip starts again in under an hour. Through the scratched Perspex of the rain-flecked windows more orange lights illuminate a point arrival that is not much prettier than the point of departure. None of this is helped by the fact that we are still two hours ahead of an Irish February dawn. In fact, Kind and Bullet Train are probably the chirpiest on board. Life in the stall of a horse box is not so different to that in the stall of a horse barn. Admittedly it is smaller, but all the comforts of home – hay, water and warmth – are there, with the little foal suckling on his mother's milk.

Ahead of the Dublin rush-hour traffic the run to Coolmore, 115 miles to the southwest, is quick. The high windows of the horse box wouldn't have afforded our pair the view that intrigued me so much as they drew close to their destination. In fact, they would have seen nothing until the side ramp was lowered, the internal panels swung back and they were led to their new, albeit temporary, home. Kind was back on Irish soil for the second time in a year.

Even though Lakeview Yard is reserved for the best broodmares visiting the best of the Coolmore stallions, it lacks the grandiosity of Kind's regular home. It is functional rather than fancy. On three sides of a square are ranged twenty-five stables built of breeze blocks painted white with a low-pitched slate roof that surround a plain courtyard with a square of grass and a tree at the centre. The fourth side is half filled by a squat bungalow of similar construction in which the Lakeview Yard manager lives.

But nobody is here for the architecture. The beauty lies in the location. It is a quiet corner away from the hustle and bustle of stud life. All around are horse paddocks that run down to the lake, interspersed with clumps of woodland. There is not a public road in sight. The only people you'll ever see are working or visiting the stud. You are largely sealed away from life as most people know it. Here, mothers fresh from giving birth have time and space to recuperate. Newly born foals are introduced to the world ever so gradually. It is all about calm. Routine. And care.

However, for all the wondrousness of this lifestyle, Kind is not here to raise her foal. She is here to create her next. Who will be the greatest of all time.

3

Creation day

I am no bioethicist. I can't cogently argue when life – human, equine or any other for that matter – truly begins. The last time I visited Tipperary, it was a question exercising and dividing a nation. The lampposts of Fethard were the placard poles for the abortion referendum posters. The images were not always good to look at, the words designed to compel an opinion. But there did seem to be a certain democracy about the debate, alternate lampposts pro and anti, while the conversation, apparently more heated elsewhere, seemed to have largely passed by the regulars of McCarthy's bar.

I think we'll take our lead from them and not worry too much about a higher debate. Let's simply assume that the Frankel story truly begins in a covering barn, somewhere in rural Ireland, with the union of Kind and Galileo on a first Saturday in March. Reproduction doesn't take the weekend off.

There is nothing very romantic about the covering barn at Coolmore or any that I have seen for that matter. If I called it what it is without euphemism – the mating complex – you can draw a better picture in your mind. None of it would win architectural prizes; this is essentially a series of agricultural steel outbuildings. At the unloading bay, Kind and Bullet Train are led from the horse box into the pre-covering shed, their arrival eye-balled every step of the way by the teasers who occupy three stalls along one wall.

One will be brought out for the final affirmation that all is well. It will be. Away in the corner is the veterinary bay where Kind is washed, prepared and most importantly checked to prove she is who she's supposed to be. Horses, like people, have passports. Satisfied, a handler clips a leather fob, with a brass tab engraved with the name GALILEO, to Kind's head collar. All that remains now is for her to await her suitor, which she does with Bullet Train, under the only concession to prettiness, a rose-covered arbour.

Coolmore is a busy place at the height of the breeding season; there is not just one covering shed, but two, one to the left and one to the right of the atrium into which Kind and her foal are led. Each shed is pretty big. I guess you'd easily fit two tennis courts inside. It is hexadecagonal, with a skylight set in each of the sixteen sections of the domed roof that give the place a light and airy feel. Each wall section is padded, as are the doors. The floor is fibresand mixed rubber chippings, raked flat with the exception of a small coconut matting dais at the centre which is about the size and elevation of a flat-topped road hump, a step up when the respective heights of mare and stallion are out of kilter. Like everything else, it is calm and ordered and, at this precise moment, empty of horse and human.

Kind's day had started much like all the others since she and Bullet Train had arrived two weeks earlier, brought in from the paddock just before sunrise to their stall in the Lakeview Yard after the night outside. On a typical day, the foal will snuggle down into the deep straw to sleep, while Kind, relieved of the duties of motherhood for a few hours, eats her feed and relaxes. But this early dawn morning will not be typical. For Kind this will be the day: pronounced ready for the stallion by the vet who has been checking her ovaries daily since she came into season. Mares have an oestrous cycle of fifteen to twenty-one days which divides into two parts: the bulk of it, roughly fourteen days, will be the dioestrus, the period of sexual inactivity. That for the stud manager is relatively easy to pick. However, knowing when not to mate your mare is of limited use. What you really need to know is on which of those remaining five or so days she will be on heat and ready to mate. At this point, human knowledge and science is only of so much use. Enter the teaser.

If you had to conjure in your mind an image of the teaser, forget all ideas of some equine lothario, with chiselled looks and a demeanour honed on the memory of a thousand conquests. Rather cast your mind back to those Norman Thelwell cartoons and the recalcitrant, world weary and forever scruffy pony, where life would be easy but for the daily demands of others. That is the teaser, the pony stallion, whose job around the stud is to detect when the mare is in 'heat', ready for a stallion a good deal further up the pecking order than him. It takes the old expression 'forever the bridesmaid but never the bride' to a whole new plane.

It would be easy to stereotype Padraig, Kind's teaser (I've made up his name as the otherwise impeccable Coolmore records don't record which teaser was in what barn in what year), as a randy old so-and-so, frustrated in every aspect of his life, mooching from one ultimately unavailable female to the next. But under that cascading fringe hides a more sophisticated animal than you might imagine. To start with, it is not always about detecting heat. In the wild, in running with the herd a maiden mare, one still to be covered, would have witnessed the act of mating many times. By the time her turn comes, she would at least have some idea of what was about to happen. But a newly retired racing mare? Probably not. So the teaser takes to 'bouncing', mounting (without penetrating) the maiden mare until she accepts, or at least understands, what is going on and has confidence in the presence of a stallion. A patient teaser is important, because this is meant to be a gradual learning process rather than some kind of sexual shock and awe.

Of course, for Kind, she is no longer a maiden – this is second time around. Padraig's job is to detect that change in her cycle that is beyond any human. So, as the calendar ticks around to that moment, Kind and Padraig are brought together each day soon after breakfast in the Lakeview Yard. It is tempting to see Padraig as a catalyst in the process, but he is not that at all. His job is rather, just by his very presence, to elicit a reaction from Kind for others to gauge. And that I suspect would have been pretty definitive. For Ed Murrell says she quite gets her blood up when something upsets her. An unwanted stallion at the wrong time would certainly fall into that category as she'd clamp down her tail, put back her ears and attempt to bite or kick an unwelcome Padraig, who would be swiftly led away for another try a day or two later. That's even assuming she'd even let him near her, which is by no means a given. Sometimes, he never even gets close.

But the change from no to yes is swift. One day, snarling dismissal. The next, acceptance. Instead of moving away from Padraig, Kind lets him nip and lick along her body starting at her neck, down her shoulders along her side and to her tail, his head constantly moving. Probing. His whole body aquiver at the sign of a receptive mare. She relaxes, leans towards him, straddling her legs, lifting her tail to allow him to sniff, and again lick and nip, at her genitals. For a mare that so often knows her own mind, Kind becomes placid. That is the final tell that her time has arrived.

However, before we follow the short journey Kind and Bullet Train took early on that Saturday morning to meet with Galileo in the covering barn, it is worth asking how exactly we have arrived at this point. In hindsight, the pairing looks both brilliant and obvious, but the who and the why deserve both credit and explanation. For the Frankel story started longer ago than you might imagine.

Prince Khalid bin Abdullah, a member of the Saudi Arabian Royal Family, first visited a racecourse just shy of his twentieth birthday in 1956. Though Longchamp in France was to become the scene of some of his greatest racing triumphs including the consecutive victories of the filly Enable in the Prix de l'Arc de Triomphe of 2017 and 2018, the day obviously didn't spark any immediate passion, for it was not until the late 1970s that he began to buy racehorses. He was one of that group of Arabs who at that time, took the international racing scene across the UK, France and the United States by storm, upending the old order. Success came quickly. The Prince had his first winner of any kind in 1979 (at Windsor), and when Known Fact won the 2,000 Guineas at Newmarket the following year, he became the first Arab owner of an English Classic. Now you might say he bought success. He, and others, did indeed pay outrageous prices. But what choice did they have? They didn't have the studs. They didn't have the bloodlines. Prince Khalid set out to change that.

I could try to paraphrase the Prince's thinking, but his words taken from an interview for the *Racing Post* in 2010 pretty well tell it all: 'When I was at the [bloodstock] sales I realised that it would be easier to buy horses and race them, but I got the feeling that this was not enough, that it would be more fun to do what people like the Aga Khan and Lord Howard de Walden did and build up your own families.'

He chose the breeding above buying route early on, with his first home-bred winner coming in 1982. The properties soon followed, with horse farms in England, Ireland and the United States, all of which come under the Juddmonte Farms banner. He calls Juddmonte his 'only hobby', run for the pleasure of breeding and racing the thoroughbred horse rather than a business. I had no special access to the financial side of the operation during the writing of this book, but in my gut that chimes true. All the places of his that I visited that touched the life of Frankel – Banstead Manor Stud in Suffolk, New Abbey Stud and Ferrans in Ireland – felt like homes, a fact not just reflected in the places but in the people as well.

Henry Ford once said, 'The harder I work the luckier I get.' I think we can reasonably apply that epithet to the Juddmonte racing empire. They don't shout their extraordinary success from the rooftops, so perhaps we don't entirely realise their achievements. When the Prince mentioned the Aga Khan and Howard de Walden, he was referencing families who have been breeding racehorses for generations. He has achieved the same in three decades. And how? Well, it is very much by the Arab way of building up what has been described on occasion as, 'one of the greatest broodmare bands in the history of breeding'. The results are amazing. By 1997, all the five English Classics had been won by home-bred horses. Prince Khalid has in numerous years before and since been the leading owner, mostly with horses he bred himself, in Britain and the United States. I won't rattle off all the statistics, but you'd be right to assume it is impressive. So, this is the heritage of Kind, a second-generation Juddmonte mare. That is to say, Prince Khalid bought her grandfather Rainbow Quest and bred her mother Rainbow Lake.

The decision to mate Kind with Galileo was made by Prince Khalid the previous November prior to plotting out the covering programme. It is a big task, the aim being to plan on somewhere over 200 foals to be born in eighteen months' time that will race in the Prince's green, pink and white colours three years after that. You are truly planning for the future. Inevitably, with that number of mares to place, some decisions are more debated over than others. Kind, even though she was just a one-foal mare, was particularly well thought of, so merited extra consideration not least because she had what they call the nick.

Thoroughbred racehorse breeding is high-octane stuff. Not much is left to chance and such is the huge volume of statistical data from both breeding records and racecourse performances that every Juddmonte decision, certainly at this level, is based on quantifiable facts. Naturally, today the amount of information is huge, but that is not a strictly modern phenomenon: Kind's family tree, and that of every thoroughbred, can be traced back with certainty to the seventeenth century thanks to the publication of the *General Stud Book* by James Weatherby in 1791 who set to record 'the pedigree of every horse, mare etc. of any note, that has appeared on the turf for the last fifty years, and many of an earlier date …' He was well placed to do this, as the Weatherby family were publishers of the *Racing Calendar* that had been recording all horse races and matches since 1727, something they continue to do today with the annual publication of both books.

It all looks so easy now, but when Prince Khalid, assisted by Juddmonte's general manager, Philip Mitchell, sat down at Banstead Manor Stud, with background analysis done by pedigree experts Andrew Caulfield and Claire Curry, as the beech tree leaves started to curl brown with the first frost of autumn, Galileo was not the potent force we know him to be today. He was still up and coming. Likewise, Kind was unproven. Even little Bullet Train was still two years away from his racecourse debut. But the reasoning was not overcomplicated: Galileo was a proven middle-distance performer. That is to say, he was at his most effective between a mile and a quarter and a mile and a half. Kind, as a sprinter, could provide speed.

Prince Khalid and Philip had some other salient facts to draw on: Although Kind's dam Rainbow Lake had plenty of stamina, Kind herself had sprinting speed through her father Danehill, whereas her half-brother Powerscourt demonstrated the middle distance class of the pedigree, having recently retired with a gilded reputation after winning his final race, the Arlington Million. (This was one of the leading turf contests in the US, so called as the first ever TB race to offer a purse of $1,000,000 when inaugurated in 1981.) And finally there was that nick.

I have to confess I had never come across the term the 'nick' until I began to research this book. If you do some googling, you will discover that vast amounts of cloud space are given over to this concept, as algorithms are deployed to drill down into every breeding permutation there has ever been to discover those that work best. It is a sort of genetic prospecting, trying to discover a new vein of equine gold. Summarised in a few words the nick is when the offspring of a particular stallion and the daughters of an unrelated stallion produce a higher than expected proportion of good performers. In our particular case, the two in question are Sadler's Wells, Galileo's father and Danehill, Kind's father, with one such 'nick' being Powerscourt. Now not everyone is entirely signed up to the nick theory. Horse-breeding writers Matthew Binns and Tony Morris, who provided the summary you just read, are less convinced. They contend, without absolutely coming down on one side of the fence or another, that if you mate superior individuals the probability over time is that you will produce a higher than average number of superior offspring. But that is enough of the theory; what Kind and Galileo were about to do was put it into practice.

* * *

It is still dark as the horse box rattles down the estate road to the Lakeview Yard. Kind had been allocated the first slot of the day, 7 am. Her reaction to Padraig had pronounced her ready the previous day. The vet was satisfied. That combination of old-fashioned breeding lore and modern science told the Coolmore team that her time was upon them.

Kind and her foal are loaded together into the box. There is no question of them being separated even though this will take under an hour. Separation would cause too much distress for both; after all, in the wild, in a herd, the foal would be at his or her mother's side during mating. Why should this be any different?

The journey is not long. Ten minutes at most. Back up the estate road, across the public road and into the home grounds of the Coolmore stallions, which is altogether more grandiose than that of the mares. The gate man, from inside his temple-style, Portland stone gate house pushes a button to allow the huge, black wrought-iron gates to swing open. Along the drive of mature trees and manicured grass, the statues of the Coolmore greats pay silent heed to our early-morning arrivals. Ahead is the Magnier home, largely obscured by a high hedge above which peeks a fancy Swiss Family Robinson-style treehouse that reminds us that this is still, for all the bloodstock high finance, a family business.

Around the back, among the complex of stables, barns and offices it is altogether more workmanlike. Kind and her foal are unloaded and led into the pre-covering shed. The horse box remains, ramp down. This should not take long. The shed is cream-walled with a corrugated-iron roof and a large, blue-black sliding door that opens into a double-height shed lit by halogen lights high up in the rafters that counter the morning gloom. The floor has a deep covering of fine shredded rubber that muffles all sound. To the side are the three teaser stalls; behind the mesh door of one, the nose of a shaggy head moves from side to side, tracking every movement of the incoming occupants. At the opposite end is a rubber-floored, brightly lit veterinary bay that has the air of a surgery. Into here is led Kind; her foal, still in sight of mother, is gently held outside by two stable hands.

None of this would be unusual or unsettling to our pair; being handled, put in and out of horse boxes, moved to unfamiliar places and meeting unfamiliar people is part of the daily fabric of their lives. As the team wash her vulval area and bandage her tail to avoid any stray hairs interfering at the moment of covering, Kind thinks little of it. If nothing else, she has gone through precisely all this a year before. The hand-held scanner is passed over her neck, bringing up her ID number on the display from the microchip that was inserted soon after birth. A check against her passport confirms she is indeed who she is purported to be. It is not always that easy: American horses are identified by a tattoo on the inside of the lip which is notoriously hard to read, and Australian horses are branded. Again, not always easy to read. That is not to say high-end technology has all the answers. The Coolmore way of reminding everyone which mare is destined for which stallion is the leather fob bearing the stallion's name, which is attached to the mare's head collar. Simple. Effective.

Back out among the fine shredded floor covering of the shed, there is one last test. A stall door swings open to reveal our moving nose which is attached to a Padraig lookalike. Different barns, different teasers, but let's call him Nosey. In half a dozen of his very short strides he is upsides Kind who doesn't move at his approach, and almost without breaking stride he rears up to mount her, not from the rear as you might suppose but from the side, draping his front legs across her back where a saddle might be. It is practised and smooth. Almost balletic. Kind's compliant acceptance of this act is the final confirmation she is ready. From the moment the door opens to Kind shrugging him off and Nosey on his way back to his stall – both seem to accept this for what it is, a final unrequited affirmation – takes no more than twenty seconds. As the stall door closes shut and Nosey is shrouded from view, Kind and Bullet Train leave the barn. Outside, in the pretty arbour, they await the call to attend Galileo like brides before the door of the church.

Galileo doesn't need a horse box for his thrice daily journey to the covering shed; there is a private back route that takes him from stable to shed in a minute or two. No distractions. Nothing left to chance. This is a stallion prepped and ready to go. He knows the walk. He knows the routine. He knows what lies at the end of this particular yellow brick road. This is, after all, his job.

It is hard to overstate how very simple Galileo's life is. Wake up. Have some food. Take a bit of exercise. Relax between two or three bouts of servicing your ever-changing harem. Retire for the night. That has pretty well been the sum of it for fifteen years; yesterday the template for today and today the template for tomorrow. For the highest paid athlete on the planet it is all remarkably, well I want to say boring, but that is not the correct word. People sometimes worry that horses get bored, but that doesn't seem the case to me. As long as you attend to their essential needs with kindness, food, warmth and care, the passing of the days seems not to matter to them. They are, in the best of ways, simple souls. Shall we agree his life, of which a human might have much to envy, is comfortingly routine?

Galileo starts his day with what all horses crave: food. He has five meals a day, plenty to look forward to though they are smaller than your average stallion portions. A few years ago, he had a colon operation so for his own well-being he has a special diet of five reduced-size meals rather that the more normal three. Horses this valuable have nutritionists too. On the stable floor are wood shavings, not the favoured bedding of Coolmore as they can be dusty which gets in the lungs. Most animals have straw but Galileo would eat it – a tender colon and roughage-rich straw has all the potential for disaster. But he won't go hungry by choice; there is always a pile of home-grown hay in the corner to pick at.

Like any horse he gets his exercise. Noel, his groom, lunges him each day in his paddock, trotting him in a circle controlled by a lunging line that is about 10 yards in length. Round and round they go for twenty or thirty minutes like some kind of human/equine whirligig, burning off energy until the pair have had enough. A bit later on, weather permitting, there will be a two-mile power walk. In the end, it is a toss-up who is the fitter – Noel or Galileo.

Galileo, along with the other five leading Coolmore stallions, live apart from everyone else. Their stables, two blocks of triple stalls, stand at right angles to each other overlooking a courtyard with a little park beyond. Each individual stable is big; if you are familiar with horse stables think at least twice the usual size. If not, think one half of a tennis court. The walls are whitewashed, the barrel-shaped double-height roof lined with cedar wood, with a large, half-moon-shaped window in the end wall with about a quarter of the roof given over to two enormous skylights. In the ceiling are water sprinklers and smoke detectors, no doubt the requirement of some ultra-cautious insurance company who carries the risk of these super-valuable residents. An infrared heating lamp hangs down ready to take the chill off a cold night.

For the top half of the stable door is never closed. Horses like the comings and goings of stable life. They must see the same things a thousand times or more. Still they stand and watch, those brown eyes tracking every small movement. Familiar figures confirming all is well. Strangers the subject of particular interest. At night, they are mostly awake; horses only need about three hours' sleep in every twenty-four and largely do it while standing up. But at night there is still plenty going on. Mice scurry about gathering stray corn seeds, often shadowed by the stable cats never shy of spotting an opportunity. Occasionally, a fox pads on through, sliding through the shadows, curious but furtive. Bats flit. Owls hoot. The darkness provides a soothing blanket. Every hour a human figure appears, the shielded beam of a torch checking the occupants of each stall. And they'll tell you that on a clear night, Galileo stands for hours staring up, his skylights a window to the stars. Maybe like his namesake, the father of astronomy, he sees things in the galaxy that are beyond our knowing?

The clatter of food bins brings all six residents to their doors. Night is over. It is day again. About the time when Nosey was slipping off Kind, Galileo was chasing the last few oats around his feed bin. The bolts of the door clank. He turns to Noel, slightly inclining his head, allowing the head collar, with brass chain and leading rein attached, to be slipped on. The pair head for the door, across the yard, down the hedge-lined path between the stallion paddocks before turning left up the short incline to the covering barn. With well-timed precision, as the doors of the barn slide open for Galileo, Kind and the foal enter from the opposite doors. The foal is peeled away, stiff limbed in the restraint of two stable hands who gently hold him up close to the wall, far enough away but still in sight of the soon to be coupling pair.

Jutting out from the wall, in direct line between the two entrance doors, is the teasing rail. It is here, for the first time, that Kind and Galileo come together. The rail isn't a rail at all. It is a barrier. A reinforced, padded board that is 5 feet high and 12 feet long. In other words, about the height (to the neck) and length of a horse. Just enough to allow division with the opportunity for union.

At first, the pair start head to head. There's a brief shaking of heads, a meeting of eyes, but like the teaser Padraig, Galileo's interest lies elsewhere. As Kind is held parallel to the rail he turns towards her tail end. His head slides down her mane, his nose then rubbing against her spine, sliding up, then down her rib cage, inexorably moving rearwards, nipping at her flesh. Snorting in appreciation of what is to come. Kind stands rigid, all four legs slightly splayed. As Galileo reaches her rump she lifts her tail to expose herself. He lets off a deafening retort as he sniffs and licks and nips her vulva. Kind's tail rises further, fully posed. Galileo kicks and thumps at the teasing rail. It is not natural and it should not be there. He lets his displeasure be known. Kind quivers as a stream of hot, odourful urine waterfalls out of her. She is staling, proof that she is ready.

As the two are backed to the centre of the barn the pheromones from her steaming urine reach Galileo, triggering the Flehmen response. This is really quite frightening to behold; the German origin of the word *flemmen* that means to look spiteful is not far from the truth. Here's the side of Galileo rarely seen. A horse defined by what he now is. A stallion ready for his mare. His otherwise placid face contorts as he stretches his head high in the air, curls back his upper lip, exposes his front teeth and white gums, narrowing his nostrils to suck in the smell of Kind. When the scents hit his nasal organs in the roof of his mouth he holds the pose for a few seconds, as if he was a sommelier savouring the bouquet of a rare vintage. As he lowers his head the handler leads him, erect and ready, towards Kind.

She sees nothing of this; Galileo is away and behind her. Her movements are restricted by not only two handlers at her head but giant soft felt boots that engulf her rear hooves. Her hobbling gait looks uncomfortable but it's necessary; a single kick can inflict great damage on both horse and human, so the boots are put on soon after she arrives in the barn. Like at the teasing rail Kind stands legs splayed. Braced. At her head one handler takes the reins, while the other stands by with the twitch in hand, which is nothing more than a stout broom handle with a loop of rope at the end. A few yards away the foal looks on, eyes fixed on his mother in a scene that must be totally incomprehensible, leaning hard against the handlers as if to take comfort from their grip.

Kind is allowed to look around to see Galileo is approaching; it is important she is not caught unawares. The twitch is applied to her upper lip, the rope loop twisted around to cause a certain amount of pain. At first, this is both a distraction and a restraint. Then a rush of endorphins kicks in, dulling the pain before creating a feeling of calm. The moment has nearly arrived. Galileo is ready. Anyone can see that. But Kind's signals are more subtle. She lowers her rear in a very slight squat before raising her tail and winking to her stallion, the vulva turning outwards to expose her clitoris.

Galileo raises himself up on his hind legs, pausing for a moment in mid-air before, with remarkable poise, he lowers himself slowly down, his front legs sliding either side of Kind's back before gripping at her belly. He doesn't slump over. He uses his colossal strength, aided no doubt by pumping adrenalin, to hold himself above her. Beneath, his rigid penis sways from side to side. The stallion manager steps forward, guiding Galileo into Kind. At the moment of penetration Galileo arches his back, leans forward to bite her on the neck, gripping her mane and a roll of flesh in his mouth, the combination of legs and teeth giving him enough purchase to start thrusting into Kind.

The mating is not as violent or as animalistic as you might imagine. Kind is ready. Compliant. Relaxed, even. Galileo by contrast is the picture of concentration, his tail stretched downwards to the ground in perfect alignment with his back, his neck and head curved, his eyes gone to another place. While he thrusts and thrusts and thrusts. There is very little noise. Some deep sucks of air. Hooves readjusting on the floor. The smack of flesh on flesh. Spittle trails appear down Kind's neck. A patch of her mane becomes matted wet. Nobody talks.

It doesn't last for long. I didn't time it, but I counted the seconds in my head. Maybe twenty-five or thirty from penetration to ejaculation. Everyone turns to stud manager who nods. It is over. He has felt the sperm pulsing through the urethra at the base of the penis. It is important to know that it has truly happened. Galileo pauses for a few seconds further over Kind to allow his engorgement to subside before he slides back, off and away.

Relieved of the pressure, Kind straightens her legs and stands upright again. She pricks her ears at the sight of the foal, the two led on converging paths meeting just before they go out of the door. Bullet Train skips with joy at their reunion, giving his mother a gentle nudge to the belly. Kind turns her head to him ever so slightly, as if by way of grateful maternal acknowledgement, before they disappear from view. Across the other side, Galileo is leaving. There are no backward or lingering glances. It is most definitely over. Within a minute or two the barn is empty of both people and horses. All that is left is a few damp patches on the floor from the wash down water and, lying at crazy angles and in random spots, a pair of discarded felt boots.

Creation day has lasted less than an hour.

4

Day 343

You are probably asking yourself at this particular moment why the bloodstock industry goes to all this trouble of bringing horses together from all corners of the globe for a physical mating. As you will have gathered, it is a huge and expensive logistical jigsaw. Have they not heard of artificial insemination? If it is good enough for cows, pigs, polo ponies, sheep and just about any other animal or even bird you care to name, why not horses? For goodness sake, we humans have been at it since the London surgeon John Hunter carried out the first documented insemination and subsequent successful birth in the 1770s. As ever with all things horse racing, the answer is, all at once, that complex mixture of tradition, rules, money and hard science.

Tradition is the easy one to tick off. I like the fact that horse racing embraces tradition. Maybe furlongs are today only ever used in ploughing matches and on racecourses, but doesn't that make it interesting and different? We like our conversations a little odd. Okay, when you say, 'I got 6–4 about that horse' a little mental agility is required, but it slips off the tongue better than any metricised 1.5–1.

Of course, we could take the bulldozers to the switchback Derby course at Epsom to reduce it to a perfectly flat and uniform oval, but where would be the unique test of the racehorse in that?

If you are thinking, well, I don't give a damn about tradition, I'm going to be progressive about all this in embracing modern science, then you will find your foal forever excluded from thoroughbred horse racing around the globe which requires all horses to be registered in the *General Stud Book*. The wording is definitive: 'Any foal resulting from or produced by the processes of Artificial Insemination, Embryo Transfer or Transplant, Cloning or any other form of genetic manipulation not herein specified, shall not be eligible for registration in The General Stud Book.' That closes the door on anything produced other than by what the rules call 'natural service', as we just witnessed between Galileo and Kind.

Then, of course, there is the money thing. The most productive bulls are inseminating over fifty thousand cows a year each. It doesn't take a Nobel prize-winning economist to work out the supply and demand implications. Not only would there be a flight to a very few top stallions (only 95,000 thoroughbreds are registered worldwide each year) but the market would entirely collapse for everyone else. It is no exaggeration in saying that thousands of stallions would cease to be. Nobody would want them in physical or test-tube form.

But aside from the money, the flight to a very few stallions would be a slow-burning disaster for the thoroughbred breed. Interbreeding, in horses and animals or even people for that matter (think *The Madness of King George*), eventually causes the bad, or more correctly recessive, genes to crowd out the good. Within a matter of generations, fewer and fewer foals would reach the racecourse as birth abnormalities became more commonplace. The racehorse as we know it – lithe, fit and fast – that began with those Arabian stallions all those centuries ago, would soon cease to be.

On something of a tangent you might be wondering, as I did, why those recessive genes haven't taken hold in cattle. Fifty thousand sounds like an awful lot of offspring. Well, it is and it isn't. There are currently 1.5 billion head of cattle on the planet (the most are in Brazil at 210 million, in case you ask). So, Galileo is fathering about one in 325 of the worldwide crop of foals each year, whereas Toystory, the most productive bull in history with roughly 500,000 calves to his name in nine years (he died in 2014), was producing a 'mere' one in 6,000 annually.

An in-foal Kind returned to a different Banstead Manor Stud than the one she had left. Two months on from the bleak of February, spring had come to the Suffolk countryside. The beech trees were in vivid green leaf. Birds were nesting among the hedges that separate the paddocks. The farm tractor was rolling the fields, the broad striped grass adding a certain gaiety to the morning turn out. Kind was paired with Prove in the Blackthorn paddock, a more experienced mare who had raced in France, the two mothers-in-arms with foals to care for inside and out.

Kind had stayed at Coolmore for a while subsequent to her time with Galileo. Two weeks after her covering she was confirmed as pregnant by a scan, an ultrasound that creates that same fuzzy black-and-white photo expectant parents hang on the fridge door. The egg, a single cell about the size of a grain of sand when fertilised by that one spermatozoon, was already multiplying rapidly by division, having spent a restless two weeks in the womb, moving around, until finally fixing itself in one of the horns of the uterus at the end of that first fortnight. A week later, the first heartbeat was detectable.

By the time she had her third scan two further weeks later the miniature foal was visible in outline. Seven weeks after covering, a manual inspection by the vet confirmed all was well. The yolk sac that had sustained the embryo had shrivelled away, the umbilical cord formed, tethering foal to mother. Now was time for Kind, Bullet Train and an embryonic nine-gram Frankel to head for home.

The Victorians liked to term pregnancy as a period of 'confine-ment', as if all activity was to be kept to a bare minimum – if that was the case it certainly didn't apply to Kind. Or even her kind. Not all broodmares are retired racers – some are still in training, racing for the first third of their gestation. That will be for potentially as long as 100 days, as full term for a horse is generally regarded to be around 340 days or 11 months. And that time was to be spent largely unconfined.

I imagined that the Juddmonte mares, with their valuable cargoes, would be kept in light, airy boxes monitored 24-7 by both people and science. After all, one in five pregnancies don't end with a live foal. Should there be twins (a rarity in itself at 2.5 per cent of all pregnancies) the chances are grim, with only one in six resulting in the live birth of both foals. But for all the attendant risks, my imag-ination is way off-beam; Kind and Bullet Train live the life outdoors, in the quiet paddocks that stretch away and out into the far corners of the stud. They are not alone. The Banstead Manor team group-up mares and foals at similar points in their respective lives. It is part social – horses like it that way. If you ever catch a glimpse of the wild ponies on the heather heaths of the New Forest, you will see a simi-lar thing as the herd divides into groups, grazing together with the immediate companions defined by age and disposition. It is also practical; pregnant mares are the adult group most susceptible to infection.

It is hard to make the life of Kind and Bullet Train complicated. It is also hard not to think of it as idyllic as the spring became summer. Long, warm days spent cropping grass. Dozing in the shade. The foals gradually finding their independence. If they want to run, they run. If they want to roll, they roll. Nuzzling. Suckling. Little foals doing that strange hoppy, skippy leap as they run forward and then jump, spring-like, all four feet simultaneously in mid-air before bouncing back down onto the ground. Mother and foal do quite precisely whatever their nature tells them to do. They spend nearly all their time outside; close to twenty-two hours a day. It is a routine that doesn't change, regardless of the season or the weather. There is no shelter as such, simply high corner panels in each paddock and tree lines that provide protection in the lee of any wind.

Each morning they wait by the gate, not for the dawn but for food. Breakfast is the highlight of the day, followed by a couple of hours in the stable. A chance for the broodmare team to handle the foals. Check on their physical development. Pick up their feet. Trim their hooves. Adjust the collar to a growing head. This is the time to cement that physical bond between man and horse that will be so important through any racing career. Trust is long won. And when the morning routine is over, Bullet Train lies down in the deep, long-stranded oat straw to sleep. But soon it is out again, and if it's a Friday that is it until Monday; the entire weekend, night and day, will be spent outside. As Ed Murrell so insightfully observes: the stable is entirely a human construct. No horse has, as yet, mastered bricklaying and carpentry.

By the time the centre court at Wimbledon has turned from verdant green to scuffed brown and the final ball of the Championships is struck, Kind's broodmare group is halved in number. All the foals are weaned and gone. But life carries on much as before. There are few outward signs to suggest the months are marching on, because the foal in the womb grows very slowly in the early stages; by month six most veterinarians will tell you it is no bigger than your average cat. So that is around 10 lb, less than one-twelfth of Frankel's ultimate birth weight. With Kind due sometime in February, it is around November that the growth spurt begins. As Christmas comes and goes she passes the critical 300-day point; from here on in, the foal is a viable being. Our Frankel is, to all intents and purposes, a horse but no longer in quite such minia-ture form. Body, legs, head, ears and hooves are all fully formed. The mane and tail are visible. That bay hair we will grow to recognise covers his entire body. Actually, we don't know he is a 'he' at this point, as Juddmonte do not sex test the mares. So make no mistake, the team at Banstead Manor seek out this news at the moment of birth as much as any excited human parent. Like you they have plans to make. Dreams to fulfil. Aspirations. And fears. And doubts. For, despite every technology known to equine science (and believe me, if it exists Juddmonte has it), you will never truly know you have a fit and healthy foal until it lays bloodied and breathing in the straw of the foaling box.

Foaling box number 5 looks much like the other four foaling boxes in the foaling unit at Banstead Manor, except for one thing. It bears a green plaque which reads:

FRANKEL
b.c. Galileo – Kind (Danehill)
Winner of 10 Gr. 1 races and
first unbeaten champion at 2, 3 and 4
Timeform 147

I know that reads like poetry for anyone in the racing game, but not everyone speaks racing. The term 'b.c.' is shorthand for bay colt, bay covering a wide spectrum of reddish-brown body hair with a black mane and tail. A colt is an entire, or uncastrated male horse, gener-ally less than five years old. Older than five, an entire male is called a horse and will stay that way unless gelded or used for breeding; in the latter case he becomes a stallion. As you know, Galileo and Kind are Dad and Mum. Danehill is Kind's father.

'Gr. 1' refers to Group 1 races. There is a hierarchy of all racing competitions and Group 1 races stand at the very pinnacle. These are the best races in which the best horses compete. They are to racing what the Grand Slams are to tennis or the Majors are to golf. To even compete in ten is extraordinary. To win ten? Well, that is remarkable.

The fourth line needs some unpicking. 'First' seems almost insignificant but put it in context: that is the first horse in the history of European horse racing. So we are talking centuries and millions of horses. Fortunes lost. Dreams busted. Stories of what might have been but for a little bad luck are legion. Such is the enormity of what our about-to-be-born foal will achieve, I'd be tempted to defy the Gods of Fate by adding a little graffiti to the plaque in parentheses: (and only).

'Unbeaten'. That word is the elixir of sport. Turning great men, women and teams from just being great to being truly great. The comparators by which every performance past, present and future will be measured. Now there have been unbeaten horses in the past, but in truth not many. It is an unusual thing even at the lesser levels of horse racing. That said, some good horses have retired unbeaten, but often they have been whisked away after a handful of races to lock in their stud value rather than test them further. Because so much can go wrong. Injury. Bad luck. Come up against one better on the day. Poor tactics. Feeling a bit under the weather. Just a bad day at the office. We all have them. Horses are no different. But Frankel was and is different, because not only was he unbeaten in the three prime years of any flat racing career but he beat every rival sent out to take him on. And here we are not talking about an average crop; a simply okay generation. Many of Frankel's contemporaries were brilliant horses in their own right that simply had the misfortune to come up against him. In any other year, in any other era, they would have been the crowned champions. To be the best, you have to beat the best. Frankel was to achieve that in spades, winning even when the cards of fate dealt him the harshest of hands.

And finally 'Timeform 147' – that is really a bit of racing techie speak. It's thanks to Phil Bull, son of a Yorkshire coal miner, school-teacher turned professional gambler who along the way to amassing a multi-million-pound fortune from betting on the horses created an internationally acknowledged and respected rating system – Timeform – by which all horses, past and present are measured. And 147 is the highest rating ever achieved.

I wish I could tell you something romantic about the moment of Frankel's birth, maybe coinciding with a beautiful sunrise goldening the sparse countryside of a Suffolk February dawn. But, to be blunt, it was at 11.40 pm. It was dry and 4° C outside. If you like your bed, I don't recommend working on the foaling unit of a busy stud farm. From January to the second week of May, Simon Mockridge, the then stud manager, Jim Power, the stud groom and Ed Murrell become night owls. They live on the stud farm for good reason, as 90 per cent of foals are born under the cover of darkness, with a majority of those clustered around the two hours either side of midnight. It is, of course, a throwback to the wild when the dark offered respite and protection from predators.

Number 5 foaling box is bigger than the everyday stables, with extra-wide stable doors and, unusually, a small, human-sized door set in the back wall. Around the ceiling are an array of night cameras that monitor every square inch of the stall, the live feed piped back to the office of the night team who have a wall of TV monitors as impressive as any high-security bank vault. Kind may think she is alone, but she isn't really.

Right up to the last 30 days of the 343 of pregnancy, the team maintained Kind's routine, out day and night except for that morning interval. Then she became what is termed a 'heavy mare', and was brought in at night for those last four weeks. Until the final week of pregnancy, there are not many outward signs of what is happening inside. The mammaries begin to develop six weeks out but even that is not a continuous process, the enlargement plateauing until resuming in the last week. Jim knows her time is fast approaching, as the bags get large and the teats secrete milk the consistency of translucent candle wax. Drops of milk appear, first clear, then thick and creamy. As the foal moves towards the birthing position within the womb, Kind's belly drops. All the signs are there of an imminent birth, but this time is all about the mare; human contact is kept to an absolute minimum. Kind stands alone in the box. The night crew scan the monitors.

Soon after ten o'clock, Kind starts to become restless, moving around in her box. Dripping milk. She is hot, sweaty and steamy. The uterine contractions are starting. Think of her womb as being the shape of an avocado, with the stem end the birth passage. In the midst is the foal, almost crouched down, hind legs drawn up under his stomach, his rump and tail backed up against the bulbous end. At the front, Frankel's head is laid on top of his two front legs, nose and hooves together, as if he is preparing to dive out of the stem end. He is ready and so is she. Kind becomes incredibly docile – laid back, as Ed describes it. As she subsides to the ground, her waters break. Jim, Simon and Ed quietly slip in through that back door. Jim is in charge of the delivery; he needs to check the foal. The clock is ticking now. For a successful live birth the foaling must be completed within half an hour. Jim slides his hand inside Kind to feel for two front hooves and a muzzle. All is well.

The second stage of labour is starting, the abdominal muscles exerting more pressure on the womb. It works. Quite suddenly, a single hoof appears. Then a second and then the muzzle. The team are there to gently assist, offering comfort and soothing words but Kind can, and should, do this on her own. There is no hauling at the emerging foal; nature and the mare must do the work. Pushing. Gradually the legs, neck, shoulders and body are out. The hind legs remain in the birth canal for a short while further as Frankel takes his first breath, moving his forelegs like a chick pecking the shell to break open the white amniotic sac, in which he has lived for nearly a year, and that Jim then gently peels away to expose him to the world. The question then hangs in the air among Simon, Jim and Ed: they have a healthy foal, but is it a colt or filly? For at this point they have absolutely no idea. Among the blood and fluid Jim seeks out the answer. Colt! Smiles break out. Knowing nods of congratulation, for, however unfair it might seem, the possibilities for a colt seem so much more than those of a filly. Twelve minutes after her waters have broken, Kind's foal, the great Frankel, is already a notable being.

Soon she is up on her feet, nuzzling and licking at her foal. Kind is a good mother, recognising her foal by taste and smell. Frankel sits up, taking in his new world – horses see from the moment of birth. And what he sees is a small circle of faces, Jim, Simon and Ed, as he is cleaned and dried. But soon they retreat through the rear door to the office behind, dimming the lights to almost darkness as they go. It is time for mother and foal to bond.

As the guys relaxed with tea and one eye on the monitors after another successful birth, did they speculate that they had just delivered the greatest racehorse of all time? The truth is, and Ed admits this, no. Banstead Manor Stud breeds many beautiful colts and fillies; Frankel was one of thirteen foaled at Banstead that year. But he was more than noteworthy. Beautifully marked with strong colour. This excited Simon – from the very outset he had high hopes. The comments in the birth book show these observations to be more than just braggadocio hindsight. Let me quote in full:

Comment: Quality colt, tall with size and scope. Adequate bone. Slight medial deviation of the left knee. Strong hind leg. Very good foal. Rating: 7+.

In case you are wondering, 7+ is pretty much as good as it gets on the Banstead scale – nobody wants to make him or herself a hostage to fortune. After all, there are plenty of very good foals who don't necessarily make very good racehorses. But this time, that was to prove one of the greatest understatements in the history of horse racing. It is not always bad to be wrong.

It is coming up to 2 am as Simon heads for his bed; the night team will be on duty until he returns at 7 am. Outside the confines of the foaling unit, nobody in the world knows of Frankel's arrival and that is the way it shall be until Prince Khalid is told. Reporting the news will be Simon's first morning task, as across the dawn of Frankel's first day on earth and several continents, the wires hum.

5

More Irish than English

I find myself in something of a quandary at this point of the book when I call our newly born colt Frankel and you, no doubt, think of him as Frankel. But that, in fact, is not his name. As of now, he has no name. And he will not have a name for another two years. He is referred to by everyone, from stud hand to Prince Khalid, as the Kind colt. It took me a while to get used to this, for the people who knew him well at his various homes and in his various guises until he went into training still, years after he retired to stud, refer to him as the Kind colt. Or sometimes '*that* Kind colt' with heavy emphasis on the 'that'. But in a good way.

I did wonder why he wasn't the Galileo colt; more deference to the female line, I thought. Until the penny dropped. There are numerous Galileo offspring of the same age, give or take a few months. There were in fact six in the Juddmonte crop of Frankel's birth year. To refer to them all as the Galileo colts or foals would be plain confusing. So, as mother and foal are pronounced healthy and well by the veterinarian, the sign on the door announced the occupants. There would be a green plastic door card with white lettering which would have read:

BAY COLT
11. 2. 08
GALILEO – KIND

Even though we might be slightly breaching horse-rearing protocol, let's stick with Frankel, the name others will come to know him by in the years to come.

Young foals, even ones an hour or two old, have a remarkable survival instinct. As he lies in the straw accepting the licks and nuzzles of a nursing mother, Frankel, like all horses, knows he is vulnerable and exposed. He needs to stand. And he needs food. Horses are animals of flight. Should the worst occur in the wild, Kind would have few ways of defending Frankel. He needs to be on his feet quickly. At 1.10 am, just ninety minutes after birth, he is up. And he is not sea-legged or uncertain. Ed Murrell describes him as balanced. Coherent. Organised. Eleven minutes later, he is at his mother's teat suckling for the first time. He drinks down what is known as the colostrum, the milk of the first forty-eight hours that contains disease antibodies, with a higher than usual protein and fat content. Without it, his survival would be compromised. For he and his breed are precocial. Born into this world relatively mature and mobile, ready to take on the rigours of life. Even fresh out of the womb, Frankel's legs are already 90 per cent of their eventual length. On the open plain, he would now be ready to run beside his mother. Keep up with the herd. Cover dozens of miles in a day.

It is still dark at 7 am as Ed swings back the wide stable door, and for him it is the perfect sight under the dim lighting of Number 5 box: mother with nursing foal. Frankel is bright and alert. Kind is ready for her morning feed; she'll be having extra to help her milk production. At 8.30 am the veterinarian Professor Sidney Ricketts (FRCVS) arrives. This is always a nervous time for the broodmare team. Sometimes the night-time optimism is burst by the report of some previously unnoticed flaw, but as Frankel is meticulously examined – head, mouth, body and limbs – all are ticked off as sound. Heartbeat is strong and regular. Breathing is good. Frankel's weight is 123 lb, almost bang on par for his sex (the average Juddmonte birth weight was 126 lb that year) and exactly one-tenth of what will be his adult weight.

As he stands tightly close to his mother, almost leaning against her belly, Ed slips on, for the first time in Frankel's life, a head collar, something he will now wear every day, forever. With its leather straps and brass buckles it is slightly oversize, hanging loosely, accentuating the soft hairs of his muzzle. He waggles his ears, adjusting to the new sensation. But Frankel is too young to question or fight against this new addition; after all, his mother seems to approve and at this age her consent and protection is all he asks. And that is rather the point.

Kind is accepting of the stable life and all that goes with it. That trust in the people who care for her, built up not just here at Banstead Manor but all through her racing life, is now being passed to her son. The truth is that the collar is not strictly necessary this early in life; it will be a little while before it is used to lead him. But it is an opportunity to handle Frankel. Stop him becoming head shy. Get him used to people up close and personal; invading if you like, in the loosest sense of the word, his space. For him to understand that there is more to the world than just his mother. So each morning, the collar will go on. Each evening, it comes off. It is a routine, along with the people who do it, that Frankel will always accept as normal.

And that, with one small exception, is about as dramatic as Frankel's first day on earth gets. The one exception being his first steps outside the box. A short walk to the indoor schooling barn. The transition causes him no angst for, wherever Kind goes Frankel will follow, trotting along beside her, barely a hands breadth between them, as he looks more towards her than towards where they are going or where they have been. Around the soft polytrack of the barn, Kind is briskly led for a few circuits, Frankel keeping up without breaking sweat. Well, it is hardly the Wild West plains where the mustangs roam. But it serves a purpose, though perhaps more for the benefit of mother than foal; a chance to discharge some redundant fluids and, to put it crudely, rearrange her insides. And after that it is back to the box to complete his first twenty-four hours of life.

It might be easy at this point to jump the next two years of Frankel's life. To take you to the day he first arrived into the care of trainer Henry Cecil at his Warren Place stables in England. Or maybe to go directly to that wet Newmarket August evening when Frankel made his racecourse debut. But that would be to miss out. For when we see a racehorse in the parade ring for that debut race, we rarely ask: how did you get here? Where have you been since birth? Who made you the horse you are? For there is a hidden world that is glimpsed by very few. Down narrow lanes that take you to out of the way places that you probably never knew existed. It is there, by people the names of whom you have likely never heard spoken, that Frankel was moulded from gangly foal to the fantastic beast that did indeed come down the ramp into the gaze of Henry Cecil.

For making it successfully through this largely unseen period in a racehorse's life is far from being a given. Plenty will fail. Peeled away as growth exposes an inadequate equine athlete. Birth defects hidden in the early weeks and months are horribly exposed by the evolution from young foal to adolescent yearling. Sometimes it is physical. Sometimes it is in the head. Sometimes it is just sheer bad luck – a career-ending injury. These things happen. Think upon the next two years a bit like the schooling system, with Henry Cecil the

Oxbridge or Ivy League attainment: nursery, primary and then secondary school. But tested and tried at each level with little room for sentiment. The wheat separated from the chaff. The weak. The lame. Those simply not even as good as average consigned to a different life. This might sound a little harsh; Darwinian in fact. Perhaps it is. The survival of the fittest. And the fastest. Only the horses with both the physical and mental attributes to perform will make it to each new level.

Foals develop rapidly in the first month of life. They need to in captivity as much as they would do in the wild, as they are not shielded from the realities of bloodstock life. At just twenty-four days old Frankel, like his half-brother Bullet Train the year before, will be on the Irish ferry with his mother as she returns for another date with Galileo. In that time, Frankel has gone from stable to paddock, spending each day with Kind in a small, nursery field set aside for just the two of them. He stays close to her. Feeding every hour. Sleeping for long periods, lying down both in the stable and out in the field. With each passing day he becomes stronger. More curious of the world around him. He is a fine foal who gives little trouble, soon familiar with the people who handle him. Grooming becomes part of the routine. Again, there is no strict purpose or reason; foals look cute enough without our brushes and mother attends to his basic needs. But it is part of that handling thing. Another reason for Frankel to understand the human routine that will be imposed upon his life.

One morning, there is a new figure in the box with Kind and Frankel; mother barely gives him a second glance. The leather apron and the box of tools he sets down in the straw she has seen a hundred times or more before. The farrier has arrived to check Frankel's feet. It is not yet for shoeing, that is a full twenty months away, but for the horse equivalent of a pedicure. Hooves, like our nails, grow – in fact they completely regrow every nine to eleven months – but in the confines of stables and paddocks they are not worn away like they would be in the wild where typically the herd will travel fifteen or twenty miles a day. So it is up to the farrier to trim and rasp the growing hooves. Today there is little to be done, the farrier visit as much to ensure Frankel becomes accustomed to having each of his four feet picked up as anything else. But over time this will change, the monthly visits an opportunity to trim the hooves to remedy any imperfections in Frankel's gait. As the old saying goes, 'No foot, no horse', for if you can't walk right you won't run right.

At the end of the second week, Frankel's world opens up a little further as he and Kind are joined for the daily paddock turn out with another nursing pair and for the first time, emboldened by the company of kindred spirit, the apron strings are slowly stretched. To start, it is a matter of feet. Then a few yards. But the two foals never go very far, an eye and an ear always on mother. The slightest out-of-the-ordinary thing, even something as small as an inquisitive bumble bee, is enough to send them scurrying back to the side of mother. In truth, it might not seem a great adventure to us – the paddock is not very big, maybe half an acre – but it is the start of an independence that will eventually lead to complete separation in five or six months' time. Still, a few things have to happen between now and then; notably a journey to Ireland and a meeting with his father.

It always astonishes me how young foals take so much in their stride. Imagine how alien all this must have been to Frankel. Not just the people and how they intertwine themselves into his life, but the logistics of how his life unfolds. Mounting the ramp into the horse box for the first time, uncertain legs slipping this way and that as they adjust to a slope for the first time ever. The sensation of gravity with the motion of the wagon as it gently yaws through corners. The noise. The smells. The unfamiliarity of it all. But Kind is the key.

When Frankel is untroubled he stands a little way apart, bold enough to take on the world on his terms. But when the unfamiliar comes along the distance closes, his side touching her side, a small shiver through his body telling her as much. Kind turns her head to him, an exhalation of warm hay breath or a soft whinny enough to reassure him that all is well. Then he'll linger for a while at her side, sometimes leaning, other times rubbing his head against her until the crisis, imagined or real, is past before he moves ever so slightly away again.

And so, like his half-brother Bullet Train before him, Frankel took that journey to Ireland. To Coolmore. To the Lakeview Yard. To the covering barn.

It might be tempting to tell you that this second Galileo–Kind mating was as a result of Frankel, such was the impression the just-born foal had made on the Juddmonte team. But that would be stretching the truth to breaking point. Indeed, there were to be six more similar matings which might be attributed to the success of Frankel. But not this one. It was planned closer to Frankel's conception than his birth. However, it does beg the question: were Frankel's siblings as good as him and if not, why not? After all, if the Galileo–Kind combination has worked once, why not again? It is a commonly held misconception that breeding is that simple. The reason why it is not lies in probability.

Every horse has 32 pairs of chromosomes; we, by the way, have 23 pairs which makes them considerably more genetically complex than us. Incidentally a potato has 24 pairs and the creature on our planet with the most (at least so far discovered) is the hermit crab at 127. But I digress.

When a stallion produces sperm, one chromosome from each of his 32 pairs is randomly introduced into each sperm. So, the chances of another sperm containing precisely the same 32 chromosome mix is 2^{32} (i.e. 2x2x2x2 with x2 added another 28 times) which is, to put it mildly, a pretty big number of possible combinations. But if that has left your head swirling, it gets worse. Exactly the same random chromosome distribution happens in the creation of the egg, so when mating takes place the number of possible combinations doubles to 2^{64} (i.e. 2x2x2x2 with x2 added another 60 times).

Now this number, despite its mind-boggling hugeness, has a name. It is the chess number, so called because an ancient emperor, as the legend goes, was so delighted at the creation of the game of chess that he invited the inventor to name his reward. The man asked for rice, the amount determined by the number of grains required to put one grain on the first square of the board, two on the second, four on the third, eight on the fourth, and so on, with each square having double the number of grains as the square before, until the sixty-fourth square. The Emperor acceded to this apparently modest request, not understanding that the total number of grains required is 2^{64} or 18,446,744,073,709,551,616. No such amount of rice exists in the world. The legend is unclear whether the man was lauded or executed for his cleverness.

It is hard to put this probability in any sort of reasonable context but let's try: the chances of getting Frankel's exact genetic match second time around is roughly the same as every single human being on the planet winning the lottery fifty-four times each. Or the world could exist for roughly another 4 billion times over, and that number of years still wouldn't be as big. Or Galileo and Kind would have to produce a foal every year for the next 18 million, million, million years for another Frankel to come along. I think we can safely assume we won't see his like in our lifetimes.

It might also be tempting to tell you that Frankel's meeting with his father was a watershed; that moment when the great and the would-be great came together in communion. One recognising the other. Some acknowledgement of shared blood. A union in equine wisdom. But of course no such thing happened. For that is a strange thing about animals – they have no sense of genetic connection. They are, of course, protective of their young, but beyond that the connection dies. Fathers kill sons. Sons mate with mothers. Siblings fight to the death. Love and rivalry perpetuates regardless of relation. So the meeting was as you might expect. Galileo was prepped for his time with Kind. A foal, his or any other, was of simply no importance. In those handful of minutes in the covering barn, Frankel would have been all but invisible to his father. If he registered him at all it was simply as a scared, forty-day-old foal that was being kept out of the way. That suited Galileo just fine. He did not want Kind distracted.

As for Frankel, well, he really had no idea whether the scene unfolding before him was something to fear or not. Maybe there is something deep inside the head that tells him this is fine. Part of the natural course of life. That is probably true. In the wild, the herd mill around while mating happens. It is too routine – sometimes as often as a dozen times for a single mare in a single day – for it to be too disruptive. So Frankel accepted the restraint of the stud hands, their soothing words and calming hands easing the tensions away.

And that I have to tell you was the total sum of the day when Frankel met his father. They have never met since. And they likely never will. They are too valuable to move around. An actuarial risk too far that would keep even the bravest insurer awake at night. That there would be no practical purpose to the meeting is a shame – it would be quite the photo opportunity.

I think it is fair to say that most people think of Frankel as English, or maybe British. But really the Irish deserve more than a little credit. After all, he was conceived in Ireland and spent the bulk of his early life until he went into training in Ireland. First at Coolmore and then at the Irish bases of the Juddmonte empire; those places few people see, New Abbey Stud and Ferrans. In fact, his entire yearling year was spent in Ireland, and if you add up his one hundred weeks of life from birth to training, all but fifteen were spent in the land on the west of the Irish Sea. But why?

It took me a while to find New Abbey Stud, which is not far from the Curragh racecourse in County Kildare, eighty miles northeast of Coolmore. For the umpteenth time in my pursuit of Frankel's past, an electronic gate swung open on my arrival. But this one was apparently in the middle of nowhere. This gate had no sign or notice, so I simply assumed the best. I didn't know I was in the right place, but I sort of guessed I was. It was all so very immaculate. I'd arrived in late April. Spring was in full flow. The grass was into its third or fourth cut. The yellow dandelions had figured that stunted growth was the best way to avoid the mower blades. The maintenance crew were out repainting the black paddock fencing. I assume they have a job for life – there is mile upon mile of it. Happy to be distracted they give me a friendly wave, unconcerned at who I might be.

For a while they were the only souls I saw as I drove around what I assumed was New Abbey. One private road branched into another. I came across a large stable block deserted of both people and horses. In the distance I saw a 4x4. Ah, I thought, I have either been rumbled or someone has come to find me. But it veered away, speeding in the opposite direction. Eventually, I came into a cul-de-sac of farm sheds, a car park for tractors, balers, trailers and mowers. Stacks of golden straw bales stood ready. The soft green hay smelled sweet. Used straw was gently rotting in tidy bays. Wherever I was, I had clearly reached its furthest extent. And then it struck me. For the past half hour, I had seen all those things you might associate with horses: paddocks, stables, food and bedding. But of the horses themselves I had not seen a single one. With that I concluded I must truly be in the wrong place.

It was time to head off, but that 4x4 had a different plan as it had returned to seek me out, the two of us drawing to a halt, the road too narrow to pass, driver door to driver door. As we buzzed down our respective windows I expected some kind of almighty bollocking for my trespass. Instead, a hand shot out in greeting, 'You must be Simon. I'm Barry. Sorry about that earlier. Saw you but then had a small emergency. Didn't think you'd come to any harm.' This was Barry Mahon.

As we chatted, I felt impelled to ask, why no horses? Barry seemed to think this the funniest question in the world, providing the less than helpful reply, 'Well, it is nearly May.' I have to confess that didn't help me much. I'd have thought May was the perfect time for a stud farm to have horses. But apparently not and, as is the case for so much in the Juddmonte empire, there is an astoundingly logical explanation.

Prince Khalid has owned New Abbey Stud for a long while; he bought it back in 1990. It is worth saying to avoid any confusion that New Abbey Stud is not a commercial stallion operation like Banstead Manor Stud. It is, in another meaning of the word, a collection of horses belonging to one person, in this case more of a horse rearing farm.

If you ever have the chance to visit you will notice, like I did, that it is laid out in a seemingly random fashion. At the top end, and highest point, you have the main house, a small Georgian mansion, offices and the fillies' stable block. But as for the remaining 550 acres the roads snake here, there and everywhere, skirting around clumps of century-old oaks. The paddocks are random in size and shape. The stable blocks are in unexpected places. I suspect if Capability Brown, landscape gardener to the eighteenth-century

English aristocracy, who bent his design to the will of the landscape, had ever designed a horse farm this is what it would have looked like.

But this wasn't created by any fancy designer but rather herds of beef cattle who were given the run of the estate by the previous owner, Mrs Kenneth Urquhart. She didn't believe in fencing. This was free-range cattle ranching Irish style. And cattle being what they are they have a sixth sense for picking out the driest ground, so they created the paths which later became roads. The trouble is, nobody ever told the cattle that the shortest route between two points is a straight line ... It is all very random. However, New Abbey works so well not due to its haphazard layout but because the land is dry and free draining, sitting as it does on a sandy base. Combine that with the temperate Irish climate and you have the perfect winter quarters for growing foals who do best if they are able to live outside. There is a flip side; from May onwards the ground is too hard and the grass too sparse so everyone ships out. It is perfect logic once you know it, which is why I guess Barry laughed at my question.

After Kind had been pronounced in-foal to Galileo for the second time, she and Frankel had travelled to New Abbey for a six-week layover en route back to Banstead Manor. John Glennon, the stud groom, remembers the three-month-old Kind colt (he is one of those who still refers to Frankel that way) as one of just a small band he had passing through that spring. But he recalls Frankel in a way you might not expect, because as John says, 'good horses have a knack of not needing very much'. So, as one of a group of six mares and foals, Frankel passed largely under the New Abbey radar, spending twenty-two of twenty-four hours a day out in a paddock. In the morning, they were led in for a couple of hours but for the most part that May and June was spent outdoors.

Like all colts Frankel was boisterous and fun, enjoying a life of freedom under the watchful eye of mother. He had already passed peak milk at two months of age when he'd have been suckling at Kind twenty-plus times each day to take the thirty-two pints (yes, four gallons) of milk he needed to keep him on what John describes as the 'heavy side', the perfect condition for a growing foal. The volume, large though it may seem – imagine four good-sized buckets – is actually not such a dramatic increase on his first week of life when he was already taking twenty-four pints a day. But now he is drinking water and eating solid food. At first, he picked at Kind's food. Then he was given a double handful of his own oats each day. Gradually, his nutrient intake becomes more solids than milk. By the time Frankel leaves New Abbey, taking the lead from his mother as he does on so many things, he is foraging on the paddock grass for half the day, his dependence on his mother's milk gradually diminishing. And that is how it has to be, because as the pair return to Banstead Manor in late June, Frankel has just another three weeks at her side. For he is about to experience what has the potential to be the most traumatic time in his young life. Weaning. The separation of mother and foal.

In the wild, Kind and Frankel would have stayed together for almost a year, more or less up to the day Kind's next foal was born. It is true that by that point the bond would have been more emotional than physical, the requirement to suckle long gone. But nonetheless it demonstrates how against the grain of nature our human-imposed separation in his sixth month of life is.

In times gone past, weaning was almost seen as a rite of passage. A dramatic moment when, without warning or preparation, foal and mother were separated. The mare would be moved out of earshot. The foal confined to a stable which was sometimes shuttered dark. It was traumatic for both. The mare whinnying in distress. Sometimes attempting to jump or break down fencing to return to her foal. Pawing at the ground. Rushing from one corner of the paddock to the next in search of a foal that was not there. The foal in turn would cry. Kick out against the sides of the box. Become frantic in attempts to free him or herself. This might last for days. Anything up to a week. Not eating. Until exhaustion and hunger dulled the memory. Fortunately, there are gentler, kinder ways.

Our pair returned from Ireland as the last of the crowds had deserted Royal Ascot. It was high summer. The time of year when the days are longer than the nights. Darkness rarely complete. The night times inky blue rather than dark black. The morning dew reveals the dawn tracks of the eight – four mares, four foals – as they graze the Banstead Manor grass. But the time for mother and son is soon to end. The final seperation, weaning, was just a few days away.

The truth is that weaning is as much social as it is physical. The food bond is already tenuous; 95 per cent of Frankel's protein is from hard food. The foals and mares have split from one mutually supporting, cohesive group into two. Foals in one. Mares in another. Mother and son are spending less and less time together. They have, without knowing it, made it easy on themselves. On 17 July, the day arrived.

Jim and Ed had already picked out the two foals for that warm, summer morning; as they say, the oldest and the boldest. Frankel was decidedly both. The plan, as followed a thousand times before, was to distract the foals with breakfast and lead the two respective mares away. It was something the foals had become well used to. Oftentimes their mothers had departed in this fashion. The difference today was that they would never return.

And Kind did not return. Sometimes the foals do take fright, running up and down the paddock rail, whinnying as they go. This kinder separation is not always perfect. But for Frankel the moment came and went without a murmur. At 150 days of age, he was on his own.

6

The Pick

It was mid-September when Frankel returned alone to Ireland and New Abbey Stud; he would not return to England for another sixteen months. The dry summer had broken, with mist and rain a daily occurrence. The cracks in the arid Kildare ground were healing. The hardness was becoming soft. The grass was growing again. Life was slowly returning to New Abbey as the cohorts of weanlings arrived by sea and horse box from the many outposts of the Juddmonte empire. The work was just starting for stud groom John Glennon and the New Abbey team that numbers just a dozen. They would have until the spring to turn one hundred of these tall, gawky and uncertain individuals into confident, strong yearlings that could in turn be broken in, readied for training proper to compete on the racecourses of Europe.

We have to be honest here. Frankel did not depart from Banstead Manor Stud with a special asterisk by his name. The crew at New Abbey Stud didn't line up to see him walk down the ramp of the box. That is not to say he wasn't well thought of; nobody as yet had reason to question that 7+ rating. He was clearly, as they all say with terrific understatement, a 'nice colt', readily regarded as one of the better members of his generation. But, and I don't want you to think I am accusing anyone of cynicism, they had seen it all before. The slightly sad thing about raising horses is that so many flatter to deceive. Bred in the pink. Raised in the most perfect manner. With confirmation and looks to die for. However, until you put a rider up and ask the question of a horse … well, it is all hope, dreams and speculation. And that question was all still a year away.

Weanling – it is a great word. For me, it evocatively sums up that half a year between being weaned and becoming a yearling. That time when foals have both the innocence of youth and the frame for the perfect athlete. For at this moment, Frankel is already at 80 per cent of his mature height but he is still slight. Look at him head on and his shoulders are narrow; he sort of tapers backwards to his hind quarters. His legs remain impossibly spindly, the knee joints exaggeratedly large. From the side, he is more of the horse he will become, with his deep chest and powerful rear end already apparent. He might be eight-tenths his eventual height but he is still only half his final adult weight. It is a small body in a big space. And all is wrapped in that soft brown coat with fuzzy-furred ears, wispy black mane and a stubby tail that would look more in place on a fox.

Frankel was one of the early arrivals that autumn, largely by virtue of the fact that he was a February birth, so a few months advanced of those who might have been born as late as May. One companion on the journey from Banstead Manor was a bay filly, born just four days after him, who was to race as Exemplify. She didn't scale great heights in a four-race career in France, but she stayed within the Juddmonte fold as a successful broodmare and is the dam of Breeders' Cup Mile winner, Expert Eye.

As one of the first groups to arrive, there was no great method as to where Exemplify and Frankel were put. As it turned out, they were in the Newtown Villa Yard which is the most isolated of the three stable blocks, at almost the furthest extremity of New Abbey in a quiet glade of tall beech trees. However, as September rolled into October and then became November, New Abbey was filling up; it was time for division. Exemplify as a filly headed to the yard by the main house. Frankel, as befitted his 7+ status, took up his place in Box 21 of the Green Field Yard, the stables reserved for the best twenty-five colts of the Prince Khalid crop for that year.

Did he recognise what was to be his home for the next six months? The long rectangle of boxes. The tall entrance arch topped by a clock tower. The concrete rendered walls, framed by lichened, faded yellow brickwork. The brown paint of the stable doors. My guess is yes. Horses tend to remember the familiar, for it was only back in June that he had been lodged in the Green Field Yard with Kind.

And the routine would not have been so radically different. Turned out all day, every day, regardless of the weather with a group of similarly matched colts in Paddock 12d which is just out the front of the Green Field Yard. The only difference is now that with winter approaching, they'd be coming in at night to what must be said would turn out to be the perfect box for Frankel. He is without a doubt an inquisitive horse. He likes to be amid the hustle and bustle. Activity stimulates his brain. He likes to observe the comings and goings of the yard: human, equine and mechanical. And Box 21, located in the corner by the main thoroughfare was, by happy accident, ideal.

I stood for a while in Box 21 to get some sense of how Frankel saw the world as he grew from weanling to yearling. I can see how he might have liked it. Leaning out from his stable door, he has a panoramic view to just about every other stall in the yard. Across and opposite is the hub of Green Field; the tack, feed and lads tea room. It gives him great delight to see buckets of food en route, a gentle tap-tap of his hoof against the tin lining on the inside of his door a reminder that he should be first in line. The box itself is large, about 16 square metres, with the lower part of the walls to horse shoulder height painted dark green, the remainder white to a vaulted, varnished wood ceiling. In opposite corners are his feed bin and a self-filling water trough. The door frame goes full height, floor to high ceiling, with a window above it that pivots for ventilation. But most of all, with the top half of the stable door permanently open and with windows both back and sides, I was struck by how incredibly bright and airy it is. The back window looks onto an estate road (yet more activity to eye up) and then directly onto Paddock 12d and the fields beyond. The side windows, which are called companion windows, are actually barred openings that allowed Frankel direct contact – sight, noise, smell and touch – with his neighbours to the left and right. As John Glennon, the stud groom, reminded me, horses are herd animals; they crave the companionship of each other and will grow up better horses for it.

It was the simplicity of life at New Abbey that was so striking to me. Wake up. Have some food. Spend the day with your mates outside. Watch the world go by. Come in at dusk. More food. Lie down in a deep bed of golden barley straw. Wake up and do it all the next day with equal pleasure. Horses don't seem to resent what humans might see as the monotony of the same routine day in day out. Indeed they seem to relish it. And so the team at New Abbey pander to this. It is all about allowing these young colts to naturally grow and develop into themselves.

Frankel's growth spurt of the first sixth months of his life with Kind is slowing down, from two to three pounds of weight gain each day to about a pound. Counter-intuitively, the quantity of food measured in sheer poundage increases as the pure protein of milk is replaced by roughage; when Frankel arrived he was on three pounds a day of Juddmonte Special. When he leaves he will be on ten pounds, plus a square of hay morning and evening, with as much water as he wishes to drink. The one thing everyone will agree on about Frankel is that he loves his food. It was then, and remains now, the highlight of his day. He eats far more than any horse of equivalent age or weight, a quarter to a third more food than a regular racehorse. But it is not gluttony. You would never have called him fat. He clearly just has a metabolism that burns up the calories.

I don't entirely blame him for tucking into the coarse mix which at first sight I thought I'd happily take as my breakfast muesli. It is a mixture of rolled oats, corn, peas, grains and supplements with bright yellow sweetcorn kernels that shine with the slick, sweet molasses that gives any handful that gorgeous sense that if-I-don't-eat-this-I'd-be-insane. Actually, it looks and smells better than it tastes, but I'm not a horse.

You'll notice that there is no mention of exercise in the New Abbey day. That is because there is none, at least not in any formal training sense. The most any of the horses would experience at a human hand would be the fifty yards on a lead rein from stable to paddock. I must admit this surprised me. But the fact is that too much exercise is detrimental to the growing colt. What they do is up to them. All exercise is self-exercise and indeed, they do take off around the 12 acres of Paddock 12d, cantering and skittering about, but all or any effort is entirely of their choosing.

So if New Abbey isn't about training, what is it all about? If you talk to John Glennon it is very much about building a strong, fit, well-balanced yearling with a good temperament. He is very clear about the latter. 'You can't', he says, 'have a great horse without a good temperament.'

Does he remember Frankel? Of course. From the day he arrived, when John rated the 'Kind colt' for size, shape, walk and pedigree, he had him noted down as an exceptionally physically strong colt. You'll sometimes hear it said that Frankel was always pushing himself to the head of the queue. Always wanting to be the first. But John recalls him differently: stand-offish and apart from the rest. But what all the New Abbey team agree on was that Frankel was no trouble. No sickness. No injury. No bad habits or incidents. He just sailed through his time in the Kildare countryside unremarked, his 7+ status intact. As Dominic, the horse box driver who ferried Frankel around Ireland and across the Irish Sea says with both pride and admiration, he was 'remarkably unremarkable'.

As the clock in the tower above the Green Field Yard struck midnight to mark the arrival of the New Year, Frankel was now officially a one-year-old. A yearling. This may seem a little odd for a horse who was actually only ten months and seventeen days old when measured by his true 11 February birthdate, but all thoroughbreds registered in the northern hemisphere *General Stud Book* are deemed to have their birthdays on 1 January, regardless of whether they were born in January or June. (It is, by the way, 1 August in the southern hemisphere.) As you may well imagine, this artificial age construct has an impact on the progression of horses through their two- and three-year-old careers in much the same way that a summer-born child is perceived as being disadvantaged by the timings of the academic year. All that said, it probably evens itself out in the end, with April or May foals and mothers making up for lost ground with the benefit of young grass and better weather. On a human scale, an August birthday didn't seem to hold back a certain Barack Obama. If you are good enough you will succeed regardless, which is more than proved by Frankel's great-grandfather Northern Dancer. He who won the Kentucky Derby and Preakness Stakes after a success-ful two-year-old season, going on to become one of the most influential stallions of modern times. And all that after being one of the latest of the late, born on 27 May.

The odd thing about Frankel in this first period of his life, from birth to coming of yearling age, was that though he was notionally under the care of Juddmonte, he wasn't really owned by anyone. By virtue of a rather unusual my-mares-for-your-stallion exchange between Coolmore and Juddmonte, Frankel was one of seven foals occupying a sort of ownership limbo land, awaiting a decision as to their fate. This is how the day of the Pick arrived.

There are a great many threads to Frankel's life and eventual success, but part of both the thrill and difficulty of writing this book is that so much of his life beyond the racecourse has gone unrecorded until now. That's for many reasons, not least because nobody foresaw the future and as a result there is, for instance, not a single photo of Frankel at New Abbey Stud. It is also because Prince Khalid runs a very understated operation that discourages too much hullaballoo. Of course, Frankel was always marked down as a 'nice colt', as they like to say, but he wasn't singled out for special attention; all Juddmonte foals are lavished in equal measure with love, care and attention.

Much of this was down to Philip Mitchell. Today Philip is retired, living on the outskirts of Newmarket; he relinquished his post as general manager of Juddmonte Farms three years after Frankel's last race, having been with the Prince since the early days. He has, in common with the horse he created, the perfect pedigree for the career he pursued. Brought up in a horse breeding family, Philip's résumé reads like a racing *Who's Who*: Sir Victor Sassoon, a stint at Normandy Farm in Kentucky, Captain Marcos Lemos and the Duke of Devonshire are just some of the great owner-breeders he worked for before arriving at Banstead Manor Stud in the 1990s.

One of the great delights of working for an owner-breeder is that you are planning for the long term. Less prone to the fashions and fads that sometimes sweep horse racing. Insulated from some of the pressures of commercial breeders. Able, in the case of Juddmonte, to build up over many decades a band of mighty home-bred brood-mares and stallions. Have the satisfaction of knowing that the horse standing in front of you is the result of a bloodline that you have helped create over many generations. But, for all the benefits and satisfactions, no stud farm exists within a vacuum. From time to time you have to look outside for new blood. Experiment as you probably did in the early days.

When the idea of the Coolmore–Juddmonte swap was first floated, it seemed the perfect solution for both sides – the intermingling of the bloodlines of two of the great global breeding operations, without a penny piece passing hands. Prince Khalid would provide the mares and John Magnier the stallions. It suited Juddmonte because the likes of Galileo commanded a stud fee they would prefer not to pay, while Coolmore would end up owning a group of foals from broodmares to whom they would otherwise be denied access. I suspect, though it has never been said, that there was another element at play – the what-if factor. The pure possibility and the sheer randomness of the selection process that gave the whole arrangement a certain frisson.

For this was the essence of the deal: each year Prince Khalid sent a group of his mares, of his choosing, to be covered by a single Coolmore stallion, with the resultant offspring split 50–50 between the two operations. Now foal sharing, where you supply the dam or stallion and I provide the other component part, with the resultant horse racing in our joint names, is fairly common. But where this particular arrangement departs from the norm is that outright ownership of each yearling was granted by way of an alternate picking process whereby one side had first pick of the crop, the other second and so on. If the matings had resulted in an odd number of offspring, that final one would have indeed been a foal share. In the first year of the deal, when twelve Juddmonte mares went to Sadler's Wells, Coolmore had first pick. In the second year, Frankel's year, when ten Juddmonte mares went to Coolmore (only seven produced a live foal), that first pick fell to Juddmonte.

You will often hear it said and written that Frankel would, but for the fate of the Pick, been an Aidan O'Brien horse, trained at Ballydoyle in Ireland. And had that been the case, might he have achieved as much, or perhaps even more? Of course we can never know, but what does seem certain is that Frankel the foal and yearling would also have been top of the Coolmore list. But they were content with their second choice, a Montjeu-Prove (Kind's paddock mate) colt who was to be called Malinowski, a horse who was never to set foot on a racecourse. But they weren't alone in admiration for this colt – Philip Mitchell freely admits that he thought a lot of him. But more than Frankel?

Try to put yourself in the shoes of Prince Khalid and the Juddmonte team that January. This decision has been two years in the making. You have before you a list of foals sired by some of the best stallions in the world, to mares you have known since birth. Numerous expert opinions have been sought. Data and reports have been analysed. Many discussions have been had. But in the end it is down to a few to divine the future. To commit to paper a list that ranks the crop from one to seven on which Prince Khalid would have the final say. And sometimes history turns on the smallest of details.

Philip was well placed to advise the Prince. After all, it was he who had drawn up the original list of mares to send to Coolmore, though ironically he admits that had the team known then quite what a superb broodmare Kind was to become, she may well have never gone, remaining instead at Banstead Manor to be covered by one of the home stallions. But, and such is the happenchance of Frankel's very existence, being young and yet to have her offspring tested on the racecourse, Kind had made the list.

Philip was also the only person to have seen Frankel at every stage of his life. First a few days after his birth. Then in Ireland. Then at Banstead Manor. And then back in Ireland again. For Philip's job was to continually assess the Juddmonte European crop. And that is not something you can do by Facetime. You have to get on a plane. Look at the horse. Talk to the people. Make judgements. And every six weeks that is precisely what he did.

The reports were unwavering. There was never any questioning of Frankel's 7+ status – remember, in Juddmonte terms this is as good as it gets – but it is the words that stand out for me: Strong. Uncomplicated. Correct. Good walker. Straightforward, ordinary colt. Looks to have speed. (How prescient was that?) Nothing wrong with him.

Taken at face value these might not sound like a ringing endorsement – hardly the stuff of champions – but you have to understand the reports tend to highlight flaws. Weaknesses. Things that need attention. And neither do you, as the reporter, want to make outrageous claims. Hype is discouraged. The simple fact is that Frankel was essentially the ideal horse. Now whether that would translate onto the racecourse, nobody as yet knew. The worst Philip wrote was 'not matured yet'.

When I press Philip as to whether he always thought Frankel was something special, I can see he is conflicted. To say yes seems immodest. Boasting with the benefit of hindsight. But I can see in his body language, and the way he carefully phrases the reply, that that is the truth. 'It was the way he walked,' said Philip, 'moving effortlessly and quickly from where he is to where he wants to be in the blink of an eye. I'd never seen anything like it before. Or since. Rather like …' We both struggled for an analogy, finally arriving at a panther, but we both know this is inadequate. Frankel moves like Frankel, with a fluidity of action and power you will never see in any other horse.

So when it came to the Pick, it was, without doubt or demur, Frankel.

It always had been.

7

In training for training

If New Abbey is the primary school where everyone plays nice, then Ferrans, where Frankel arrived in late April, is the tough comprehensive. The way it looks tells you that. There is none of the splendid architecture of Banstead Manor or the rural idyll of New Abbey. It is unadorned, still very much the place Prince Khalid had bought thirty years before. A complex of functional stables, barns and offices to house a hundred-plus yearlings. This is the nuts and bolts end of the bloodstock industry. More like the type of racing stable in which Frankel will eventually end up: functional rather than fancy. For that is essentially what Ferrans is: the training stable to life in training. It has a parade ring. It has a round course. It has a straight course. It has starting stalls. It is a bit of a cross between a small racecourse and a big racing yard. All this set in 694 acres of Meath countryside an hour north of New Abbey.

Actually, the first few months at Ferrans were not exactly boot camp for Frankel – more an extension of life before. Out all day. In at night. Grazing on the summer grass with a similar diet to New Abbey but now rising to 16 lb a day, split between a 5 am and 4 pm feed. It is a prodigious amount of food; next time you are in a super-market, eye up twenty or so boxes of cereal. The routine was only broken by the monthly farrier visits or a check over from the vet, but there were few concerns. Like all yearlings departing New Abbey, he had undergone thirty-two x-rays; would that all people have such care.

But this easy life had to end eventually. On 1 September, Frankel entered a four-month period in what was to be the most critical phase in his life. Breaking in.

The phrase 'breaking in' has unfortunate connotations. The idea that the will of a horse has to be broken so it might do the bidding of its human masters. Wild West films don't help. Celluloid depictions of a Marlboro-style cowboy who steps up to lasso a mustang to the ground, straps a saddle to its back, forces a bit between the jaws and rides it until, sweating and exhausted, the horse is subjugated forever more. The truth is different. There is no earthly point to breaking the spirit of a horse, thoroughbred or otherwise. The purpose of breaking in, if we choose to persist with the phrase, is that by way of persuasion and encouragement, a horse is trained to exploit that very facet of his or her character.

Rory Mahon, father of Barry at New Abbey, has been at Ferrans for over forty years. In that time with Prince Khalid and the previous owner, close on 5,000 yearlings have passed through his hands. It is fair to say that he has seen them all: the great, the merely average and the downright terrible. 'Can you tell from day one?' I ask. Rory shakes his head but with a knowing smile utters a single word. 'November'.

The first thing Frankel noticed on that first day of September was that his routine had changed; now he was in all day and out at night. Box number 5 wasn't as spacious as his box at New Abbey, with its much lower ceiling. But it was fine, with a long rectangular window along the back wall that let in plenty of light, not that the view, a line of trees, was much to shout about. However, from his stable door he looked straight up to a bustling yard of thirty boxes. A pair of stable hands were gradually working their way in his direction, lifting a head collar from the hook on the outside wall before opening each brown stable door in turn, emerging a few minutes later.

Frankly, he didn't think it seemed very interesting – there was no food involved and intrusions into his box were a regular feature of life. Usually it was just one person, which at least broke the routine. Someone to watch and assess. Other times, with the vet or farrier or some sort of inspection, they crowded in three or four strong. This could be a little annoying. If he lifted his rear leg, twitching it fast out and backwards, that was usually warning enough. They'd back off. Give him some more space. More respect. But on the whole he was well used to being handled. Groomed. His teeth inspected. His feet picked up. More of the same, he guessed.

But today they came into his box with a head collar that was different to the one he was wearing; the replacement had rings attached either side of the noseband which were in turn connected by a steel bar. As one of the stable hands slipped off his head collar, the other held what was in fact, though Frankel didn't know it, a bridle up to his head. The metal bit was in the flat of his hand; he pressed the steel against Frankel's lips. At first he resisted but the cold taste of the metal made him curious, opening first his lips, then his mouth before letting it slide between his teeth. The stable hand put the headpiece over his ears, adjusted the buckles, slid his fingers under each leather strap and when he was satisfied that the fit was snug, patted Frankel on the neck by way of a well done. And then they left him to it.

For a while the straight metal bar of the bit felt big in his mouth as he ran his tongue along, around, over and under it. Soon he discovered that by way of his teeth and tongue he could move it up, down, sideways, forward and back. It was by no means unpleasant. Intriguing in fact, and once Frankel found the right position in his mouth he found how he was able to drink and chew hay. A few hours later, one of the stable hands returned to remove the bit and bridle. Bizarrely, it took as long to get used to its absence as it had its presence. He thought that a little odd.

The following day it was more of the same, but when the stable hand returned it was not to remove the bit and bridle but lead Frankel out of his box, past his companions who hung out of their boxes watching his clip-clop progress over the rough concrete pathway until he disappeared out of sight through the arched entrance. This was out of the ordinary. He rarely went anywhere alone. Ahead was a big shed.

It took a while to get used to the dusty gloom inside this cavernous barn. You'd easily fit a half a football pitch inside. It is hardly pretty: breeze block walls with a greying asbestos roof supported by rusted metal trusses. The dull morning light was supplemented by white fluorescent lights that did nothing to enhance the scene. The floor, a deep carpet of brown chipped wood bark, absorbed all sound, sucking up any audible trace of Frankel's steps as he was led to the centre of the arena.

The stable hand removed the leading rein and replaced it with a lunging rein, stepping back eight or ten paces, paying it out as he went. 'Walk on' came the command and a memory stirred deep inside Frankel's head. Not of this place but of somewhere similar with his mother, when he trotted beside her as they went in circles. He obeyed. Enjoying the sensation. Stretching out his legs. Feeling his muscles working. Leaning into the curve. Pressing his hooves into the bark. After five minutes they stopped, reversed direction and did the same two or three times further. Frankel headed back to his box with a light sweat. He liked that.

The lunging sessions continued through to the following week with the addition of what they call breaking tack: a roller plus side reins. Imagine a giant belt that is secured over the back, under and around the belly. Fixed to it are D-rings to which reins are attached that are in turn buckled to the bridle. As Frankel first walked, then trotted, the side reins held his head in check. His neck slightly arched. At first the reins were loose, the bit in turn loose in his mouth. But each day the reins were shortened, applying more pressure. Control was gradually being asserted.

The lunging only held so much interest for Frankel. He got it. Week three was far better. The lunge rein was replaced by long reins for walking around the roads and tracks of Ferrans with the stable hand behind as if 'driving' him, pony and trap fashion, along. They went out for an hour each day, regardless of the weather. Rain. Wind. Watery October sunshine. Frankel loved them all. Aside from food, exercise was his thing. A chance to prove his mettle. He pulled the lad along in his wake; control is sometimes a two-way street.

At the end of that week, Frankel was feeling particularly good about himself when they returned from an exceptionally long reining session; for once it was he who was exhausted. Into the box came another of the stable hands, and while one held him by the head, the other grasped the top of the saddle and with the aid of a leg-up was suddenly sitting on Frankel. Before he could react the trio were on the move for a few quick turns around the box before the rider hopped off. Frankel didn't know quite what to make of it. It was neither natural nor normal. He guessed it was something he would have to get used to; he was coming to understand how these processes worked.

* * *

There are twenty-two riders at Ferrans. They are, for the most part, ex-jockeys, strong and capable. They need to be because yearlings range from the downright surly and unwilling to the flighty and dangerous. They are each over 1,000 lb of lithe flesh that can accelerate to 35 mph or more in the blink of an eye. Lash out with razor-edged hooves. Smash paddock rails. Kick holes in stable doors. Rear up. Spin round. Not because they are inherently bad or evil. But because they are young. Untrained. High-octane animals. Unused to what is expected of them.

You don't see many young faces among the riders at Ferrans. It seems to be the job you arrive at when most other avenues for your skills have been exhausted, but you still need that daily fix of the raw, untrammelled energy of a thoroughbred horse beneath you. The conversations between mounted riders (they seem to talk incessantly) come in many tongues. Today, it is largely a few Irish and a mix of eastern Europeans. In Frankel's time, before the European Union changed the rules, the mix was far more international with riders from Asia, North America, the Antipodes and South America. That is how it was an Argentinian called Miguel that came to be Frankel's rider.

There was no particular reason why Miguel and Frankel were paired; it was just a random chance. But from the moment he entered the box on 10 October with a saddle over his arm, it would just be the Kind colt and the Argentinian from now on. The saddle and girth didn't feel so different to the roller. The arrival of a man on his back was expected. A couple of minutes walking around the box. The routine. The experienced hands of Miguel applying pressure and direction through the reins and bit until he straightened Frankel up, applied pressure with his legs and on the final rotation pointed him towards the open door. As Miguel ducked to avoid the lintel Frankel was, almost three months short of his true second birthday, being ridden. As a computer printout of the Ferrans Farm manager report blandly states: 'Broken and riding on 5 October 2009.'

As you have gathered, this whole process is gradual. Frankel didn't suddenly go from his box to lighting up the gallops. As Rory says, 'They are only babies. They aren't strong or mature enough to take much work.' It is all about avoiding too much pressure on their limbs. At first, it is just half an hour each day, figure of eights and a gentle trot around the indoor arena. Then they move outside to the outdoor ring. More figure of eights. Then to a large paddock to move on grass. But all this more about education rather than exercise.

By the time November comes, Frankel is on the way to becoming a racehorse. He starts cantering on the all-weather gallop. He is in his box all the time. He is trace clipped to reduce sweating, his winter coat trimmed in a horizontal band along his body above the legs, below the saddle line and beneath the neck. He is shod for the first time. He has a sheet, a light blanket, on at night to keep him warm. Each day work (the first time we use this word in the context of his life) is a mile at a steady canter in single file, the horses a horse length apart, learning how to follow. A different horse takes the lead each day. They all walk through a set of starting stalls every morning. As Rory says, this is the time you start to see signs of those that might not make it, be that through temperament, breathing problems or soundness.

He had no such doubts of Frankel. He even briefly moved him up to a 7++ in the 24 November report that read, 'Well balanced, athletic colt. Stands on good limbs. Walks okay. Good to follow. Pretty correct. Nice colt.' Good to follow means that when you watch a horse walk from behind you see an easy walker with good hind quarters. The work was tuning Frankel's body. He lost 60 lb between the October and November reports to weigh in at 1,106 lb, the weight at which he was to go into training. He had put on just 260 lb in his yearling year.

If November is the month that you see Rory's fissures, then December is when the cracks truly appear. Immaturity. Leg problems. Attitude. Joints and knees. Any issues the x-rays of March revealed, that you hoped time might cure, haven't gone away. But the better ones are flourishing. As Rory says, the more work you do with them the more they thrive. They are now up to four miles a day: two miles cantering and galloping, four circuits around the tight turns of the all-weather round course. Two miles a day walking to warm down.

As Christmas looms it is time to make a list; in January, as freshly minted two-year-olds, the most forward of the crop would leave for Prince Khalid's trainers around Europe. Frankel was always in that advance pack. 'Sound from the very first day he was ridden', says Rory. 'Very good action. Wonderful temperament. The sort of horse who never gave you any trouble. Ironically,' and he gives me that smile again, 'he was the one that came to your notice least as he gave you so little trouble.'

So in early December, Teddy Grimthorpe, Juddmonte's racing manager, prepared a report on all of the yearlings for Prince Khalid and the Prince allocated these horses to trainers. By January the first dozen were ready to move and as you would expect, Frankel was among them: he was on his way back to England.

On 14 January, Miguel slid off Frankel's back for one last time after the morning work. He'd be leaving soon as well, back to Argentina before heading to the United States where he is a work rider today. Frankel had passed the vet; health checked with an endoscope and blood tests to ensure he had no infections. To pass on a virus, which can lay low a racing stable for weeks or months on end, is as sloppy as horse management gets. Rory likes to see his horses leave buff, fit, well and ready. Suited and booted. Frankel is shod and clipped.

Late in the afternoon Dominic arrives with the lorry; by lunchtime tomorrow they will be in Newmarket. As Frankel mounts the ramp, he is leaving the country that he'd have every right to call home. But not any longer, for he will never return.

8

A horse by a very special name

In sport there are names that require little explanation. Lord's. St Andrews. The Kop. Wimbledon. Twickenham. Wembley. Names that instantly take you to that place. The smell and hue almost tangible. Epic matches. Towering achievements. People long gone from this world. Places where the joy of victory has erased the memory of past defeats. For horse racing, Warren Place is one such destination.

It sits on one of the highest points above Newmarket, the gallops of the Heath rolling down to the town that looks small in the distance. Further still, the stands of the racecourses are specks on the horizon. In the summer the stables capture the sun. In winter the chill winds, fresh from the North Sea, arrive unimpeded across the flat East Anglian farmlands.

Henry Cecil had come to Warren Place by way of marriage. His first wife Julie was the daughter of Noel Murless, one of the training greats of the postwar era. He owned Warren Place from 1952 when he moved to Newmarket from Beckhampton in Wiltshire, where in one of those many racing interconnections, Roger Charlton, a trainer for Prince Khalid and a Classic winner in his own right, had charge of Frankel's mother Kind.

Henry may have not been bred to be a trainer (his father died fighting in North Africa in World War II, six weeks before he was born) but he was certainly raised to be a trainer. His stepfather was Cecil Boyd-Rochfort who vied with Noel Murless in the late 1950s for the title of Champion British trainer. Henry's upbringing was typical of the time for someone whose mother was the daughter of a baronet: private schools in Berkshire and Canford public school in Dorset where horsemanship was on the curriculum. Then stints in various studs after school before completing his education at the Royal Agricultural College in Gloucestershire. Where did he go after that? Well, as Henry frequently admitted, he had no firm idea, so rather than the City or the Army he became an assistant to his stepfather who trained at Freemason Lodge, one of the prestige yards of Newmarket that today is home to one of the Queen's trainers, Sir Michael Stoute. In 1969, aged twenty-six, Henry Cecil struck out on his own.

Success came quickly. In that first year he had his inaugural Group 1 winner. The following year a Royal Ascot winner. Some of the most storied owner-breeders began to beat a path to his door. Not only was he apparently a brilliant trainer but he had a certain personal style that broke the mould. His clothing was Carnaby Street meets Savile Row. His interviews suggested a certain carelessness both in victory and defeat. He brought colour and excitement to the drab austerity of the 1970s. He was that rarity in horse racing – a name that drew recognition outside the sport. In 1975, he had his first English Classic winner. The upward trajectory seemed unstoppable when the following year Henry and Julie took over, and bought,

Warren Place Stables on the retirement of Noel Murless. That year, 1976, Henry was crowned Champion Trainer on the first of ten occasions.

For the next two and a bit decades, he was a permanent fixture in the highest firmaments of flat racing. His yard was filled for each season with over 200 of the best thoroughbreds the global racing industry could offer. He had on retainer the finest jockeys. To work at Warren Place, regardless of your position, was the apex of any racing career. Over twenty English Classics came his way. The big prizes, both home and overseas, filled the Warren Place trophy cabinet. In 1999, he won three of the five English Classics and was second in the remaining two. But that, it seemed, was to be the high water mark of Henry Cecil's training career. The dawn of a new millennium was not to be kind to him.

Plenty has been written, both in tabloid and broadsheet format, about Henry's Icarian descent, but the statistics alone will tell you enough: Warren Place went five seasons (2001–5) without a Group 1 winner. The yard was reduced to fifty horses. Henry struggled to make the top 100 trainer money list. In 2005, he won just a dozen races; in his heyday that could almost have been the tally for a single day. So, you may well ask, how is it that Frankel, the pick of the Coolmore/Juddmonte stables, ended up with Henry Cecil rather than any of the other many-talented trainers at Prince Khalid's disposal? It is about friendship, competitiveness and foresight.

Henry Cecil and the Prince went back a long way; they had shared their first winner together in 1983 with a horse called Adonijah ridden by Lester Piggott, and the first Classic in 1993 when Commander in Chief won the Derby at Epsom. Hundreds of Juddmonte foals had arrived at Warren Place over the intervening twenty-seven years. Some had been good. Some had been bad. Some world beaters. The pair had been together through the exultation of success and the misery of failed expectations. And in that time they had weaved a common thread; a knowledge of not just the horses that raced now but the generations that had brought them to this point. Horses the Prince had bred and Henry had trained. When they talked, and they often did, they referenced the past to determine the future.

It was clearly a special bond. The Prince regarded Henry as his friend. In the dark years of the early 2000s it was he who kept the Warren Place flame alight. At the nadir when the roll was barely fifty, most of those were Prince Khalid colts and fillies. And his unwavering support was to be rewarded.

For the mark of greatness in any endeavour is not how you fare when everything goes your way but rather in adversity. Henry did bring the glory days back to Warren Place. The assumption that his insouciance, that ability to accept victory and defeat with equal nonchalance, was the mark of a man without ambition, was stunningly wide of the mark. Henry hated what had happened to him. An interview with Chris McGrath for the *Independent* newspaper shortly before Frankel made it eight from eight at Goodwood in July 2011 vividly illustrates the point.

'I might not be [competitive] on the outside, but I am on the inside, definitely – underneath, very competitive. Always have been. We like winning, you know. We do like winning. It's what motivates you. Nobody likes failure. [When] Your horses are running badly, or they're no good, you get jealous of everybody else.' And with a typical Henry Cecil you-mustn't-take-too-seriously-the-serious-point-I-have-just-made, he added, 'It's not quite so much fun, is it?'

In 2007, Henry was back in the Classic winning enclosure when Light Shift won the Oaks; it was his twenty-fourth Classic. His next, and last, was to be with Frankel, for the stomach cancer that had plagued him in the mid-2000s never really left him and was to take hold again. He would die in June 2013, having seen Frankel to the end of his racing career.

If the friendship was that of the Prince and the competitiveness that of Henry, then what of the foresight? Well, that followed a suggestion made to Prince Khalid by Teddy Grimthorpe. It was in the wake of events that were happening thousands of miles away in California when on 16 November 2009, at about the time our Frankel was getting into serious work at Ferrans, the man he was to be named after, Robert 'Bobby' Frankel, died of leukaemia aged just sixty-eight.

If Henry Cecil was Prince Khalid's British ying, then Bobby Frankel was his American yang. As successful in the United States as Cecil was in the United Kingdom, Bobby is the second highest money-earning trainer of all time, with $228 million in purse money from 3,654 winners stretching back to 1966. At first glance, brought up in Brooklyn, New York the son of Jewish parents who ran a kosher catering business, there seems little reason why he should have risen to the top. If Cecil was brought up on the right side of the tracks for their chosen profession, Bobby Frankel certainly was not.

Bobby (he called himself Robert but nearly everyone called him Bobby) caught the racing bug from an early age when he went to the local New Jersey racetracks with his parents. Soon he was buying the racing papers, studying the form and trying to make a living betting at the tracks. As school and regular jobs went by the way, he became a hot walker at the Belmont Park track, the guy who cools down horses after exercise. Not only did this get him on the inside of the racing game, with all the gossip and information that came his way, but it gave him a free pass to the track; $3 saved on admission was $3 more to bet. In the early 1960s, he became an assistant to Buddy Jacobson, one of the leading New York trainers of the time, under whom he learned his trade before becoming a trainer in his own right.

Success wasn't immediate or perhaps planned. As Bobby said himself, 'Some fool gave me a horse to train.' In America it is not quite as hard to start out as a trainer as it is in the UK; the trainers are mostly based at the track. All the infrastructure is provided. All you need do is get a licence and apply for a stall, from one to an entire barn. Self-deprecation aside, as he clawed his way up the racing totem pole Bobby decamped one winter from the east coast to the west coast to race under the sun of Santa Anita. He liked it so much that in 1972 he moved to California where he was to train and live for the remainder of his life.

Bobby took to the gamble of buying horses. Placing them in races they could win. He won the mantle King of the Claimers. It suited his style and reflected his own upbringing. Seeing the potential in the underrated. Beating the odds. Tapping talent others had not seen. Claiming races are races where every horse is available for purchase prior to the start of the race at a price fixed by the conditions of the race. If you 'claim' a horse it effectively races in your name, you drive it away at the end of the day but the previous owner keeps the prize money. In the USA these races are the daily fare of regular race meetings, making up two-thirds of the races run but for less than a fifth of the prize money. They are, it must be said, the lowest grade in racing, but for someone with a sharp mind they are a pool of talent to be constantly trawled in what is effectively an ever-repeating fixed price auction.

Bobby Frankel wasn't alone in following the claiming path; plenty did then and do now, make a living that way. But what set him apart from others was his extraordinary strike rate – one winner in every three runners. Soon he came to the attention of more affluent owners such as Stavros Niarchos, who Henry Cecil also trained for, followed by, in 1990, Prince Khalid. It was to be a defining moment for both. The Jewish kid from Brooklyn saw it as such. 'Where in the world', he asked, 'do you get better bred horses than these?' But in the not-me-Guv style of Henry Cecil he added as to why it had happened, 'I was in the right place at the right time.' For that is the strange thing about the Cecil/Frankel axis; despite all their apparent differences they were quite similar.

Both were taciturn. Not always easy to talk to. Changing the subject midway through a sentence. More interested in the horses than the people that owned them. Both utterly driven by ambition. With echoes of that Henry comment about winning, Bobby said of and since his time as King of the Claimers, 'The thing then, and it will always be, was to win.' Neither particularly cared for convention; swimming against the tide gave them both an edge and satisfaction. One of the statistical absences from the horse Frankel's life is his weight. Most trainers weigh their horses on a regular basis; it is a good way of assessing health and condition, giving you data points as to how your horse is progressing physically. And once you have arrived at the perfect racing weight you are able to fine tune when coming back from a layoff or injury. But this was not Henry. I can only tell you Frankel's weight on the day he left Ferrans and on the day he arrived back at Banstead Manor two and a half years later. Bobby, never one to avoid colourful language, unwittingly summed it up for them both: '... you make your own judgements. I've heard things at the racetrack that have been passed down from era to era that are pure bullshit.'

It must be said that if Henry's owners were in awe of him, Bobby operated on an altogether different level; his were wary of him. Worried about getting on the wrong side of him. Not that it overly bothered him. One day, he was watching work at Hollywood Park with an owner, a well-respected heart surgeon, who proceeded to offer training advice. Bobby listened without comment. As they parted, Bobby shook the guy's hand, looked him in the eye and asked, 'By the way, would you let me do heart surgery on you?' Not sure where this was going the surgeon replied, 'No.' To which Bobby replied, 'Well then, don't tell me how to train your [insert expletive of your choice] horses.' I suspect there is many a trainer who might agree with that sentiment.

But despite his self-belief, and the support of Prince Khalid for whom he would eventually train all the US Juddmonte horses, sometimes the biggest prizes were elusive. At the Breeders' Cup, racing's equivalent of the Olympics, where over two days each November horses battle it out over fourteen races for $28 million in prize money, Bobby at one point stood at 36–0. In a seventeen-year losing streak of thirty-six runners, with zero winners, he finally broke his duck in 2001 with Squirtle Squirt at his racing *alma mater* Belmont Park. Not that he took the run of failure as an admission of failure. As he pointed out, of those thirty-six only one had started favourite back in 1993 and that one was beaten by, as Bobby described it, a 'freakish' 134–1 outsider. However the detail by which he remembers such things tells you something about the man.

Bobby Frankel was for both Prince Khalid, and for others, a phenomenally successful trainer. For Juddmonte he produced 507 wins over nineteen years with prize money totalling something in the region of $60 million. He was inducted in the American Racing Hall Fame. Twice leading trainer measured by prize money. Five times recipient of the Eclipse Award for Outstanding Trainer. The best way to put all that in some European context is to consider that his record of twenty-five Group 1 wins in a single season of 2003 stood until beaten by Aidan O'Brien in 2017.

So, when Prince Khalid had indicated in the immediate wake of Bobby Frankel's death that he wanted a horse to run the following season named after the trainer he most respected (he considered Henry Cecil a friend), the pressure was on.

But whichever horse was to be designated the Frankel name, Prince Khalid had let it be known that he was to be trained by Henry Cecil; a denouement to the lives of the two trainers who'd had such a profound impact on his racing empire. With the trainer picked, one half of the decision was in place. It now just simply fell to the team to pick the best horse. Divine the future. Avoid a dud. Find the horse who would be worthy of his namesake. It is to their enormous credit that they chose the Kind colt.

Stable staff are a competitive bunch. Everyone wants first pick of the arriving two-year-olds. But they, as much as Prince Khalid, Henry Cecil or anyone for that matter, are spinning the wheel of fortune. As the list of the incoming arrivals goes up on the office wall at Warren Place, the speculation begins. The guesswork. The jostling for position intensifies as arrival day approaches. Dee Deacon, Henry Cecil's head girl, the keeper of this particular deck of cards is variously cajoled, coerced and lobbied. In the end, it is she who deals out the selections. It is a big moment. The beginning of an intense relationship that can stretch for years. Every day the stable hand, be it man or woman, is the constant in the life of the racehorse. The smell. The sound. The habits. The touch. The morning greeting. The goodnight pat. Man and horse existing together in mutualistic symbiosis. It is a relationship where each benefits from the activity of the other.

Strangely, the still-to-be officially named Frankel (that would happen in May) didn't excite much comment or interest among the Warren Place stable hands. Clearly neither had news of the Coolmore/Juddmonte pick filtered through, nor that the racing manager had put his neck on the line. Others were preferred that had some bloodline or an association with previous Warren Place favourites. Continuity is popular. That constant reference to horses past. And Galileo was yet to become the stallion we know today. Kind was virtually unknown. True, her sole offspring to date, Bullet Train, was at Warren Place, but his only two-year-old race, a win the previous October in a minor maiden at Yarmouth, was good but hardly blew the doors off. Of course, he was to become the best lead horse in the world; Frankel's daily training companion at three and four, leading him up the gallops until his half-brother, one year his junior, put on the gas to pull away each and every time. If only they'd known what was to come, poor Dee Deacon would have been knocked down in the rush.

But they didn't. Nobody did. The only clue was the Departure Report of Rory Mahon that had travelled with Frankel from Ferrans. It read:

Broken and riding 5 of October 2009
Scopey, well balanced, athletic colt. Stands on good limbs. Good
mover.
Good temperament. Rides well. Nice colt.
Trots one mile
Steady canter one mile.
Has walked quietly through the starting stalls
No quarter sheets used.
Results of the blood sample taken are attached

In case you were wondering (as I was) a quarter sheet is a light blanket that covers the back and sides of a horse from the saddle to the tail to keep the horse warm and/or dry going to and from the gallops. So the note is a heads up that Frankel won't be used to cantering while wearing one.

Aside from this, I think you'd agree that the report was, as a clue to what was to come, not much of one. But as Frankel, still the Kind colt, was led down the ramp for forty-five minutes of walking to loosen his limbs after sixteen hours in the horse box, at least one person was impressed. And that wasn't Henry. At least not yet.

9

Warren Place

As you leave Newmarket and the Heath behind you travelling on the Moulton Road, you'd struggle to miss Warren Place on the left-hand side. The main stable block, long and redbrick with an imposing arch in the middle which is topped by a clock tower, faces the road, barely concealed behind a row of tall fir trees and stubby pleached limes.

To the right is a dusky-pink mock Tudor, faux Elizabethan house that would not look out of place in the Surrey commuter belt. It is looking a little sorry for itself. Clearly nobody lives it in now. It was once the home of Henry Cecil. To the left is an entrance flanked by what were originally Edwardian cottages with fancy brickwork and those high gable ends so typical of windswept East Anglia. They rise above the line of the slate roof, though these have fancy castellations that ladder upwards with the pitch of the roof.

Today the cottages are offices. You might, if you feel inclined, pull over, knock at the window and ask to see the box Frankel once lived in. Stand where he stood. Take in his daily view. Smell the straw that has seeped into the walls over generations. Wonder if the tooth marks on the door are those of the great one. Rub your hand along the greasy corner of the wall to take just a tiny fraction of him away with you. Admire the commemorative plaque on the wall that reads:

Frankel, the greatest horse
that ever raced, lived here.
15 January 2010–8 November 2012

Of course, you will take the obligatory selfie. Well, who wouldn't? Sadly, the truth is that no selfies will be taken. Not because you won't be allowed in (though you probably won't) but because his box has been demolished. Erased from history. Much has changed at Warren Place.

The best way to picture Warren Place as it was the day Frankel arrived, is from the air. Imagine a rectangle of land. What will strike you first with your bird's-eye view is the trees. About a third of the 20 or so acres that make up the main body of the place is thick woodland, the three sides other than the road screened from the wind by ragged pines that long outgrew their natural span. The cottages, entrances, main stable block and house that are ranged along the road hide a hotchpotch of buildings behind – more stable blocks, houses for the staff, the canteen, barns, exercise yards, steel caged paddocks, patches of grass, the horse walking machine, the indoor ride – all connected by what I might be tempted to describe as a spider's web of paths and roads if it was that logical. But they cross, turn and interweave every which way. It is clearly a working place. Built for horses, not show. You would never describe Warren Place as uber smart. This is no Banstead Manor. It is clean. It is tidy. But it is pared down to the essentials of horse training.

This is Frankel's new home. And as he and his companions on the journey from Ireland stood and unloaded from the box on that January day in 2010, Sandeep Gauravaram, along with assistant trainer Mike Marshall, were comparing his shortlist of two. Sandy, as everyone calls him, was short of a horse, his regular three reduced to two on a retirement. He had a fancy for a handicapper that had arrived but Henry had laughed at the idea. 'Why would you want a handicapper when you can have a Group horse? Hang on for a couple of weeks for the pick of the Prince's new arrivals.' It seemed wise advice and as Sandy reflects, 'All the Abdullah horses are bred in gold.'

Sandy, who had just turned thirty, had been with Henry for four years despite having only come initially for three months. He had been born and raised in India: racing had been his life since the age of thirteen and he'd been a race rider since seventeen. Hyderabad, the fourth largest city of the nation, was both his home and home track, which tends to be the way in India, the size of the country mitigating against moving between the tracks. And Sandy was good, becoming champion apprentice in 2001. But injuries set him back, which meant long periods off the track. A friend of his at Warren Place said he'd ask Henry if Sandy could come over for a working holiday. That was in 2006. I asked Sandy whether he'd ever considered returning to race riding. He laughed. He loved the English food and 'once you discover three meals a day your time as a jockey is over'. Though looking at his stick-thin build you'd never know it. And so he stayed, fortunate to always have good horses in what was clearly an easy and relaxed friendship with Henry.

His first impressions of Frankel? Of all the words Sandy ever said to me, the phrase that rings out was, 'All there.' He used it often. He was all there. Well built. Muscled. With something about him. As to the future? 'You don't expect a horse like Frankel.' Sandy's hopes seemed remarkably modest. Maybe some black type. When Sandy says this he means a horse that wins (or is placed) in a Listed or

Group race, the two highest classifications of race, the form from which is printed in bold black ink in a sales catalogue. Or trips to the good race meetings like Royal Ascot or Goodwood. 'It is pointless dreaming of a Classic winner', he said with a smile.

Much though he liked the other colt, it was always going to be Frankel. He immediately impressed. He was all there. Sandy recalls how he said to Mike Marshall, 'I'd like to do [racing speak for look after] the Kind colt.'

'I'll ask the Guv'nor this evening', came the reply.

So Sandy led Frankel on the weaving path to the grass at the back of Warren Place. For a while he walked him around, stretching those travel-tight limbs. Letting him breathe in the Suffolk air. Absorb the taste and smell of his new home. Pick at the grass. Paw and sniff at the unfamiliar earth. The two communing with gentle pats, softly spoken words. Creating a togetherness that was to endure. For there would now be barely a day at Warren Place that the two would not be together. Later I asked Sandy if Henry would have turned down his request. He thought this was funny, laughing as he replied, 'No, Henry would never have said no.'

It was a good pick by Sandy, not least because the other horse on his shortlist was to die on the gallops of a heart attack. Such is the precariousness of racing.

As for Frankel, you do wonder rather what he thought. Still short of his second (true) birthday but already arriving at his sixth lodging: Banstead Manor twice, Coolmore, New Abbey, Ferrans and now Warren Place. As he was led into yet another unfamiliar box, by my estimation something like his fifteenth or twentieth, there was no shock of the new. Horse boxes may vary in terms of luxury but they are essentially the same the world over. As long as horses have bedding, water, warmth and light they tend to be happy. But not Frankel. He soon came to loathe the House Barn.

The House Barn is an L-shaped stable block that is tucked away at the far end of Warren Place, so called because it is close to Warren House, the home of Henry Cecil and Jane, his wife since 2008 who was very much part of the team. It houses a dozen newly arrived colts. It is quiet and isolated, so you would think the perfect place to acclimatise these fresh young things to the rigours of a professional racing stable. You'll often hear the stable hands say they are all, despite massive price tags and owner expectations to match, still babies. Both in awe and inquisitive of a world they do not truly yet understand. Walk down the row and they are still naïve enough to be curious of your arrival. Ceasing whatever they are doing, including eating, to emerge over the doors so you have to run the gauntlet of stretched necks and heads, the mouth extremity nipping or licking if you stray too close. It is not a vicious thing. It is just something they do. A sort of greeting. A throwback to suckling.

But Frankel was clearly taking no joy from this colt nursery. By the end of the second week, he was kicking seven bells of hell out of his box, reserving particular ire for his manger which he destroyed. When he cut his foot one night Henry decided it was time for a move. He was banished to the Garage which was, in many respects, the polar opposite of the House Barn.

The Garage was the worst stable block at Warren Place. It was, as the name suggests, carved out of an old machinery store. If you were being generous you'd say it was an American-style barn, the stalls ranged along each side within the building. But instead of wide doors, usually slid open at either end, the main entrance was in the middle. There were three boxes to the left of the entrance, two to the right, in the first of which lived Frankel's half-brother and eventual lead horse, Bullet Train. Along the opposite side were six more boxes to make up the Garage posse. As you came in the doors Frankel was allocated the second box on the left.

Whether Henry moved Frankel to the Garage simply because it was the place he was least worried about being kicked to hell, or for some other reason, we will never know. But one way or another it proved to be a decision of genius, for within minutes of arrival Frankel's rage against inanimate structures vanished. He simply turned it onto people.

Something had changed in Frankel since Ferrans. You have read the report, heard what Rory Mahon said. He was as good as gold in Ireland. Never gave a moment of trouble. But at Warren Place he became the beast of the box. Sandy is probably being kind when he describes him as being 'a bit of a boy'. Essentially, Frankel had a simple mission in life. If you came into his box he was determined at best to prove he was the master of this particular domain or at worst get you out. He only really tolerated (and this is a wide stretch in the use of the word) four people: Sandy, Dee, Mike and the farrier Stephen Kielt. Everyone else was fair game for a bite until they made a swift departure. Even Henry took the flak, so much so that some days Sandy would say, 'Guv'nor, don't go in. He's got a head on him.'

But even the favoured four took punishment. Dee describes him as having a particularly bendy neck. When you thought you were out of range you weren't. For Frankel the whole thing was a giant game. A tussle for superiority. The box was his territory. Bullying everyone around suited him just fine. But it was poor Sandy who took the daily brunt, raising some questions at home from his newly married wife who worried about the bruises on his body and who, once she found out it was work related (heaven knows what she thought before), urged him to find a 'safer' horse. Sandy maintains, as do the others (and I believe them), that there was nothing innately malevolent about Frankel's behaviour. He just needed to make his point. It was all very measured. He wouldn't kick a man when he was down but he would take him down. His favoured trick to play on Sandy was the trip up. Waiting until he was distracted carrying a water bucket or some such, then sticking out his leg to trip him over. As Sandy lay in the dusty shavings Frankel would nod his head as if to say 'Gotcha' before peaceably resuming whatever he was doing.

So what brought on these changes? Clearly he was growing up, the adolescent genes as disruptive to the psyche of a horse as a human. But that alone doesn't explain it. It all happened too quickly. The dislike of the House Barn seems pretty clear: Frankel has a brain that doesn't do well with boredom. Staring out at precisely nothing is his idea of hell. He likes to see the world, such as it is in a racing stable, go by. Frankel is essentially a nosy horse. What he sees might not necessarily hold his attention for long, but he demands the ability to at least give it his consideration.

Despite its ramshackle air, the Garage was at the nexus of Warren Place. Pretty well all roads led to or past it. Nearly every person and horse would have cause to come past numerous times each day. And Frankel watched it all, with vantage points in all the important directions. His back window, which opens like the top half of a stable door, looked out onto the main entrance road. Such was the proximity he'd almost be able to brush the passing cars and lorries with his nose. In a 180 degree sweep he could take in the road in all directions: the indoor ride, two cottages, numerous stables, the staff hostel, the canteen and some of the offices. On the inside he could see most of his neighbours along the aisle; and thanks to an extra set of sliding doors in the end wall to his left that were almost always open, he had, if he positioned himself just right, a direct line of sight to the gates and the Moulton Road beyond. If a particular arrival, be it a person, horse or vehicle took his interest, he would track them all the way, reappearing in his rear window to complete his observations. He simply loved the Garage.

But his interest in the interesting still doesn't explain his change to becoming the beast of the box within a matter of a few weeks. The biting. The territory thing. The truth, I suspect, lies not in the people or the place, but in the horses. During life as a foal, and then as a yearling, Frankel had always been among his contemporaries. Now he suddenly found himself among older, bigger and at that point at least, faster horses. He might not have been going upsides those horses on the gallops just yet, but he saw them. Watched them. Walked beside them. Considered their traits and conformation. For one of the things that sets Frankel apart from ordinary horses is his extraordinary competitive streak. The desire to separate himself from the everyday. To assert himself. This was simply the first manifestation of that trait.

Life evolves quickly for a two-year-old in a racing stable, but none of it would have come as any great shock to Frankel. The routine is not so wildly different to Ferrans – food, exercise and relaxation – but the intent is more serious. Expectations are ratcheted just a little higher with each passing day. Plans are gradually formulated. The good ones compared with the not-so-good. The pressures on body and mind are not unique to human athletes; horses feel them as well. The trick, of which Henry was a master, was to waft those pressures away. Life was, in what must be regarded as one of the world's most celebrated racing stables, remarkably relaxed.

I am not going to draw you a management hierarchy flowchart for Warren Place but it is worth knowing how all the people, with their respective tasks, fit into this particular pyramid. At the top, naturally, was Henry, known to all as the Guv'nor. His second in command was assistant trainer Mike Marshall. Below him were four head lads or girls (for good or ill, racing still hasn't entirely adapted to modern terminology) who each had charge of roughly a quarter of the horses that divided into various groups which occupied the various stable blocks. Mike Marshall's wife, Aideen, for instance, looked after the fillies in the marvellously named Hovels. Dee Deacon, head girl for the Garage and another set of stables, was in charge of the colts with her group of stable hands, who, including Sandy, 'did' (looked after) three horses each. Added to the mix were the work riders, self-employed men and women who arrived each morning with the sole job of riding the horses on the gallops and at exercise. Sandy, despite all his riding heritage, only sat on Frankel's back on two or three occasions. The other regulars in Frankel's life were farrier Stephen Kielt, who re-shod him every three weeks or so, and travelling head lad Mike McGowan who was in charge of his trips to the races. In passing we should mention the Warren Place vet Charlie Smith, but that is not to diminish his role. The simple fact is that Frankel rarely had a day of sickness or call for veterinary care.

As you can see it was a pretty big organisation, which, by the time you add in all the backroom staff, took about fifty people to keep the entire Warren Place show on the road. And it was growing all the time. When Mike Marshall arrived in 2007, the year Henry was back on the Classic trail with Light Shift winning the Oaks, there were sixty horses in the yard. Henry wanted a few more; success, after all, begets success. 'Let's aim for eighty or ninety', he said. By the time Frankel left they were at over 150. Henry was, in many respects, a soft touch. He never liked to say no. He wanted people to enjoy Warren Place as much as he did. Mike said he'd often find people wandering around the yard looking a little lost. 'We bumped into Henry at the Moulton village store', said one visitor (the village store was a favoured retreat of Henry's where he'd hide out for a quiet smoke and a cup of coffee). 'He said come on over to see Frankel.' So Mike added to his already heavy roster of duties the label of regular tour guide.

* * *

The day starts early at Warren Place; at most times of the year it's 4.30 am, long before sunrise. The clank of bolts and opening doors. Scoops sliding into grain. Feed poured into buckets. The clack of wooden sticks against plastic sides as breakfast is mixed. Taps running fresh water. The line of lights beneath the Garage roof flicker into life, banishing the darkness. Dee lines up the feeding pails. Horse heads appear above stable doors. She inspects each horse in turn; another night safely negotiated. In all probability, Frankel will have cast off his night blanket, with it lying scrunched up in some corner of his box. He was then, as he is now, a hot horse with a tendency to feel warm regardless of the prevailing temperature. It is, no doubt, a metabolism thing for such a high-energy horse. So during the night, with hours to kill and little else to distract him, Frankel would dedicate his time to shedding the blanket. Using that bendy neck to reach the straps. Rub and rotate against the walls. Agitate and squirm until he was eventually able to slough it off. He seemed to take great pleasure in these small equine victories, watching Dee as she gathered up the blanket as if to say, 'I told you not to bother.'

Food is the passion in Frankel's life. He would eat, given half the chance, morning, noon and night. His consumption, even going back to the Ferrans days, is prodigious (a meal is three bowls of corn, one of bran and one of chaff, supplemented with a teaspoon of calcium, cod liver oil and glucose, total weight some 11 lb). It is not that you'd ever call him a fat horse. Big and muscled, yes. Fat, no. But he just simply burns it off. And he scoffs it all down fast. Most horses eat a bit. Then stop. Eat a bit and so on. But not Frankel. It is head down until the bin is licked clean. Then his head comes up looking for more. Not that he is going to be instantly rewarded with more. Food is the fuel that powers the horses. Give them too much and they become over-revved. Regulating their intake is as important to their fitness regime as the exercise itself. Dee might not go by a fancy title like nutrition manager that you might see in, say, a Tour de France cycling team, but matching Frankel's food to his workload is one of her most important daily tasks. She also soon learned that life was easiest when he was fed first of the Garage posse: it fed not only his stomach but his ego. He always wants to be first in everything.*

Back at Warren Place, Sandy's day starts around 6 am; he has plenty to do to prepare Frankel and his other two horses in time for the first lot to roll out around 7 am. He 'mucks out' the boxes, removing the droppings and any soiled straw from the stall. It is important that it doesn't hang around for long; the ammonia that emanates is bad for the respiratory system of a horse, not to mention just being generally unpleasant. Then he changes the water and gives each a slice of hay. This might sound like an odd amount, and it is in truth rather random, but hay when baled in the meadow is compressed by the baling machine into layers about the thickness of your open palm, the whole bale squeezed together tight by twine. In the yard when the twine is cut, the bale springs open like an accordion, releasing a series of 'slices'.

Frankel, as do most horses in training, had access to pretty much unlimited hay and water – they are after all grazing animals. It is what they would do all day every day in the wild unless distracted otherwise. As much as providing them with nutrition you are

---

* Not that Rob Bowley, Frankel's stud hand at Banstead Manor, took quite the same tack when the stallion arrived to take up his stud duties. On that first November morning Rob came into view with a feed bucket in each hand, one for Frankel and the other for his neighbour and stud senior of some eight years, Oasis Dream. Rob deliberately placed Frankel's bucket outside his stall while he went to feed Oasis Dream first. It was a subtle message to Frankel that in this particular new home he wasn't top dog. In time it might be different, but for now he was to defer to others. Rob and Frankel have never looked back from that day.

keeping them occupied with a natural activity. As a distraction activity hay suited Frankel very well, though it was soon apparent that his heavy consumption of the soft, green, Canadian hay often favoured for racehorses was too rich for his digestive system. So Dee switched him to the coarser, more roughage-heavy, English hay.

At a quarter past the hour Mike Marshall shouts, 'Pull out.' Stable doors swing open. Work riders appear from all manner of crevices, often followed by a fug of last-minute cigarette smoke. Horses are brought out onto the hard standing outside their respective boxes. Sandy will have groomed all three of his horses in preparation. Checked and picked out their hooves. Swapped the head collars for bridles. Put on a quarter sheet if the weather demands it. Saddled them up. Not all the horses leave the yard at the same time – there are three or four lots a day, anywhere up to fifty horses at roughly two-hour intervals, the next lot going out when the previous one returns. The board is brought out from the office, which matches the work-rider names to their mounts in each of the lots. It is a crucial part of the Warren Place synthesis, much fiddled with by Mike and Henry in pursuit of the perfect combinations. As Sandy gives the work rider a leg up, he has his own breakfast in mind; he has an hour to kill.

It is fair to say the dress code at Warren Pace is casual, the riders wearing just about every conceivable combination of boots, long and short, riding trousers (some even jeans), shirts, gilets, wind cheaters and helmets. The only absolute given is that a safety helmet must be worn along with a body protector, a sort of armoured waistcoat that protects the spine and torso in the event of a fall. Not all trainers were as sartorially *laissez-faire* as Henry; Newmarket is smattered with yards that turn out on the gallops like a royal pageant, with all the riders in matching attire mimicking racing colours or making some other branded statement.

From your aerial view of Warren Place, you could not have failed to spot the biggest single building, the indoor ride. It is not the prettiest thing in the world with its dirty white sides and grey asbestos roof looking a little like a down-at-heel football stadium. When Noel Murless built it in the late 1960s, the covered, oval track was quite an innovation. No longer were the pre-gallop preliminaries subject to the vagaries of the weather. You could, for at least a little while longer, be shielded from wind and rain.

As the lot file in, always colts first and fillies behind, Henry appears to take up position just outside where he and Mike are afforded a view of the trotting horses circumnavigating the dirt ride through the open side door. Why be outside, you might ask. It is a chance to smoke and think. As each horse comes past, Henry is afforded a shutter's-eye view as the six circuits are completed in turn. Six times around equals a mile. This is his chance to assess the condition of every horse close up and in movement. It is a critical moment in the training day. Sending out a horse to the gallops with a small niggle or injury can clearly have calamitous implications. Some are turned back for a day of rest or a visit from the vet. Frankel? He never missed a day.

As they file out of the indoor ride, a little cameo is played out with each rider. Mike asks a single question, quietly spoken such as, 'Alright, Ray?' 'How is he, Julie?' 'Everything good?' Back comes an equally short reply. 'All good.' 'She's full of beans.' But this is more aimed at Henry who stands directly behind Mike, the reply often accompanied by a little tap of the whip handle to the peak of the helmet by way of a respectful good morning. Mike then issues the gallop instructions such as, 'Twice half-speed up Warren Hill.' All this is done with remarkable calm, paced by the speed of the horses walking by, without the aid of any notes, simply the summation of what Henry and Mike have agreed the night before, adapted by what they had seen and heard that morning.

There is a back route onto the gallops from Warren Place, a short, white-railed path through a stand of trees. As Frankel emerges from the cover to the open expanse of the Heath, his new workplace is spread out all before him, the grassland spotted with pockets of trees and railings leading down to the town of Newmarket a mile away. Had he let his eye follow the town to the horizon beyond, the stands of the two Newmarket racecourses, the respective homes of his first race and 2,000 Guineas Classic victory, would have been faintly visible. In one sweep of his head, much of his destiny was there to see.

In his early days at Warren Place, before he started to show evidence of the potential some had already seen in him, Frankel would have gone out with the second or third lot. It would be easy now to rewrite history to tell the tale of a horse that scorched the gallops from the get-go, who was allowed to let rip from the very outset. But that was not Henry's methodology. The cream of the world's thoroughbreds had come his way over the previous four decades. However brilliant they may have ended up, in the beginning they were all without exception, and that includes Frankel, unmoulded in that potential. Still babies. They needed to become racetrack fit. Learn the racing game. Understand what was expected of them. Cope with the alien and unfamiliar. In short, be transformed into honed, equine athletes. And that doesn't happen overnight. And it doesn't necessarily happen quickly. It would be a full seven months before Frankel set foot on a racecourse.

10

Getting into his head

Newmarket is a horse town. There are not many places in the world where you will find a high street with parallel footpaths, one dedicated to humans and the other, with a dirt surface, to thoroughbred horses. Pelican crossings where the lights are changed with the flick of a whip. The morning rush-hour traffic, such as it is in rural Suffolk, that patiently backs up as the horses stream across from stable to gallop and then back again. There are no such problems with the local train; the Victorian railway engineers, faced with the might of well-connected racehorse owners, were forced to put the track in a tunnel.

Horses are the life and blood of Newmarket. There are 80 trainers, 73 stud farms and up to 3,000 horses. That is one horse for every six people who live in the town. One in three jobs have some connection with the horse business. It is the world centre of thoroughbred horse racing. In fashion a trio of names roll off the tongue: London, Paris, New York. In horse racing it is a single one: Newmarket.

The connection goes back a long way, in fact four centuries, to the early 1600s when Charles I inaugurated the first Cup race. But it takes more than royalty to sustain a place for such a long time, and in Newmarket's case it certainly wasn't the physical location. We have to be honest, it is in the middle of nowhere, not really on the way to or from anywhere. And in the depth of winter it will put you in mind of Macbeth's blasted heath. But the secret of Newmarket's success lies not in what you see but what you feel underfoot. The turf.

For the gallops are the thing. Grassland as pure as any on the planet. Cosseted and teased over those centuries for the sole, single purpose of providing the most perfect training grounds for preparing racehorses. It is easy today, with all manner of artificial surfaces and monstrous irrigation machinery, to bend nature to our will, but until very recently you were largely reliant on the hand Mother Nature dealt you. The sward on Newmarket Heath has never seen the plough. It doesn't look entirely green or have that softness of manicured turf. Stoop down to part the growth and it will feel rough. A mixture of slightly browned grasses, weeds and tangled herbaceous plants that compress grudgingly. Depress a portion with your foot and it will spring back a moment later as if you were never there. That is the trick that allows it to survive the pounding of thousands of hooves, every day of the year, regardless of the weather or season.

It also helps that Newmarket Heath is huge, with 2,500 acres of gallops to ease the pressure and another 1,500 acres thrown in for good measure. There are fifty miles of turf gallops, a watered turf gallop, five peat-moss gallops that date back to the early twentieth century and the late-twentieth-century additions of fifteen all-weather tracks that cover fourteen miles. And if you are a Newmarket-based trainer, all that is available to you. Not that it comes free or easily. You have to pass muster by way of an interview with the Jockey Club who own and administer the gallops, and pay a monthly Heath Tax which is around £120 for each horse in your stables. But once in, you have virtually exclusive use. It is one of the great closed shops, visiting trainers or non-natives restricted to just a very few of the gallops and then only by special permission, not to mention the payment of a Links Tax.

In broad terms the Newmarket Training Grounds, to give them their official title, divide into two parts: Racecourse Side and Bury Side. If you have watched the racing on television from either of the two courses you will have seen part of the former stretching away in the distance sandwiched between the racetracks proper. If you have visited the Rowley Mile course, the Back of The Flat gallops behind the stands doubles as a car park on race days. In case you are slightly confused Newmarket actually has two racecourses, both dedicated to flat racing, within a direct eye-line of each other, the stands no more than two-thirds of a mile apart. The Rowley Mile is the one with the soaring Millennium Stand and the prestigious races such as the 1,000 and 2,000 Guineas, with racing at the beginning and end of the annual calendar. The July Course takes over for the summer. It must be said its stands have seen better days, but what it lacks in shiny buildings it makes up for with a charming mix of happy-go-lucky holiday crowds and hardened racing regulars, the raggedness disguised by the overflowing red geranium festooned hanging baskets and the quaint thatched roofs. Just to make things more confusing still, the racetracks themselves are joined together. Picture a 'V' with a long tail emerging at right angles from the base. Each course has its own straight, the respective stands at the top of each arm on the 'V'. However, for races over one and a quarter miles they share the track that runs along the route of the tail. It doesn't always make for great viewing. The Cesarewitch, at two and a quarter miles one of the longest handicap races in the flat year, effectively starts on the July Course and ends at the Rowley Mile finish, making tiny specks of the horses which are one and three-quarter miles distant when the starter drops his hand.

Not that Frankel would ever come into the orbit of such a distance. In seven months' time, he was to make his debut along the straight of the July Course. A year and a bit on, he would set the racing world alight with one of the most astounding Classic wins of all time on the Rowley Mile. But for now the Bury Side, on the other side of the town, was to be his natural home.

If you have ever read a Dick Francis novel, the names of the Bury Side gallops will be familiar. They are the stuff of flat racing legend. Where the first whispers of greatness emanate. The Limekilns. Side Hill. Railway Field. Bury Hill. Warren Hill. All wrapped up in the sad mysticism of the Gypsy Boy's Grave that lies in the northeast corner of Bury Side at the Well Bottom crossroads. The tale goes that many centuries ago a young lad was tending a flock of sheep when one went missing; fearing punishment from a harsh master, the boy hung himself from a nearby tree. As a suicide he could not be buried in consecrated ground, so as was the tradition of the time, he was interred beside a road junction, the crossing roads as close to a symbolic crucifix as could be, to be laid to rest. But for horse racing the story doesn't end there. Should flowers appear on the grave during Derby week, the belief is that the winning horse will be from a Newmarket stable. And the colours of the graveside flowers on the day of the race itself will foretell the racing colours of the winning horse.

On that first morning Frankel would have taken in his Newmarket panorama from the top of the gallops they call Long Hill. From there, in a ragged group, the string headed ever downhill along the sandy pathway for almost a mile to the outskirts of the town itself. I say ragged because the riders ebbed and flowed between those ahead and those behind, just ever so slightly speeding up or slowing down the walking pace to come upside to chat. Henry liked it that way. It was all very companionable and convivial. Not for him the regimented single files of other yards. He saw that as unnatural, nothing like the herd instinct that horses find so comforting. Likewise, it was a chance for the work riders to catch up on the gossip. The conversation was rarely about anything other than horses or racing. You can catch snippets of it if you wish, for the gallops are more public that you might suppose. About halfway down Long Hill, as the Warren Place lot appear from behind the Claypit Plantation, the sand track runs beside a long parking area that in turn runs parallel to the Moulton Road. It is a stopping area for all sorts. Dog walkers. Van delivery drivers sneaking ten minutes' rest. Bemused tourists with number plates indicating all manner of European countries. The plainly curious. And the plainly interested sporting binoculars. If you leaned against the rails you would almost have been able to touch Frankel. On a cold morning you would have certainly felt the backdraught of his warm breath.

At the bottom of the hill the string crossed the Moulton Road, the tarmac at the crossing point replaced by a special surface. Horses in aluminium plates and regular road surfaces don't mix; it would be like you and me trying to walk on ice.

There is oftentimes a queue of lots waiting to go up Warren Hill; the different stables patiently waiting their turn to head up one of the two five-furlong all-weather gallops that run parallel to each other. It is a busy spot. A place where everyone watches everyone else. It might just be training but it is the only window to the quality of your rivals until you meet them on the racecourse. To the uninitiated this is simply a melee of horseflesh, where discerning the good from the bad is close to impossible. But for the tribe, those who live, breathe and attend every day, it is an open book where every word is read. Each turn of phrase scrutinised. And hidden meanings sought in every possible manner.

It was here, at the base of Warren Hill, that took place a twist in this particular Newmarket training dynamic that was unique to Frankel; nobody had seen it before or since, but many of the work riders I spoke to relate the same story. As the Frankel legend grew, his daily arrival on the gallops became a moment, eyes turning to track the progress of the Cecil string. As they came close, chatter would stop. Like the parting of the Red Sea, the other lots would clear the way for Frankel, each head, both horse and human, following his every extended stride. He was then, and is now, a stunning example of the thoroughbred breed. All muscled. Primed for that explosive burst of speed. Like a sleek Formula 1 car on the starting grid waiting for lights out. But it was more than that. It is not often in life you get to be that close to the truly great, all relaxed and informal. Him or her just going about those everyday things that you are doing as well. Sharing, albeit just for a moment, the same air and view of the world. And it was a chance to be both part of, and be witness to, a tiny bit of history. Not that I think Frankel quite saw it that way. He is an impatient horse. A free pass to the front of the queue suited him very well. And he loved and loves the attention. But on that frosty February morning when he looked up Warren Hill for the first time, nobody knew that any of this was to come.

There was a tradition at Warren Place that winter quarters, the downtime between the flat racing seasons, came to an end on 1 February. For the old hands and the newly arrived two-year-olds, this was the time when training proper began. Actually, as Mike Marshall admits, it wasn't a date that was absolutely set in stone, but it was the touchstone by which the new beginning was denoted, all winter roads leading to that departure spot. So on a Monday morning, sometime in the early February of 2010, Gemma Flack, Frankel's first work rider, paused him at the base of Warren Hill.

Frankel the stallion, retired from racing at his Banstead Manor home.

(Asunción Piñeyrúa / Juddmonte)

Frankel's dam, Kind, photographed at Banstead Manor Stud, Newmarket in 2012. (Steven Cargill / Racingfotos.com)

Frankel's sire, Galileo, had a successful racing career, including winning the Derby and the Irish Derby, before retiring to stud in 2001.
(Trevor Jones / Racingfotos.com)

An idyllic mare and foal paddock at Coolmore, where Frankel spent two months as a foal.

An aerial view of Warren Place. The large, white oval is the indoor ride, and the brown rectangular building south of that is the Garage stable block where Frankel lived for most of his racing life. (Cambridge Aerial Photography / Alamy Stock Photo)

Sir Henry Cecil became Frankel's trainer in 2010 and would be an essential part of the racehorse's success and his legacy. Newmarket, 2 May 2011.
(Chris Smith / Popperfoto / Getty Images)

Frankel wins his first race at Newmarket in 2010, narrowly defeating Nathaniel in the European Breeders' Fund Maiden Stakes, Newmarket, 13 August 2010.
(Steven Cargill / Racingfotos.com)

Henry Cecil and Frankel's owner, Prince Khalid Abdullah, watch the three-year old's fifth race at Newbury on 16 April 2011. They know they have something special on their hands. (Alan Crowhurst / Getty Images)

Frankel wins the Qipco 2,000 Guineas, Newmarket by a country mile. 30 April 2011. (Alan Crowhurst / Getty Images)

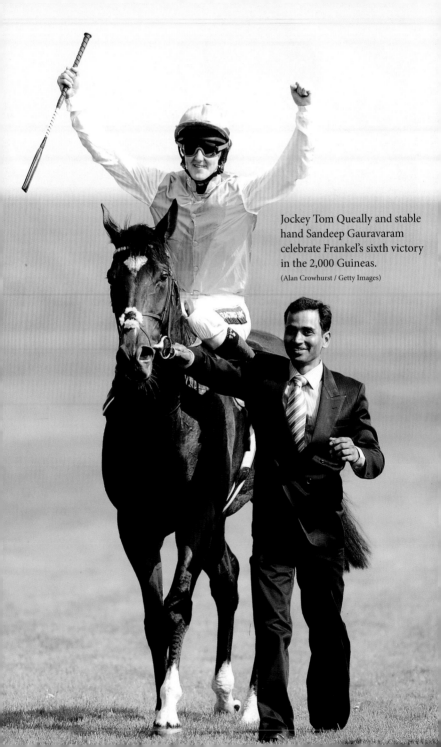

Jockey Tom Queally and stable hand Sandeep Gauravaram celebrate Frankel's sixth victory in the 2,000 Guineas.

(Alan Crowhurst / Getty Images)

After winning the 2,000 Guineas, Henry Cecil's twenty-fifth and final classic, Frankel becomes a media sensation. Tom Queally with Frankel, as owner Prince Khalid Abdullah holds the horse along with trainer Henry Cecil (right).

(Alan Crowhurst / Getty Images)

The life of a racehorse begins early. Tom Queally riding Frankel out on 23 September 2011 at Newmarket on exercise prior to running at the Champions Day meeting at Ascot racecourse on 15 October.

(Alan Crowhurst / Getty Images)

Tom exercises Frankel in September 2011, in advance of his ninth race at Ascot. (Alan Crowhurst / Getty Images)

Frankel wins the Queen Elizabeth II Stakes Sponsored by Qipco at Ascot on 15 October 2011. (David Ashdown / The Independent / Shutterstock)

Warren Hill is far from being Mount Everest but after a flattish start it is a long, steady, relentless climb of just over half a mile. If you were treating it as a brisk walk, it is the sort of incline where you might pause halfway to 'take in the view', i.e. catch your breath. If you were an occasional cyclist, you would definitely get off to push the final third. Henry put great store by Warren Hill. Of all the huge array of gallops he had at his disposal, it was the one he used most often. It gave him the opportunity, from his viewpoint at the three-and-a-half-furlong marker, to see how each horse made use of himself. That connection between physique and stride. Ignoring the pounding of hooves to minutely listen out for every breath as each horse arrived, drew level and then passed on by. The effort of the hill creates tell-tales. A horse at full gallop takes in fifteen litres of air with each breath, as much as ten times that of a human athlete, breathing between two and three times each second. It is a huge effort. Any weakness, be it fitness or congenital, will be exposed. As Teddy Grimthorpe, the Juddmonte racing manager and a regular on the gallops, succinctly sums it up: any horse that reaches the top comfortably is either fit or good. Or in Frankel's case both.

Quite what Frankel thought of Warren Hill that morning we cannot know, but it is an absolute certainty that he had never seen such a steep slope, let alone be asked to canter up it, in all his life. New Abbey Stud and Ferrans are essentially flat. But as he cantered up in single file, the first of many hundreds of climbs he would complete over the next three seasons, he clearly found it easier than most. For the one thing he loved above food was running. And running fast. But that is not always such a good thing in the untrained and untested.

The training schedule of a racehorse, Frankel included, looks surprisingly simple. In writing this book I sought to find comparisons in the training of human and equine athletes, but in reality there seem to be very few with Henry Cecil. I looked in vain for blood tests, regular weighing, stopwatch timings and all the other things you might have expected in the armoury of a top trainer. Detailed assessments. Intensive veterinary supervision. If modern practices such as the aggregation of marginal gains theory as propounded by cycling guru Dave Brailsford was taking place some-where in Newmarket, it was certainly not at Warren Place. Nobody was striving for that one per cent margin of improvement in everything they did. I never came across an ice bath. Ever. Nor a motivational coach. I say all this not by way of criticism but really in awe. For I think you'll agree, a typical week in the life of Frankel was simple, but in the best of ways and to devastating effect.

You've already seen Monday training. A total of about an hour out the box; in aggregate three and a half miles made up of two miles of walking, a mile of trotting and a half-mile easy canter up Warren Hill. And that would be it. Prison inmates complain of being 'banged up' for twenty-three hours a day. For a horse it is seventh heaven. As long as they have all their creature comforts – a homely stable, food and water – they are happy. In the wild it wouldn't be a lot different; just a bigger space for much the same outcome.

Tuesday would not be so different to Monday but with two canters this time, either up Warren Hill or the Long Hill, another uphill all-weather gallop, which ends just beside the back way into Warren Place. But Wednesday is altogether more serious, a proper 'work' day with a strong gallop over five or six furlongs in pairs along the grass of the Limekilns or the Al Bahathri polytrack, another all-weather surface variant.

It is probably worth defining what a gallop is in relation to all the other speeds that horses are set to move at. A walk is 4 mph, so a brisk human equivalent. The trot is twice that speed. The canter is around 15 mph, which you'll sometimes hear referred to as 'half-speed', as a full gallop is 30 mph. Not that that is anywhere close to the top speed of a horse at racing pace – sprinters will cruise in the high 30s and low 40s, with the thoroughbred record standing at just below 44 mph. However, getting Frankel to go fast was never the problem. In fact, it was quite the reverse.

There is no doubt he was, especially as a two-year-old, a difficult horse to train. You'll often hear the word 'exuberant' used to describe him by those who largely viewed him from a distance or only knew him by repute. For anyone who had to work on or with him the same word was equally well used, but either with heavy irony or a certain sense of exhaustion. Life on the gallops was a trial of strength. And when you have a seething, one-thousand-pound-plus ball of over-eager equine flesh, that is no easy task. Gemma Flack soon had to give way to a heavier, stronger Dan de Haan.

Frankel's problem was that he would not settle. He was never content to lob along, keeping stride with his galloping companions until asked to quicken or, heaven forbid, slow down. There are not many videos of him during those first few months, but those that there are, and recollections of the work riders, tell of this horse that he fought the bridle. Fought the rider. Reins strained tight. White spittle flying every which way. His head held in uncomfortably tight to give the rider some semblance of control. Somehow, he had to be taught to turn himself off. Conserve his energy to use his turn of foot when it mattered most. And for that Henry had a plan.

I think it is fair to say Henry had a way of getting inside a horse's head, and in Frankel he saw the desire to best his rivals, not just on the racecourse but in the everyday as well. So he used that knowledge to tame Frankel's headstrong side. Henry's instructions to Dan in the early days and Shane Fetherstonhaugh latterly, were simple: tuck Frankel in behind the lead horse, get him settled and when the moment comes give him his head to surge on by. Oh, that it would be so simple. Settle? You must be joking. Day after day Frankel fought every effort at restraint but, and here was the trick, Dan kept to Henry's supplementary instructions: if he won't settle don't let him go on by. Keep him tucked in behind the lead horse until you pull up at the end of the gallop. Coming second to anyone? Frankel absolutely hated that. Eventually the penny dropped: settle and you'll be rewarded with want you want. It took time but it did indeed work, though not every day or every time. Frankel was too independent minded, or maybe just cussed, to fall for Henry's physiological trickery all the time. But it worked enough of the time to start to make a racehorse of him.

The Thursday routine was largely a repeat of Monday excepting one important addition: starting stall training. Anyone who has ever watched a flat race will have seen the stalls in action and know that not every horse likes them. This is not altogether surprising. They are intimidating structures made of tubular steel, with a padded compartment for each horse which has, front and back, pairs of spring-loaded gates that look a bit like the doors of a Wild West saloon bar. The front pairs are all sprung open simultaneously to ensure an even start. But not every horse enters the stalls at the gentle behest of the jockey. Some have to be led by a stalls handler; others inched forward by a pair of handlers who push from the tail end. Sometimes a blindfold is used; other times a special blanket. There are all manner of tricks to encourage the recalcitrant.

But even once loaded the potential for trouble is far from over. Some horses rear up. Others kick and push. Some even go down on their knees to crawl out underneath. Often there is as long as two or three minutes between the first and last loaded. Jockeys become fractious. The stalls sway and clank. The noise is terrific. The starter on his rostrum, impatient to get his race away on time, shouts instructions above the din. And among all this is a young horse who has to be ready to burst from the stalls the moment the gates open, accelerating from nought to 35 mph in a matter of a few strides. Miss the break and you'll usually lose the race. Hence stalls training.

As you'll recall from Rory Mahon's Ferrans report, Frankel had walked quietly through the starting stalls. In truth it is not quite the test you might expect, simply a set of three stalls without the front or back gates through which the horses routinely passed on the way to the gallops each morning. The early sessions at Warren Place were not a lot different, with a similar wooden mock-up. But as the Thursdays progressed so did the familiarisation with a real set of stalls. In progressive weeks Frankel walked in, through and out. Then he walked in, stood and walked out. Then the back gates were closed behind him. Then the front gates ahead of him. Then both front and back. Then he was given time to stand as others were loaded beside him. Finally the front gates were sprung open, at first by hand but eventually with the full clanking suddenness of the automated mechanism. How did he take to this? Well, by all accounts, perfectly fine. One of the contradictory things about Frankel is that for all his less-than-welcoming antics within his box and his rebellious attitude on the gallops, when it came to the everyday stuff he was, mercifully, close to being a model racehorse. Not everything was a fight.

Maybe that was something to do with the routine – Frankel absolutely loves routine, so he must have relished the fact that the second half of the training week was a facsimile of the first half. Friday was a repeat of Tuesday with a couple of canters, which will probably lead you to conclude that Saturday would be a repeat of Wednesday. You'd be right; a work gallop at nearly racing pace over six or seven furlongs. As for Sunday, that was always a rest day. The horses didn't even leave their boxes, content to eat, rest and sleep. As for Sandy,

Dee and Mike they would have much the same thing in mind unless they were on the roster as part of the Sabbath skeleton crew.

As the summer drew on, Henry's thoughts turned to Frankel's first race. When was it to be? Where was it to be? Over what distance? What standard of opposition should he face? His fitness was never in question, but that temperament? It was always the needle that pricked. These are all questions that are never easily answered. It is the ultimate judgement call that, for all the opinions and advice of others, rested solely on the shoulders of Henry Cecil. Frankel was good. That much was clear. But try him, or any horse for that matter, in a race too long or too soon or too hard and the spirit can be broken forever. As Philip Mitchell observes, horses don't have great memories except for the bad things that happen to them – those they remember for a very long time.

So, as the turf of the Heath took on its brown, dusty August tinge, Frankel underwent a final stalls test which was as close to the race-course experience as Mike, Dan and the team could make it. An eight-berth set was towed onto the grass of Long Hill, the horses ridden down as if cantering to the start of a race. They were loaded. Paused for a short while to absorb the tension before they were jumped out. It was a proper race start. Accelerated to full pace. Racing in earnest for fifty or sixty yards before pulling up to repeat the whole process a couple of times further.

Frankel was ready.

11

The 6.35 at Newmarket

Henry Cecil could have run Frankel well ahead of his eventual mid-August debut, but he chose not to. One of the privileges of training for a great owner-breeder such as Prince Khalid is that you have time. The economic imperatives that bite at the heels of smaller or less established trainers don't have to apply to the likes of Henry Cecil. That is not to say that Juddmonte is oblivious of the bottom line. Far from it. With upwards of 250 horses in training around the globe at any given moment, financial discipline is properly exercised. Horses are bought. Horses are sold. Everyone is expected to add value as they can and should. But there is also a longer view of things. Time is not always measured by the simple matter of a few weeks or months. Or sometimes even money. If a trusted trainer judges something to be in the best interests of a horse, and by association the best interests of Juddmonte, so be it. Thus it was that Frankel was steered away from an earlier run, over a shorter distance. Henry stayed his hand, despite an ever-growing weight of expectation.

That said, by the time Friday 13 August came around, Henry might have been wondering if that earlier debut may have been advisable. It had rained solidly all Wednesday and Thursday. But come the dawn of the only Friday the 13th of that year, it was all blue skies and sunshine. The going looked set to be on the soft side of good but nothing to worry about. However, it didn't stay that way.

Warren Place used to operate a just-in-time operation for their Newmarket runners, which was quite different to other race meetings. Usually, all the runners for that given day would travel in a single horse transporter, arriving at least five hours before the first race. But for a July Course meeting, the Warren Place lorry would ferry the runners race by race; after all, the journey time is just nine minutes. Or eleven if you get caught on red at the only traffic light on the high street. The procedure was so slick that the horses didn't even enter the racecourse stables, going directly from the horse box to the pre-parade ring. In theory, and in fact in practice, a horse could depart, arrive, run and return in under an hour. In terms of a stress-free racecourse debut, it is hard to do much better. This was precisely the plan for Frankel; the only problem was come that evening (the race was scheduled for 6.35 pm) the rain came down. And came down.

I must confess I have a particular weakness for the summer meetings on the July Course at Newmarket. There is something wonderfully transient about a racecourse that only operates for a few months each year. You do pay a price, however. The stands aren't quite as smart, or for that matter weatherproof, as you might hope or have a right to expect. Whether it is that, or the apparent isolation of its East Anglian location, but somehow Newmarket seems to be outside the orbit of the London crowd who flock to Ascot and their like. Here they are noticeably absent, drawn instead to their villas in Tuscany or their yachts on the Mediterranean. I am not sure they are missed. No, this crowd is a gathering of the Fen folk. Some are the racing regulars: the tribe who make their living by the sport or call it their number one pastime. The others are the occasionals: the people who come racing for a treat. The office outing. Loud hen parties that, after a certain amount of jousting, will join forces with equally loud stags in common purpose – fun and a last hurrah. Family groups where two or three generations, from Grandpa, the knowledgeable racing sage, to the latest arrival in a pushchair, are camped out on a bench at the one-furlong marker. The tweeded and the suited. The smart and the everyday. Somehow racing has this special way of embracing all sorts. All classes. All wealths.

It also embraced Sandy's shoe. The route from the unloading area to the pre-parade ring takes you directly across the track. Such was the ever-increasing softness of the turf that his shoe sank into the ground, pulling it off, a bemused Frankel having to halt to witness Sandy hopping around on one leg while he retrieved it. Finally back on six legs the pair continued, the officials holding back the crowds – all 22,500 of them (many there to watch Irish boy band Westlife provide the after-racing entertainment) – that were still arriving through the turnstiles (remember this was only the third race on the card) to allow the runners into the pre-parade ring. As in the town, horses have the right of way.

For those unfamiliar with the rituals of a horse race, there are two stages before the horses finally set off for the start of the race. The pre-parade ring which they enter and circle about thirty minutes beforehand and the main paddock where they circle again about fifteen minutes ahead of the start. Most people head for the paddock; it is the one area really designed for viewing but the pre-parade is the most informal, where you can get up really close. And at Newmarket you can get extraordinarily close, standing in the middle among the owners and trainers while the horses circle around you. It was here that Henry and assistant Mike Marshall joined Sandy and Frankel.

It was this small group, plus Jane Cecil's daughter Carina McKeown, that headed from the pre-parade to the paddock, the absences almost more notable than the attendees that evening.

Prince Khalid wasn't there. Neither was Jane Cecil herself, who was in France at the Deauville races and sales along with Juddmonte racing manager Teddy Grimthorpe. Even the crowd looked absent, the paddock viewing rostrums almost empty as everyone sheltered in the bars, content to watch the preliminaries on TV.

As Henry stood in the paddock, as ever doing his permanent trick of talking while forever watching, the twelve runners circled. Did he look agitated or ruffled? No. He had been to this point so many times, with so many horses – I want to say hundreds but it was probably thousands. Well-bred horses that had shown promise at home. Arrived at the racecourse with a reputation founded on rumour, speculation and some indication of talent. Just maybe this was 'the one'. And oftentimes it had been 'the one' for Henry. The best of a generation. A name that still resonates years or decades after it last departed a racecourse. But more often than not, the dreams turn out to be precisely that – dreams. The brutal truth is that only one horse was going to win the European Breeders' Fund Maiden Stakes (Class 4) one-mile race for two-year-olds that evening and claim the winning prize of £4,533.20. For the other eleven, beyond the hard luck stories and 'we'll do it next time' optimism, was the realisation that you simply might not be that good. It is a horrible reality check. Two and a half years of hope shot down in 103 seconds.

There was no doubt that Frankel had talent. The Newmarket rumour mill was in full overdrive about him lighting up the gallops. Chris Cook, racing correspondent for the *Guardian*, had mentioned the Kind colt in his gossip column the previous Saturday. Chris's source was very clear: this was the best horse Cecil had had for a very long time, which well might have come as news to a more sanguine Henry. But talent is only part of the racing trick. The other is temperament. The ability to cope with the unfamiliar. To be calm in the preliminaries. Settle in the race. And then turn on the tap when the moment is right. It is not as easy as it sounds. Anyone who has ever been racing will have seen the horse that sweats and jiggles, expending so much nervous energy that the race is lost even before he or she reaches the starting gate. And if Henry had a worry it was that this difficult-to-train two-year-old would lose his head amid the swirl of the race meeting.

But Henry need not have worried; as least as regards to the preliminaries. For Sandy's observation that Frankel is the most nosy of horses was so evidently true. He took in every little thing. Every person. Every building. Every movement. The colours. The noise. The activity. This was a year's worth of looking out the Garage all rolled into one. He absolutely loved it. And as Tom Queally, the Warren Place stable jockey, joined the group in Prince Khalid's green, pink and white racing colours, the riding instructions, such as they were, were easy: race behind the leaders, get him settled and then go when the time is right. Sound familiar? Yes, just like those Wednesdays and Saturdays on the gallops.

For all Henry's relaxed demeanour and the certain knowledge that he had trod this particular path before, there was definitely more than your average level of expectation swirling around Frankel's debut. Frankel had, as we know, been regarded as the cream of the Juddmonte 2008 crop for quite some while. After all, he had that burden of the name. But more importantly he hadn't really put a foot wrong, even at this young age. If you ask Teddy Grimthorpe what in his mind marks Frankel out above mere 'ordinary' champions, he'll point to his continual improvement. He never plateaued. He never went backwards. Every time you asked more of him, he gave you more. That is unusual in a racehorse. Teddy, sequestered in France, admits that he had never, ever been so nervous in his life before a race. Any race. He even slipped away from the Juddmonte party to watch the race alone.

As Mike gave Tom a leg up onto Frankel and Sandy led the pair out the forty yards from paddock to track, there was one oddity as they disappeared into the gloom, eventually obscured from sight by distance and the driving rain. This alleged flying machine, the one Warren Place thought so much of, was only just favourite in the betting ring. Not everyone shared their confidence. In times of old a Cecil hotshot, on his local course, against a bunch of mostly untried maidens would be short odds-on. You'd probably have to stake five pounds to win just two; be content to lay your money down entirely on the basis of Henry's reputation rather than that of the horse. But that same bet five minutes before the start could win you ten on this particular Friday evening. 2–1? Was this a reflection of how much the shine had come off the Warren Place name? In fact, the answer lay in another name: Nathaniel.

It is hard not to feel a little sorry for Nathaniel who was jousting for favouritism with Frankel in the betting market on that particular evening. Today he is an established stallion, his progeny much sought after. Actually, in one of those odd twists of fate, when I went to New Abbey Stud recently one of his offspring was occupying Frankel's old number 21 in the Green Field Barn. He, like Frankel, was a Newmarket horse but trained by John Gosden whose rise filled some of the vacuum left by the barren years of Warren Place. So when Gosden had a 'talking' horse people listened. And Nathaniel, with a breeding heritage every bit as blue-blooded as Frankel's, was such a horse. It was clear there was something to note about this other bay colt, another son of, you guessed it, Galileo.

The betting market was reflecting the rumours of some great training gallops. The big bets were going down for Nathaniel. He was, in short, fancied to win. Frankel's apparently generous price (he would never, ever go off odds-against ever again) was due to the weight of money piling in for Nathaniel. But it was to be the misfortune of Nathaniel – later a Group 1 winner and sire of Prince Khalid's twice-winning Prix de l'Arc de Triomphe filly Enable, who in another time might have been the champion of his generation – to come up against one greater still. He was to lose not just once but twice to Frankel in one of those weird twists of fate, as they were destined to compete against each other in the first and last races of their respective racing careers.

It is a long, long way down to the one-mile start of Newmarket if you are trying to subdue and relax an eager two-year-old racehorse. Once you leave the stands behind you, the expanse of the Heath is huge; the most visible point is the horizon. If your animal takes hold, there are few natural obstructions to halt a helter-skelter runaway. Next stop is pretty well Six Mile Bottom, which is as far as it sounds, the start of long-distance races in centuries past. But the driving rain and the wind that drove it dampened all exuberance, the jockeys bunching their mounts in a group, as much in an attempt to use each other as a shield as by way of any companionship. It was one of those moments when you understood why, regardless of the weather, good or foul, Henry insisted the lots went out every morning. Get used to it. It will happen.

Should you ever have a chance it is worth walking the July Course; or in fact any racecourse for that matter. For what television or the view from the stands rarely gives you is a true sense of the roller-coaster undulations of a racetrack. This might be called a one-mile flat race over the straight course but it is far from flat or straight. The white plastic running rail snakes and weaves like a loose thread of wool. The course is lower at the start than the finish. The track cambers different ways at different points on the course. But for Frankel this wasn't so different to everyday life; the look and feel of Newmarket Heath was already woven into his psyche.

* * *

A furlong shy of the start, at what will be the seven-furlong marker on the way back, the jockeys collectively ease their horses up as they breast the final undulation. It is a strangely isolating moment. The purpose of racing – the public and the adulation – all but disappears. There is nobody here but those who need to be here: the stalls handlers who number eight, the starter and his assistant. I'd like to tell you that all is beautifully quiet, just the sound of the birdsong and a ruffling breeze. But it is not. An earth dyke that borders the Heath shields from view the rush-hour traffic on the A14 Newmarket bypass; the continual roar ensures all conversations have to be shouted.

In a loose group the runners walk down towards the stalls, disappearing from the view of those in the stands. Frankel and Tom look incredibly relaxed. True, Frankel had wanted to accelerate as Sandy let them go; you can see Tom leaning back, reins rigid tight to restrain him, but once out in the country he takes the hint, lobbing along with the pack. In front of the stalls this is no evening for chatting or dawdling; they don't circle for long, just a minute or two as the clock counts down to 6.35 pm. With nothing much to do, Frankel inclines his head every which way, taking it all in. Staring down horses, people and inanimate objects in turn until his curiosity is sated. I am not entirely sure whether Tom thinks this a good thing, for ahead of most of the others, one of the loaders comes forward to thread his leading rope through the side rings of Frankel's bit, keeping him from then on in tight check. Or maybe Tom and the loader are friends – they seem to have plenty to talk about.

'Round the back, lads', shouts the assistant starter. Nobody needs much encouragement. The sooner they are loaded the sooner they will be back in the dry of the weighing room. Circling behind the stalls the roll call accounts for all the runners; hardly necessary you'd think but the loaders delight in telling tales of the ones that were forgotten. They are, almost to a man (I didn't see any women) all ex-jockeys or stable hands, so gossip is in their DNA, this job as close to racing as their oft-battered bodies will allow. Experienced hands slide beneath the belly of each horse, checking the saddles are secure. 'Let's go!' shouts the assistant when they are ready to load.

I have to say this now for it is true. The television archive from that evening is hardly HD quality. It is grainy, dark and with the pre-race action obscured by the rain. But every time Frankel comes into view, he fills the frame. He walks and looks different to the rest. Compact. Assured. Muscled. Your eyes are inevitably drawn to that head with the white star. If you didn't know better you'd have thought he'd done this a hundred times before. And this wasn't to be any ordinary maiden. Nathaniel, now 3–1 having opened at 7–1, was to win the King George VI and Queen Elizabeth Stakes the following year. Genius Beast would be in time ante-post favourite for the Derby before getting caught up in a doping scandal. Colour Vision would win the Ascot Gold Cup. Between them all they would go on to contest 245 races, winning 49 of them with prize money of over £5 million. As I said, no ordinary maiden.

As the handlers start the loading the commentator asks, 'Surely it is not possible for the rain to get any heavier?' His colleagues in the stand have already lost their umbrella to the wind but continue to talk through the attributes of the runners for what they consider the most fascinating race of the evening. As one of them presciently concludes, 'We might end up with, who knows, an impressive winner … in a really good looking field.' The conditions are getting worse and worse as the loaders shorten the lead rope, take a firm hold of each head, leading the horses into the allocated stalls, ducking away out and away under the front gates as colleagues close the rear gates to lock each one in. Frankel, wearing the number 6 cloth (the horses are numbered alphabetically in maidens), goes into his drawn number 10 stall which puts him on the left-hand side if you are look-ing from the stands. He loads in seventh without trouble. There was no reason why not; this wasn't so different to those sessions on Long Hill. But as ever there are the dawdlers and the nervous. As the wait-ing time lengthens, Tom Queally leans up against the side of the stall, hanging his arm over the partition, levering himself up to take some of his weight off Frankel. On their left Bonita Star goes in easily enough but on their right Breton Star is playing up – Frankel, ever inquisitive, keeps craning his neck, twisting around 90 degrees or more to see what is happening alongside and behind. The assistant chivvies the last of them along: keep walking boys. When they are nearly all in, the starter mounts his rostrum. 'Last one coming!' shouts the assistant as Breton Star, one of the eight racecourse debu-tants that evening and destined to be plumb last, thirty-three lengths adrift of Frankel, is levered in from behind. The assistant raises his arm to indicate to the starter that the loading is complete. 'Blinds off!' shouts the starter. Jockeys with horses who needed the blindfold to assist with the loading lean forward, tear them off, fling them backwards over their shoulders, and while they are still fluttering in the air the starter presses the button. As the gates spring open there is a wave of sound that pushes forward. It is the supreme effort of horses accelerating from no speed to fast speed in a matter of strides. The enormous intakes of breath; you can hear the sucking of wind. Hooves cutting wet turf. Jockeys shouting for room. Horses colliding in the melee. The reverberations of the stalls themselves.

Frankel made two really bad starts in his fourteen-race career and one not so good one. It was that not so good one today. The race report says he dwelt, which pretty well says it all – you stay while the others leave. We are, of course, only talking fractions of seconds, but with the sort of acceleration a racehorse is capable of, those millisec-onds soon translate into yards. Actually, as it turns out Frankel's less than stellar start is probably a good thing, as the horse to his left, Bonita Star, breaks fast and cuts straight across his path – had he been half a stride quicker they would have collided. Bonita Star's move leaves Frankel behind his biggest rival, Nathaniel, which is pretty well perfect for Tom Queally who, just like on the gallops, settles Frankel in behind him.

Not that Frankel takes it that well; for the first two furlongs he is nodding his head left, then right, as if to see a way past Nathaniel. But those hundreds of training gallops are not in vain, for in the middle four furlongs Tom has Frankel switched off. Just moving along, even letting Nathaniel stretch the lead between them. As they pass the three furlongs from home marker, it is seven runners, almost in a line, spread across the track, with Frankel eighth. It is about here that the track rises, not Warren Hill steep but distinctly noticeable for horse and rider. Tom gives Frankel an inch or two of rein, moving in motion with him, urging without being insistent. For fifty yards nothing seems to happen. Is Frankel's home pace an illusion? Does he not understand he is meant to be racing? Then as first Lemon Drop Red and more importantly Maher move to the left to give Frankel clear daylight ahead, he surges forward. One moment Nathaniel is ahead. The next they are stride for stride. At this point, with still a furlong and a half to go, you can see Tom knows he has it won. He relaxes. Frankel relaxes. They keep stride with Nathaniel whose jockey Willie Buick draws the whip. Tom doesn't bother. He doesn't have to. With hands and heels, he and Frankel do what they will always do best – go faster than the rest.

First Frankel. Second Nathaniel. Third Genius Beast. An apparently insignificant race on a wet August evening has just written itself a place in racing history.

The last past the post are usually the first to the leave the racetrack, gathering in front of the saddling boxes on the grass that goes by various unofficial names: my personal favourites are the Crying Field or the Lawn of Shattered Dreams. Whatever you want to call what is now the unsaddling area, it is here where owner and trainer gather to greet the losing jockey. The conversations are rarely long; there is little pleasure to be had in re-hashing failure. By the time Frankel arrives back having pulled Tom pretty well the full one-furlong length of the run-out (something he was to make a habit of), the losers are starting to disperse. As Sandy weaves through them, with a beaming smile that radiates both relief and delight, the glances of the vanquished vary from undisguised admiration to less-than-solicitous envy.

At the winners enclosure, a big cheer goes up; Frankel pricks up his ears and looks around as, for the first time in his life, applause becomes a currency for him. On this occasion, he is maybe getting a little ahead of himself; the Newmarket crowd have always felt a special connection to Henry, the bravos and clapping louder and longer than for anyone else. It is more for him than the horse, at least today. That might change just a little over time.

There isn't much of a press throng that evening so it falls to the guy from Racing TV to ask the questions. Henry is as diffident as ever. He doesn't feel Frankel has gone on the ground but then nothing has really been asked of him. Tom has been easy on him and he (Henry) is pleased with him as he hadn't really galloped him at home – he was just ready for a race. Oddly, he never once uses Frankel's name, signing off before joining his stepdaughter Carina to receive the trophy, uttering the less than Delphic words, 'He has good engagements. Let's hope he goes the right way.'

As the steam rises off Frankel, Tom slips off his saddle and for a moment, as travelling head lad Mike McGowan steps forward to put on a blanket, he pauses, looks Frankel in the eye, and breaks into a huge smile as he does so. Tom knows something special is going on here, and as Henry inclines his head to hear the race report, the two look like conspirators who have just pulled off a successful heist. In France, Teddy Grimthorpe feels happier than he has all day. This is important.

Soon after 7 pm, Frankel is back at home, a bucket of food and a bucket of water his reward for a job well done. Sandy is smiling still, oblivious to the fact that his smart grey racing suit is drenched. He knows. They all know. Frankel is good. The strange thing is that Frankel seems to know as well.

Everyone sleeps soundly that night.

12

Intensive training

It must have been hard for Henry to keep a lid on his expectations for Frankel. He had been here before with talented horses who had flared then fizzled. He also had a wider duty to both the horse and the people around him; hype can be corrosive. He had 154 other horses at Warren Place, with egos and expectations, however valid or unrealistic, to be massaged. But he suspected he was on to something special.

A week before the Newmarket race he was in the canteen with Stephen Kielt, Warren Place's in-house farrier. I don't think Stephen will mind me saying but he is not your usual farrier. The first time I met him I was expecting brawny arms, a hand with the texture of a chicken's claw, a battered leather apron and a hot forge. Instead he has a smart office in a Georgian building just off Newmarket high street, the windows to the back overlooking Warren Hill. On his desk are research extracts from the latest scientific journals, the paperweight a medical cutaway of an equine leg and hoof. There is not an anvil in sight. Stephen is dressed in a sports jacket, checked shirt and an immaculate pair of Australian R M Williams jeans. He is also young.

He arrived in Newmarket in 2003 from Northern Ireland, his birthplace and where he qualified as a farrier. He worked first for one of the commercial firms, then did a stint with Godolphin, where he grew to know Mike Marshall who recommended him to Henry in 2007. Farriers for the big yards occupy a rather odd position in the hierarchy: they are self-employed, on contract to supply shoeing services but they are, to all intents and purposes, full-time employees. Stephen would be in the yard every morning from half an hour before the first lot went out to well after the last horse had come in. He also employed an assistant to help him out. But he wasn't confined to the yard; Stephen went out with every lot in case a shoe came off or for any minor running repairs. As such he was probably the only person who saw every gallop Frankel ever did; even Henry missed a few through illness or travel. Stephen was impressed with Frankel (as was Henry) from the very first time he saw him gallop and he has the paper to prove it: he backed Frankel ante-post for both the 2,000 Guineas and Derby, then still a year and a bit away.

Frankel's shoeing regime was a little different to most horses; he has big feet and is a heavy horse so wore his shoes out quicker than most. Stephen would replace his front plates, as farriers like to call shoes, every thirteen to fourteen days, and the back pair every sixteen to seventeen days. Contrary to what you might expect given some of his attitudes, Frankel was always quiet to shoe and very well mannered. He didn't apparently try to take chunks out of Stephen. Later on, as the Frankel bandwagon grew, Stephen began to be aware of the part he had to play; a nail (actually they are properly called clenches) a few millimetres out of line could render him lame. The tolerances he has to play with – hard outer hoof shell through which the clench is hammered and sensitive inner core – are really very small. So Stephen began to organise his day around Frankel, picking the optimum moment when the horse was most relaxed; late morning became their appointed time as the hustle and bustle faded into the quiet of the afternoon.

Racehorses wear two types of shoe; their everyday wear are shoes made of steel that weigh 224 g each and those are the ones that Stephen routinely replaced on Frankel every thirteen to seventeen days. But three to four days ahead of his races these would be substituted with racing plates made of aluminium, which are much lighter at 101 g. These he'd wear for the race and until the next shoeing. Why the change? Well, the theory is that with less weight the animal has a more efficient stride pattern: less energy is needed to lift the feet so once set into motion the gait is more natural and efficient, less influenced by the weight of the plates. Think about kicking a ball with a heavy boot; your foot will follow through much further and be harder to stop than with a light boot. It is pretty well the same for horses. Add to that the fact that aluminium is more porous than steel, so grips the track more, and you'll see why nearly all horses race in the lighter plates despite the apparent risks and hassles involved in the fitting of them. Like all racehorses Frankel was shod cold, the plates tamped and tapped to fit him rather than hot shoeing where the plate, heated red hot in the furnace, burns a seat into the hoof. Like with people horse shoes come in sizes, but with the hind shoes slightly less rounded, a bit oval if you like, than the fore. At two and three years old, Frankel was a size seven, growing into an eight at four years which is about as big as standard racing plates come. But back to that morning in the canteen.

'What did you enjoy most about the gallops?' Henry asked.

'I enjoyed the Kind colt', replied Stephen.

'How about Midday?' suggested Henry, a filly who had just won the Nassau Stakes at Goodwood, the start of a trio of wins in the Nassau. Stephen stuck to his original answer. Henry countered with Twice Over who had just begun a similar purple patch with the

Eclipse Stakes at Sandown. Henry threw out a few other of the Warren Place hotshots, but Stephen was implacable in his support of Frankel. Henry, it seems, was challenging Stephen to moderate his view in the hope that it might give Henry reason to moderate his own. But come Tuesday evening of that same week, neither had any further reason to doubt themselves. In a special grass gallop on the round course of the Limekilns, Frankel pulverised Kings Bayonet, a horse a year his senior. That might not look much written on the page, but if you think of it as a twelve-year-old boy outrunning an eighteen-year-old man you'll get a sense of the awe Frankel was inspiring even before his debut race.

The Saturday after his victory on the Friday evening, Frankel woke up to an easy day. No gallop for him as the others headed on out. No riding at all the day after a race was a Henry thing. In fact, Frankel didn't even leave his box excepting for a pick of grass for a change of scenery. However, this was to be a brief respite, for after the Sunday rest he was about to enter the most intensive racing period of his entire life.

The target for Frankel, to which Henry had alluded in his post-race interview, was to be the Dewhurst Stakes which is run in mid-October, again at Newmarket, but over on the other course. There are certain races in the annual calendar that are milestones in the career of a horse, the outcome determining how they are regarded by the racing fraternity. The Dewhurst is one such race. The coming together of the best two-year-olds over seven furlongs in the highest grade of race. The prize money is handy at £275,000, but really this race is reputational. For the juvenile crop this is the British race to win, and should you do that you'll likely be crowned champion of your year, with a heap of expectations on your shoulders for the Classic races the following season. If Frankel was as good as Henry thought he was in his heart of hearts, then there really wasn't any other place to go. All they had to do was get there. But the Dewhurst hadn't always been a happy hunting ground for Warren Place with just two wins in thirty-three years, the last way back in 1982. And that wasn't the only monkey on Henry's shoulder; he hadn't trained the champion two-year-old for twenty-one years.

The six-day routine post-Newmarket didn't really change. Frankel had won. Everyone was relieved. But that was it. His education had to continue. You can't teach speed but you can teach a horse how best to use what they have. His work now was all about strengthening, improvement and getting inside that head to moderate his excesses. On the gallops he continued to pull the arms out of the sockets of his work rider Dan de Haan, but the suggestion by Mike Marshall that he wear a crossed noseband was helping. It might be something you never noticed but if you take a look at Frankel head-on while being ridden, on the gallops or at the races, you'll notice he has two stars on his face: the natural one on his forehead and a little sheepskin one above his nose. The latter is the pad that holds together his figure-of-eight noseband. On most regular bridles the noseband is a single band that encircles the head above the nose and bit. But with the one that was to be Frankel's daily wear, there are two cross straps: one goes up towards the cheekbone, under and round, while the other goes below the bit, under and round. You'll usually see this crossed or Mexican configuration on about one horse in twenty, but it has become something of a trademark on the sons and daughters of Frankel. The purpose is twofold: control and breathing. The lower strap, the one below the bit, keeps the bit high in the mouth giving Dan, Tom and latterly Shane Fetherstonhaugh, his work rider at three and four, more leverage and purchase, qualities they were to need in abundance both at home and on the racecourse throughout his career. It is interesting that halfway through

Frankel's two-year-old campaign Henry thought optimistically, but ultimately erroneously, that they might revert to a standard bridle at three. The cross band is also said to close the mouth and open the airways more than the standard band, something of a plus for a huge-lunged, deep-breathing animal like Frankel. However, in his box, unfettered, he remained as Dee likes to say of him 'a right so-and-so', her words amply justified when the time came to prepare Frankel for his second race and first trip away.

Henry was very old school in many respects. While the likes of Aidan O'Brien are more than happy to fly their horses in and out for the day, Henry was a firm believer that a horse should have a full five hours (excepting local Newmarket fixtures) resting in the racecourse stables prior to the race. With Frankel's next run at Doncaster some three hours north by road, this was to entail heading up the day before and staying overnight. But the troubles started before they had even set off.

There is no disguising the imminent arrival of a race day to an intelligent horse like Frankel. His life is built around routine. Everything is paced that way. Most horses like routine. Frankel positively thrives on it. You might even think he is a little OCD about it. So when Sandy was fussing around his box late that Thursday morning – bagging up the blankets, sorting out his travelling grooming kit, buzzing here and there – Frankel knew something was up. He began to get agitated. Circling round his box. Throwing his head at anyone who went by. Pawing at the floor. Moving from the back window to the front door. As Sandy would say, he was getting a head on. Now that in itself was soluble – just get him in the lorry. For Frankel, despite his headstrong nature, was always a good traveller. That would work but for one thing; he had to have his feet bandaged in a very particular manner before being loaded. Frankel. Agitation. Battle of wills. You can see where this might be going.

Horses with bandaged legs are a common enough sight but you won't often see them with all four hooves wrapped up tight, yet this was precisely the preparation required for a lengthy horse-box journey to protect the aluminium plates from becoming dislodged or loosened. Essentially, the idea is to create little booties with the bandage wrapped under and around the hoof until it is completely masked, all finally held in place with sticky gaffer tape. It is not exactly pretty but it is effective and with a willing horse easily done by one or two people in a few minutes. But Frankel wasn't willing. He was distressed and this wasn't part of his routine. It was too much for Dee and Sandy. He was jerking his leg away. Using those teeth on the end of that bendy neck. Being as difficult as only Frankel could be. The clock was ticking down. His agitation made the protection afforded by the bandaging yet more important still. He could not leave without them. Dee and Sandy called for Mike and Stephen. It was to take all four of them to do the job.

This event, which was to be repeated every single time Frankel travelled, is clearly etched into the minds of all involved. On separate occasions they all told me exactly the same tale. Sandy and Mike restraining an agitated Frankel. Stephen holding up each foot in turn. Dee wrapping as fast and efficiently as she could. It clearly became something they all dreaded; on one occasion Frankel lashed out, kicking the wall and dislodging a plate. To their credit they soon worked out that the later Frankel realised he was going racing the better, the team appearing in his box for the bandaging at the very last minute. They shielded him from any obvious pre-race activity, especially the horse lorry. The loading bay was right beside the Garage so they only drove it up when it was time to load. You might have despaired of all this in any ordinary racehorse. Given up. Passed him over as too truculent. But they all persisted with Frankel because they suspected he was extraordinary. They were right.

The Frank Whittle Partnership Conditions Stakes was due to take place at Doncaster four weeks to the day after Frankel's debut. It might not immediately stand out as a particularly prestigious race (the prize money was just £10,904.25) but Henry chose it by way of Frankel's continuing education. A longish journey in the lorry. An overnight in the racecourse stables. A different distance. This time at seven furlongs, a furlong less than Newmarket.

That said you might wonder with all the belief around Frankel why he didn't immediately step up into higher status races. That wasn't Henry's way. He didn't like to take a horse, however promising, straight from winning a maiden to taking on good horses. This was a stepping stone, if you wanted to look at it that way.

As it turns out, the morning paper showed a five-runner race that was better than your average race of this kind, but the advertised five became four when one of the outsiders was announced as a non-runner due to the ground. However, with two standout runners, both debut winners at Newmarket, Henry was excited for a good test against Farhh, a Godolphin talking horse* whose six-length July win had been written up as 'emphatic'. The expectations were justified. Farhh was to go on to win the Champion Stakes the year after Frankel and is now a successful stallion. But Frankel was shading Farhh for favouritism, the betting ring view of Frankel's first race having been enhanced the previous day when Nathaniel lost by a short head to one of Frankel's stable companions, Picture Editor. However, much to Henry's disappointment the contest didn't happen on this particular day; Farhh played up in the stalls and was withdrawn at the start, so as the bookmakers hurriedly chalked Frankel up as odds on instead of odds against, just three runners came out

---

* A tongue-in-cheek expression for a horse so talented, you'd almost think he could talk.

of the stalls to head down the straight seven furlongs of Doncaster's Town Moor course.

If Frankel had dwelt in the stalls by accident at Newmarket, here Tom made it happen on purpose. The last thing in the world he wanted was to be left out in front – the gates open and Frankel actually doesn't move a muscle, only finally lolloping out when the other two have gone a stride or two. As Tom lets him go, they insert themselves into second place for the next five furlongs, tracking Diamond Geezah with Frankel being held with his customary tight rein, but as always nodding his head left and right as if to remind Tom that this restraint both isn't welcome or required.

As they approach the two-furlong marker Frankel has his way. Tom edges them out, draws level and then, a length past Diamond Geezah, the most experienced horse in the race with seven runs and one win, he pushes the pause button. You wonder why for a moment, but then Tom lowers his head, turning to look behind under his right arm to check the position of the other two. Satisfied he gives Frankel a little rein. They start to pull away. Two, three, four, five lengths … but clearly Tom is not satisfied. As they enter the final furlong he turns around in the saddle, this time a full, long look for the disappearing pair, crouches down and lets his horse go. Frankel absolutely powers away. Tom has discovered, probably what he long suspected: Frankel has more gears than any horse he has ever ridden. Not using them would be a crime. It's like that moment in the sci-fi film *Back to the Future* when Marty McFly hits the afterburners of his time-travelling DeLorean just because he can. But this is for real.

The official winning margin is thirteen lengths, the greatest distance Frankel would ever win by. I have to say, whatever the measured distance might be, it looks further to me. It might as well have been thirteen miles for all the impact the other two were making. And as for Farhh, he didn't entirely miss out; he'd have the opportunity to be beaten twice by Frankel when they raced at four.

For a racing career that spanned just twenty-six months, it is surprising how big the gaps could be between Frankel's fourteen races; there was one of eight months and another of seven months between the end of one season and the start of another. Even in the throes of his three-year-old season when he was to sweep aside all comers, he went nearly three months between the penultimate and last race of that particular year. But that was Henry's way – they raced when they were ready, or were readied when it was time to race. There were no imperatives. No strict formula. Look for a pattern with Frankel and you'll be sorely disappointed. The breaks between races range from 217 days down to 14. The one thing for sure is that victory in the Frank Whittle marked the start of the most intensive period of Frankel's racing life, with three races in thirty-six days, which was to end with him crowned a champion.

If you were a racing journalist what would you do on your day off? Well, it's obvious if you are Chris Cook, racing correspondent of the *Guardian*. Go racing. I met Chris almost eight years to the day after he had headed to Ascot for Frankel's third race. It's fair to say that Chris wasn't the only follower of Frankel in those early days, but he was certainly one of the most enthusiastic, a quality that he retains to this day. Talk of Frankel and his whole body responds, but mostly the fingers on his phone as he digs into his personal archive for photos and articles of the horse he regards as the greatest ever. Now he is not unique in that, but he was one of the first to make such thoughts a matter of record.

We are meeting in the subterranean food hall of Kempton Park for a coffee before racing, having retreated from the sepulchral atmosphere of a packed press room. You might be disappointed to hear the press room is no hub of wine-soaked journos, sucking on fags with one eye on a deadline and another on the bookmakers' latest odds. It is deadly quiet. Two dozen bodies lined up in orderly fashion on long bench desks tapping at keyboards. The only decadences are some curling sandwiches courtesy of the management and a coffee machine that would appear to do more harm than good judging by Chris's eagerness to leave.

Chris, now forty-five years old, has been fascinated by racing since he was seven. When I asked him why, he gave me the best excuse I have ever heard for falling to this, the most deadly of all vices: 'My parents took me racing when I was young and vulnerable.' That's a lament that the woke generation might appreciate. I certainly do. I was inculcated into betting by a grandmother who waved away my parents' objections on the grounds that 'it would do wonders for his maths'. Well, I did become a bookmaker … As for Chris he did go cold turkey for a while, studying law in Edinburgh for four years before succumbing, leaving his flat, girlfriend and 50 per cent of his income behind to travel south to become deputy editor of the weekly *Racing & Football Outlook*.

In winning at Doncaster Frankel had earned, in Henry's eyes, the right to take on what he would describe as 'good' horses, though today we know he had already done that in his first race. The Juddmonte Royal Lodge Stakes, a Group 2 race at Ascot, which included Treasure Beach who was to come second in the Derby and win the Irish equivalent, fulfilled that criterion. In case you are wondering, this race is one of a series of Group races that Prince Khalid's Juddmonte sponsors in France, Ireland, the UK and USA each year. I don't suppose for one moment that Henry took this into consideration when mapping out Frankel's programme, but I'm equally sure he took a certain satisfaction in winning back his boss's money for him. It's all part of the game.

The race itself was another small field of five, though this time they were all to take part. It was back to Frankel's debut distance of a mile, but for the first time ever he'd be racing on a round course. That could make for some interest. And he'd also be racing on different ground, this time good-to-soft or as Irish readers know it, yielding.

In some ways, and especially to an outsider, this focus by racing professionals with the going borders on the obsessional. Every line of form. Every race card. Every race report. They will all mention the ground. Trainers place their horses in, or withdraw them from, races according to the predicted going. In interviews and conversations, the going is referenced as beneficial or detrimental, rarely neutral. I was recently standing with a clerk of the course (the old-fashioned name for the racecourse manager) at one of Britain's premier National Hunt tracks who was considering watering a drying track overnight in preparation for racing the following day. He took two agitated calls in rapid succession: one from a trainer imploring watering and the other not. Both threatened to withdraw if the decision went the other way.

The going, the official measure of the moisture content of the racing surface as announced at the start of each race meeting, which ranges from heavy (close to waterlogged) to hard (rock solid and usually unraceable), is one of those great imponderables when it comes to assessing a horse race. You'll often hear the commentator burbling away: so-and-so only acts on soft going. Place your bets accordingly. Trainers are similarly influenced; discovering what going your horse races best on should influence where and when he or she races. However, knowing which is largely a case of trial and error, but there are some tells: breeding, action and the physical attributes of a horse.

Certain sires acquire a reputation for producing offspring that do best on particular types of going or surface, such as turf or dirt for instance. In Frankel's case you'd do well to find any definitive pattern in Galileo's many thousands, and that includes Frankel. He was to win on all types of going, from soft to good-to-firm, rather proving one of racing's clichés: a good horse goes on any ground. The action of a horse, the way it moves at full gallop, is largely related to its physical configuration. There are, as you might imagine, many permutations to this so think about it in human terms. The next time you are on the beach with the family, experiment with everyone running along both the hard sand recently swept by the waves and the soft, dry sand. It is amazing how most will have a preference for one over the other, while a few will run equally happily on both. Horses are not a lot different.

The Ascot public were to see a great deal of Frankel. This was the only track he was to race at in each of his three seasons and the one he raced at most – five times in all including his last. It is no wonder the crowd took him to their hearts, but this, the Royal Lodge, was the first time, as Teddy Grimthorpe puts it, the wider public were to be let into the secret that was Frankel.

Though many people claim it, I suspect very few people actually saw Frankel race in the flesh for each and every one of his races. Even some of those closest to the horse missed out. Henry did; cancer kept him away from the second Sussex Stakes win. Jane was in France with Teddy for the debut. Prince Khalid didn't see him run as a two-year-old. Dee preferred to stay at Warren Place readying his stall for his return. But of course Sandy was there for them all. As was Chris Cook. From the very first time he saw him run he was hooked on Frankel, struck by what he calls the 'amazing presence' of the horse. In fact Chris peppers his conversations about Frankel with the word amazing. And he's meant to be a level-headed professional.

* * *

That said the start of the Royal Lodge, far away from the stands at almost the lowest point of the track, is far from amazing for anyone expecting fireworks. Drawn furthest from the rails, Tom chooses to deploy the same starting tactic as for Doncaster: hold Frankel back and come out last. But this time, instead of inserting himself in the middle of the pack, he tracks Frankel diagonally behind the other four horses to take up position beside the running rail, content to be five of five. And so they lob along; well, as far as Frankel is ever capable of lobbing. While the other jockeys cruise in front, Tom has Frankel under a tight rein. He said afterwards, as did Henry, that Frankel was more pliant than usual, but replays still show a jockey holding a head tight in while the horse nods to the left and to the right by way of reminder that this wasn't exactly what he wanted.

For a while the tactic works; Frankel keeps his side of the bargain but as they pass the five furlong from home marker he tries to edge right. For a few dozen strides, Tom fights the notion, trying to steer him back left, closer to the running rail. But suddenly horse and man seem to be in agreement that open daylight, on the wide outside of the other runners, is the place to be. So, as the track starts to turn towards the stands, Frankel begins his run. Chris Cook describes this as 'tactically mad'. Remember this is a horse that has never raced on a round course. Accelerating around a bend, taking the longest route around your opponents, is breathtakingly insane. But Frankel does it like it is the most natural thing in the world. He entered the bend last. And before it is halfway complete, he is first.

As the bend unwinds, the Ascot straight is ahead. The race still has nearly three furlongs to run but Frankel has already neutered his opponents. Tom shakes him up but with no great urgency and they still start to pull away. At two furlongs to go, he looks around. Satisfied with what he sees, he engages a few of those extra gears. The commentator in the stands, counting out the lengths as Frankel pulls further and further ahead, is starting to become increasingly rapturous. 'He's a class apart from the rest!' he shouts to a crowd who were probably working that out for themselves.

The winning margin is ten lengths but really that doesn't tell us much; Tom had started easing Frankel down well before the winning post and, in common with all his first three races, never picked up the whip. Tom struggles to bring Frankel to a halt (in the end he drags Frankel sideways towards the rails until he gets the hint) and into the hands of Sandy, who calls the race a complete demolition. As Henry and Jane make their way down the steps of the stands, Henry suddenly stops, turns back to look up at Jane and without prompting or any apparent prior thought says, 'He's the best I've ever had.' No probably. No I think. Just certainty. And then they started walking again.

Chris Cook pulls out his phone and blogs, 'Frankel. The most special flat horse ever.' Not a bad day at the races.

13

Economical with the actualité

All tribes have their gatherings; racing is no different. Dewhurst week in Newmarket in early October is that place. Tattersalls, the world's leading auctioneer of bloodstock, headquartered in racing's global hub, hosts the October Yearling Sale. At the racecourse they stage the Future Champions Festival, a two-day meeting which has the Dewhurst Stakes as its juvenile centrepiece. The year I was writing this book, I went along to check it out.

First of all, it is all consuming as Newmarket gives itself up to the international horse-racing elite. In an age of surge pricing, the worst hotels (of which there are many) charge outrageous rates. The bars and restaurants are packed. Owners, trainers, breeders, bloodstock agents … they are all here to tout their wares or their wallets, for this is a pivotal moment in the racing year. The decisions made over the next few days will echo forward over the coming years. Thousands of horses will be sold on the basis of hope; these are all yearlings. Unraced. Untried. Ability unknown.

In the three days before the races, it is the Book 1 yearlings that attract the attention of the high-end buyers and the dreams of the sellers. The sale entries are divided into four 'books' of descending value according to how much the auctioneer believes they will sell for; Books 2–4 will come the week after the races. For now we are just interested in the cream of some 500 lots that will collectively be sold for something over £100 million including, in all likelihood, the most expensive yearling sold on the planet that year.

You have probably seen those clips on the news where the black-tied auctioneer, beneath a glittering chandelier, with society's finest in front of him, a bank of telephone handlers to his side with a Picasso, Bacon, Koons or Warhol on the easel, who has the hushed audience in the palm of his hand as he whispers a Lottery-sized figure before slamming down the gavel. Tattersalls is not so different, except it is staged like the Coliseum, the rows of seats rising high to the roof, with a tiny ring in the middle around which the horse on the block is led beneath, of course, a giant chandelier. The sense of theatre is the same. There is palpable excitement when a fancied lot is led into the ring; today every Frankel colt or filly has that effect. The seats and the aisles fill up. The giant screen above the auctioneer is sparse on information about the horse, simply stating its lot number. The rest of the screen is all about the money, charting the rising sale price in guineas, Euros, US dollars, Japanese yen and the United Arab Emirates Dirham. That tells you something about the composition of the buyers.

As the price rises so do the increments. Early on, while our auctioneer is warming up his audience, he'll take 5,000 or 10,000 guinea bids in a wearisome manner. He knows his crowd has deeper pockets. But soon such parsimony is abandoned, as 50,000 becomes the unit of increase until, eventually, it goes beyond that. The sort of number that most normal people would consider a healthy lifetime of earnings is considered, offered then bettered in the blink of an eye. A filly turned out to be that world record yearling the day I sat beside the ring: three and a half million guineas which, once you've translated that into pounds and added VAT, is a cheque to write of £4.41 million. Three days later it looked, as far as a yearling ever can, a bargain when its full brother Too Darn Hot followed in the footsteps of Frankel, winning the Dewhurst Stakes. But back to the past.

The Dewhurst was the second race on the card for Frankel's final race of his two-year-old season. In theory it was the *hors d'oeuvre* for the third and most valuable of the day, the Champion Stakes. But in reality Frankel's race was the one everyone had come for. The high rollers who had swung into Tattersalls for Book 1 were there en masse. As Teddy had said after the Royal Lodge, the secret was out.

It is all too easy now, a few years on, to think of the Dewhurst Stakes as a one-horse race. Little more than a training gallop for Frankel. But at the time it was very different. Some were there to see him beaten. For, however good Warren Place thought Frankel may have been, there were others who thought they had one better. Three horses went into the race unbeaten, a contest some of the media were already styling as the 'two-year-old race of the century'. Only one was to go home with a reputation intact.

This was, on paper at least, the most formidable opposition Frankel had met so far. Dream Ahead was three from three including two Group 1 wins, the most recent a nine-length demolition of his opponents. Sound familiar? Frankel was of course also three from three but the best his record showed thus far was a Group 2 race. Saamidd, who made up the trio of the unbeaten, was to the Godolphin powerhouse what Frankel was to Juddmonte – the one in which they harboured dreams of greatness. They referred to him as Pegasus but most of his flying had been done away from prying eyes on their private gallops.

So why, you might ask, as Tom cantered an uncharacteristically calm Frankel down to the post past the biggest crowd of his life thus far (who he seemed quite fascinated by), was Frankel odds on at 4–6 favourite, Dream Ahead 5–2, Saamidd 7–1 and the other three 25–1 or longer? The odds seemed at odds with the form. It was because of a conversation the previous Saturday, which went like this:

Mike: 'Bloody hell!'

Henry: 'We have a good one.'

Often, a few days ahead of a big race, Henry arranged a little outing for his horses. Nothing hugely elaborate but instead of confining themselves to the gallops within walking distance of Warren Place, they'd go to the training grounds on the Racecourse Side, the gallops beside the Newmarket racecourses. It was, in many respects, a dress rehearsal for the following week. Planting a little bug inside the head of the horse that something out of the ordinary was coming up. So Frankel, along with his lead horse, was loaded into the horse lorry (mercifully no bandaging required as he was still in ordinary plates) and driven across town, unloaded onto the tarmac of what is in fact the racecourse car park.

There is no place to hide. No way, at least for Warren Place, to gallop away from public gaze. Word had got out and a crowd, including the press, had gathered to see what was in fact a trial race. Unusually Tom was there to ride Frankel; Henry never liked changing riders unless it was absolutely essential. It is back to that routine thing, so Dan stood this one out, for once able to watch what he usually had to manage.

Frankel was pitted against an older horse; Henry didn't have another two-year-old that could remotely compete so this was some attempt to create some sort of equal contest. But it didn't work. Tom tracked the lead horse for two-thirds of the six furlongs, pulled Frankel out and burst clear by ten lengths without any apparent effort. The *Racing Post* called it 'blistering' and 'breathtaking'. We know what Mike and Henry said. The odds tumbled accordingly. All Frankel had to do now was replicate on the course what he had done on the gallops.

There is no disguising how important this race was for everyone connected to Frankel. For Prince Khalid it would crown one of his most successful seasons ever. For Tom Queally a chance to cement his reputation as one of the up-and-coming young jockeys. For all the team at Warren Place confirmation that they were back. For Henry some satisfaction that he was out of the wilderness, the also-ran tag he had hung around his own neck consigned forever to that same wilderness.

As for Frankel he seemed completely unconcerned. Enjoying the crowds. The sense of occasion. Tom had never had him at such ease heading down to the start. It was just a bit of a shame it wasn't going to stay that way. The plan was that Tom was to bounce Frankel out, get to the front, make the pace, stretch the field and when the moment was right leave them all for dead. Man makes plans and God laughs.

As the starting gates open Tom does indeed bounce Frankel out but that is about as far as the plan goes. The horses drawn either side of him, the unbeaten Saamidd and Glor Na Mara, are half a stride faster, closing the gap ahead of Frankel, Saamidd in the process bumps Frankel hard which knocks him sideways from the middle of the draw to the far right, leaving him last of the six. In a matter of a few strides all the good work Tom has done to switch Frankel off is undone. He is lit up. Furious to be both bumped and behind. For the next two furlongs he fights Tom every yard of the way, trying to head out right around the pack while Tom tries to pull him left behind the pack.

It is a textbook example of headstrong Frankel. Fired up. Unwilling to settle. On course to lose the race before it is halfway done. Henry, who never carried binoculars, turns to Jane for some indication of what is going on but she can't get hers to focus. They both stare down the Rowley Mile, so many dreams blowing away across the Heath.

As the horses enter the third of the seven furlongs Tom manages to calm Frankel into some sort of order. It isn't pretty as they crab forward at full racing pace, Tom pulling Frankel's head to the left towards the pack to stop him bolting. But gradually he placates Frankel. Approaching the two-furlong pole they have both visibly relaxed. Frankel straightens up. Tom loosens the reins just a little. As they flow in that rhythm of horse and jockey, the stride of the horse matching the motion of the man, the move is made. While every other jockey is hard at it, with whips raised and frantic urgings, Tom just pushes Frankel on. Roderic O'Connor, also a son of Galileo who will win a Group 1 in France later in the month and the Irish 2,000 Guineas the following year, is the only one to put up a fight but as the race report read, 'no threat to the winner'.

In the immediate aftermath of the race, the bookmakers make Frankel hot favourite for the 2,000 Guineas and Derby the following year. Henry tries to dampen expectations: 'I am not going to do the usual thing for a trainer or tell the jockey to say he is the best horse they have ever ridden.' But we know he is being economical with the *actualité*.

Frankel is four for four. He has blown away two of the most highly thought of juveniles of his generation. Henry has his wishes: the Dewhurst Stakes and, as he had confided in Sandy months earlier, the champion two-year-old. Teddy Grimthorpe does the rounds of the post-season ceremonies, picking up the Cartier Award and the Racehorse Owners Association Award to fill an ever-burgeoning Frankel shelf in the Prince Khalid trophy cabinet at Banstead Manor Stud. Bobby Frankel would have been pleased for them all.

As to what is to become of those ante-post vouchers held by Stephen Kielt, they are beginning to look more valuable than founder shares in the Apple Corporation.

14

Winter dreaming

Hope is the crack cocaine of racing. Everyone is hopelessly addicted. During November to March, the months when the turf flat season shuts down, it provides the daily fix. When you are scraping mud from your horse. Being lashed sideways by rain on the gallops. Getting up in the dark. Going home in the dark. Paying yet another bill. It is the dreams of what may be that keep you going. Hope is that tiny speck of light on a hill far, far away by which you set your course. But that winter dreaming, in one of Henry's few missteps, didn't get off to the best of starts.

Henry didn't much like the Garage; the boxes were neither big nor airy. Dee describes it as a bit of a wreck. Mike is more diplomatic: not very nice. Hot in summer. Cold in winter. Clearly not the sort of place for a champion two-year-old. It was decided that Frankel was to be moved to one of the prestigious boxes in the main yard to join the stars of Warren Place, away from the daily distractions of the Garage. If horses reviewed on Trip Advisor, Frankel's new box would be 'OMG to die for', whereas with the Garage it would be 'Wouldn't recommend it to my worst enemy'. If Frankel had been given the benefit of such on-line reviews, he would clearly have put little store by them as he absolutely loathed his new box. After a couple of hours of disconsolate sniffing and pawing he started screaming, a sort of agonised whinnying. When that attracted little attention he began lashing out at the walls with his feet. Sandy tried to calm him down but after a couple of days he still had his 'head' on him. Angry. In a permanent sulk. He even started to go off his food, a very un-Frankel-like behaviour. Maybe he needed something more intimate? More Garage-like without being the Garage? A small square of ten or so boxes just around the corner from the main yard called the Dip was chosen. The effect was instantaneous – he stopped sulking and reverted back to kicking and screaming, trying to dispatch the Dip to oblivion. Within a few hours he was back in the Garage.

Calm restored it is worth considering how something as trivial as a box move caused Frankel such distress. Racehorses are moved around all the time. It is not a big deal for your average horse, but therein probably lies the answer. Frankel is not your average horse. It sounds obvious, but I'm not talking just about his undoubted physical attributes. I remember the first time I met him. I asked Teddy Grimthorpe to talk me through what I should look for that made him so special. Teddy, being the kind and patient man that he is, gave me the perfect '101 Thoroughbred Conformation for Dummies' talk. As we gazed on Frankel, I asked whether there was anything I couldn't see – I had read somewhere that post-mortems of previous champion racehorses had revealed extraordinarily large lungs or hearts or both. In all probability Frankel has those, but Teddy simply tapped the side of his head. 'It is in there', he said. 'He has a will to win unlike any other horse I have known.'

And that is it. Both Frankel's strength and his Achilles heel. In the Dewhurst Stakes the bump riled him up, but not in a good way. On the gallops there is the daily tussle to restrain him. Jane Cecil, who still sees Frankel two or three times a month by way of fund raising for East Anglia's Children's Hospices to which Frankel is an ambassador (yes, a horse alongside the likes of Ed Sheeran), describes him not only as exceptionally intelligent but the alpha male of all alpha males. The box move incident was all about that. In the Garage he was perfectly happy with his ten buddies, including his half-brother and lead horse Bullet Train two doors down. As they like to say in sporting circles he 'bossed' the place. Jane tells the story of when Lady Gillian, the widow of Lord Howard de Walden, came to visit her horse, newly installed in the box opposite Frankel. Naturally Lady Gillian went directly towards her horse but Frankel took this badly, kicking his door and whinnying. 'It's no good,' said Jane to Lady Gillian, 'you are going to have to say hello to Frankel first.'

The transition from racing-fit to winter quarters for 155 primed equine athletes is not quite as easy as you might suppose. You can't suddenly stop. They are too highly strung and attuned to the routine for that. During November and as Christmas approached, Warren Place was gradually wound down. No longer were there Wednesday and Saturday gallops. These were replaced with two canters up Warren Hill, the other four days a single canter. Sunday, as ever, was the day of rest. The daily feed was slowly tweaked – less calories out required fewer calories in. Come January, as Jane and Henry headed for the Caribbean, outdoor work was suspended for the entire month. When Henry was away, nobody went out. Exercise consisted of eighteen circuits, so three miles, around the indoor ride. Frankel didn't care for this much; it wasn't interesting and he acted up accordingly. Getting fresh as Shane calls it. Jinking around. On his toes. Generally just showing that he was ready for more than this.

As Henry lay in the sun did he have any reason to worry about the season ahead? Frankel was red-hot favourite for the 2,000 Guineas. Just about every sportswriter in the UK and around the globe was hailing Frankel as the racing superstar-in-the-making. Sandy, even as early as Christmas, was already getting excited. Everyone in the yard knew they had something special. The only scepticism came by way of the January publication of the *World Thoroughbred Rankings* which placed Frankel joint top of his juvenile year, sharing billing with Dream Ahead, the horse he had beaten into fifth place, seven lengths adrift, in the Dewhurst Stakes. Frankel was to dispatch him in similar fashion at Royal Ascot later in the year. Henry generously described the ranking as 'all a matter of opinion', which is probably a fair summation. But there are always doubts with racehorses. They are fickle creatures, especially as they make that transition from two years to three.

'Didn't train on.' You'll often hear this maddeningly non-specific explanation for the failure of a horse returning to the course after some stellar performances the previous season. It is the nightmare that awakens a trainer during a long winter. The knowledge that, for no apparent reason, a good horse can turn bad. It is rarely the other way around. Racing is knee-deep in these shattered reputations. Henry had experienced his fair share over the years. Horses that flared out at three when they seemed to have it all before them at two. Physically they look the same. At home their work is as good as ever. But on the racecourse the spark has gone. Sometimes the decline from champion to failure is so steep that they never race again. Whether it is in the heart, head or body nobody seems to know. Maybe it is like those contemporaries we all knew at school who seemed to be marked down for greatness but are conspicuously absent at reunions. Whatever the reason it happens, and when it happens it does so very suddenly.

As you might imagine, I spoke to a great many people in the course of researching this book; some on the periphery, some right at the heart of the Frankel story. Just about whoever they were and whatever their involvement, the conversation usually led to a single name. Not Henry. But Shane. You must talk to Shane. Have you met Shane yet? Do you have Shane's number?*

So many roads led to Shane Fetherstonhaugh who is one of a rare breed: he is a professional work rider. He is not a jockey. He is not a stable hand. He gets racehorses fit and race ready for a living. Shane, like most work riders, is self-employed, riding on contract. He arrives each morning, rides a horse out in each lot, with his day over by midday. This is a very specialist way of life. It is not without its dangers; highly strung thoroughbreds come with great risks. You need to be ultra-fit and watch your weight. The word wiry doesn't really do justice to Shane's lean frame. And then you have the hours. And weather. Of course it is life fulfilling to be out on the Heath in the warm dawn of summer, riding an amazing racehorse. There is a certain romance to it. But equally you have the dark of winter mornings: snow, Arctic winds, damp, rain and horses that you less than love. And Henry was big on that. There was no weather you didn't go out in; you can't choose your race-day weather so why choose your training-day weather? Frankel's wet August debut was a tribute to such a philosophy.

As you might imagine it is not a job for everyone; that combination of tough lifestyle and talent doesn't come together in many people, so the best work riders are in great demand, able to pick and choose the stables they ride for. Shane, though he is amazingly

---

* It is to the enormous credit of everyone I met, and the racing industry in general, as to how free people were to help. Not just with their own memories but helping me join up the dots; I rarely left an interview without two or three new contacts. Sometimes it was more instant than that. A chance conversation at a bar leading to someone I'd only just met pulling out a phone, scrolling through contacts, dialling a number and handing me the phone: you must talk to this guy. It was truly remarkable. Much of what you are reading would likely have never happened without those kindnesses. To everyone – thank you.

modest and self-effacing, is at the very pinnacle of his trade. And not just because of Frankel. In the family kitchen hangs a picture of Motivator, the Derby winner of 2005 who was one of Shane's. Today Shane is on retainer to the mighty Godolphin Newmarket stables.

Changing work riders was not an easy decision for Henry. Frankel, as we know, liked things to be just so. He didn't deal with change well. But Dan de Haan, despite doing a great job, was on the heavy side and Henry was concerned at putting undue strain on the legs and body of a thoroughbred who didn't actually grow that much between two and three; he was saving that growth spurt for the following winter. So Shane, who had impressed Henry when dealing with a particularly tricky Warren Place horse called Passage of Time, was offered Frankel. Champion two-year-old? Not a hard decision.

By the time Shane sat on Frankel for the first time in November, he had been a work rider for almost exactly half his life, having left his native Ireland at sixteen. He was no stranger to big, strong horses, having done his apprenticeship in a jumping yard; so the single word he used to describe Frankel in the early days of their relationship – headstrong – gives you some idea of his immediate thoughts. It might sound a stretch to use the word relationship but Shane was to be one of the daily constants in Frankel's life, along with Dee, Sandy and Henry, over the next two years. What he did, and how he did it, from that unique position in the saddle, was to be pivotal in unlocking Frankel's potential.

Shane would arrive in the Garage around 6.40 am. Despite this being an early hour for most people, he would be the third person Frankel saw in the morning. Dee would have been in two hours earlier for Frankel's favourite moment of the day: his first feed. Sandy would follow at 6 am with hay, change his water and muck out his box. A little while later Dee would be back to bandage all four of his legs, a process by which she wrapped each leg from the fetlock (the joint immediately above the hoof) to the knee with soft padding which was held in place by a tightly wrapped bandage. This, in contrast to his pre-race-day antics, Frankel didn't mind. It was just routine, a precaution against him 'knocking' himself as trainers call it, when the hoof of one leg hits the cannon bone (horse equivalent of our shin) that connects knee to fetlock, of another. So this was how Shane would find Frankel: fed, watered, bandaged and tied to the wall ready for work.

It was Shane's task to tack up Frankel; get him ready to ride. Most of the time Shane would use the same saddle for all his rides (the pads are never shared to avoid cross-infection), but in another sign of how Frankel was being marked out for special treatment, however much that went against Henry's grain, Frankel had his own saddle. First went on the bridle, the one with a cross band for extra control. Shane kept Frankel tied to the wall while he next went about fitting first the pads, the soft blanket under the saddle and then the saddle itself. Some horses you'd be happy to leave untied but not Frankel. It wasn't that he acted up but rather he saw this moment as an opportunity. While you were distracted with both hands committed to tightening the girth (the strap that goes around and under the belly to hold the saddle in place), it was his chance to take a chunk out of you. It wasn't the sort of early morning call Shane appreciated and it wasn't something Frankel grew out of. If anything, the older he got the more he tried to bite. All that done, two and a half hours after the start of the Warren Place day, it was time to ride.

When he was younger, Shane used to spring like a jack-in-a-box into the saddle. Not so much now, so Sandy or one of the stable hands would give him a leg up into the saddle. Actually that was another of Henry's 'things' – he disliked the riders levering themselves into the saddle by way of the stirrup; the strains and shifting of weight put unnecessary strain on the spine. Shane didn't ride work super-short like a jockey would ride a race where the stirrups are halfway up the shoulder of the horse. But with Frankel being a strong horse he always rode him with a short stirrup, shorter than he would ride anything else, whether it was work up Warren Hill or full gallops on the Racecourse Side.

In Frankel's early days, when Dan was his work rider, he went out in the third string, the late morning posse. But by the time Shane took over, he was indubitably a first lot horse. And not only that but the lead horse. He had to be first. First out of the yard. First into the indoor ride. First out of the indoor ride. The horse to lead the forty or fifty strong pack out onto the Heath. The first up Warren Hill. Or the first across whichever gallop had been chosen for that particular day. As Jane says, the alpha male. In fact the only horse Frankel ever deferred to was Bullet Train, another Garage inmate. Maybe Frankel sensed they were related?

Despite its gorgeously forgiving all-weather polytrack surface – it's like a bed of icing sugar – you wouldn't pick the Al Bahathri gallop for its ambience, sandwiched as it is between a railway line and the main road into Newmarket, with the adjacent junction of the A14 and A11 thrown in for good measure. Nor would you pick it as the venue that took Frankel off the sports pages and onto the news pages. But it did. 'HORSE OUTRUNS TRAIN' ran the headline. This was really the moment that the Frankel story broke out into the consciousness of the wider public.

The truth is that racing often struggles to grab its fair share of mainstream media attention; the Grand National, Royal Ascot and to a lesser extent the Derby will make front-page news and be the lead item on the TV news. But the horses or the people? Well, it happens rarely. In the past two decades there are probably only four flat-racing names that would strike a chord with those who politicians and pollsters like to call the man in the street. Two jock-eys, one trainer and one horse. Lester Piggott, Frankie Dettori, Henry Cecil. And Frankel. And two of those four were on the Al Bahathri on that late-March morning to make the news.

Henry had long planned to make the mid-April Greenham Stakes at Newbury the race for Frankel's three-year-old debut. It is far from unheard of for the champion two-year-old to head directly to the 2,000 Guineas two weeks later without the benefit of a preparation race, but Henry didn't trust himself. Don't forget this was to be Frankel's second longest break between races – 182 days – almost precisely half a year. So, the Greenham it was, a fairly modest race, but one that Henry had used as a stepping stone for his 1976 2,000 Guineas winner Wollow, a horse he often compared Frankel with during his two-year-old career. This Guineas trial was a Group 3 race, with just £28,385 to the winner, and as such the last time Frankel would contest anything other than a Group 1. And the last time he'd race under a mile in distance. But even the preparation race required the preparation gallop.

The sun was only just rising as Frankel led out the Wednesday lot; it is a full two-mile walk from Warren Place to the start of the Al Bahathri at the far end of the Railway Field. They had a 7 am meeting with Henry, Mike, Teddy, Stephen, plus a cluster of journalists and onlookers. Word was out that Frankel was doing some serious work. Henry gave his instructions as the horses circled; Frankel and Bullet Train were to lead off together over six furlongs. You might ask, why six? After all the Greenham Stakes is seven. Again that is a Henry thing. He rarely worked a horse over the full distance of the upcoming race, preferring to shave a furlong or two off the distance. Why? It is the easiest thing in the world to over-train a horse. The trick, which all great trainers have in common, is to bring the horse to the track at the edge of his or her ability, ready with the mental and physical fitness to produce what is needed on *the* day. You will often hear it said that more races are lost than won on the training gallops. It is one of those inelegant, throwaway lines but it contains a large element of truth.

The Al Bahathri is shaped a bit like a hockey stick: the first five furlongs are straight, then it kinks left for the final furlongs. Having puffed along its entire length (polytrack is a surface designed for the horse rather than human foot) the incline and undulations remind me a lot of both the Newmarket tracks, with a steep rise at the finish. Henry placed himself, as he always did, beneath a beech tree close to the kink with a clear view not only down the gallop but also the railway line that runs parallel to the gallop. Naturally everyone gathered around Henry, if perhaps a little upwind to avoid his ever-present cigarette smoke. They wanted to see what he saw. And what they saw was Frankel demolishing two trains: Bullet Train and Greater Anglia's Ipswich to Newmarket service.

It is one of those strange quirks. Something that happened that nobody planned. And on a day when there was a crowd to see it. Frankel and Bullet Train ran up the Al Bahathri together on dozens of occasions and never, before or since, did Shane fix the start with such perfect timing, kicking off just as the train appeared beside them. Quite what the commuters in the two-carriage train thought as the galloping pair first drew level and then pulled away, history doesn't report, but as the train disappeared into the cutting they missed the really good bit. Frankel, released by Shane from the wake of Bullet Train (remember he's a year older than Frankel, so what was about to happen should not by rights really happen), surged twenty lengths clear. As Shane fought to bring him to a halt, Frankel twisted his head to see just how far he had left his galloping companion behind. A long, long way – he could see that. Satisfied, he consented to coming to a stop. Frankel wasn't the only one that was satisfied; the bookmakers subsequently made him the hottest of hot favourites for both the 2,000 Guineas and the Derby. A horse that outruns a train? Everyone was piling aboard the Frankel express. But not everyone was in agreement as to his final destination.

The Juddmonte/Warren Place axis was aligned as to the short-term plan for Frankel: a win in the Greenham Stakes warm-up at Newbury and then Classic success at the 2,000 Guineas at Newmarket. The future thereafter was less certain. There the axis divided: the Derby at Epsom or not? The problem was that the Derby, at one and a half miles, was half as far again as any race Frankel would have run in to date. Nobody actually knew whether, with his wild ways and blistering race pace, he had the stamina to last out the distance.

Racehorses broadly divide into four groups: sprinters, milers, middle-distancers and stayers. In flat race distance terms that is six furlongs or less, seven furlongs to a mile, nine furlongs to a mile and a half, with stayers racing a mile and three-quarters up to the longest flat race run in Britain, the Queen Alexandra Stakes at Royal Ascot over two and three-quarter miles. If I'd have been writing this book half a century ago, two miles would have been regarded as the minimum distance for a stayer. But fashions change, even in horse racing. If you go back further there is a time when the racing distances were more extreme: that sign you see for Six Mile Bottom on the outskirts of Newmarket is named after the starting point for races of that distance, with eight miles the longest contested.

This ability to be effective over a particular distance is largely down to breeding; when you put a mare to a stallion it is not just about breeding a good horse. It is also about breeding a horse that will be effective over a chosen distance. Sometimes this is a purely commercial decision; today milers are the most desirable and attract the greatest stud value. Other times it is strictly emotional – you might just prefer to race stayers. Now when Prince Khalid sent Kind (who raced from five to seven furlongs) to Galileo (who raced from a mile to a mile and a half), the idea was to create a horse with speed and stamina. Now we know Frankel has speed, but what nobody knew was how much stamina he had.

Looks can only take you so far in identifying this; someone with a good bloodstock eye will tell you that the characteristics of a sprinter are a thick-set horse with a big back end and big shoulders, as opposed to a stayer with a lengthier and lighter frame powered by an easy movement. If that doesn't quite chime think of it in terms of Olympic athletes: the 100 m specialists are pumped up like body builders with calves and biceps that do justice to the strength of Lycra. The 5,000 and 10,000 m runners on the other hand are all skin and bone, their shorts and tops flapping with each fluid stride. Naturally Frankel doesn't fit easily into one or other category, which in part explains his phenomenal ability. He has not only the thick-set frame of the sprinter but a stride pattern closer to that of a stayer. Philip Mitchell has likened it to that of a panther. Jane Cecil calls it cat-like. Teddy Grimthorpe puts a number to it: 25 per cent longer than normal. In that respect he shares something in common with Usain Bolt who took just forty-one strides to win the 100 m race in the 2012 London Olympics – a great physique that eats up the ground faster than their rivals.

However, it is under the skin where you cannot see, within the skeletal muscle, that the truth behind stamina versus speed really lies. Skeletal muscle is what is known as a voluntary muscle, namely one you are able to control such as your bicep, unlike say the heart which is an involuntary muscle which we can't control. That's obvious enough to understand. But in itself it will not help you identify what distance suits your horse best, when you realise that this type of muscle is made up of an indeterminate mixture of fibres: slow twitch and fast twitch. Slow twitch are for endurance. Fast twitch for speed. This mixture of fast and slow fibres, which control how the muscle contracts, is genetically determined. You are born, like it or not, to do a particular thing. Of course natural ability and training will help exploit the muscle configuration you are born with, but in the end if nature gifts you with predominantly fast-twitch fibres in your muscles you will be, however hard you train, a sprinter not a stayer. However, the difference between sprint and middle distance has considerable shades of grey.

And therein lay Henry's conundrum – he didn't actually know how much further beyond a mile Frankel could race. His breeding raised as many questions as answers. However great a trainer Henry may have been. However great a horse Frankel might become. In the end only the racetrack could provide the answer of not just how fast but how far. That moment when Frankel strode out further than ever before. In the same way that only the return to the track would tell whether he had trained on, then only those strides into the unknown could tell how far he stayed. The truth is Henry had great doubts about Frankel running in the Derby; the distance was too far for a horse he considered still both mentally and physically unready for such a test. But the decision did not rest with him alone. As the second entry stage for the Derby closed in early April, with the Greenham yet to be run, Prince Khalid asked Teddy Grimthorpe to pay the £9,000 entry fee to keep Frankel on the list of runners. Those clutching ante-post betting slips had reason to still hope.

All manner of new and unexpected faces appeared on Greenham Saturday. Jane Cecil was surprised to bump into the *Racing Post*'s Newmarket correspondent David Milnes (who incidentally features a photo of Frankel rather than himself on his Twitter page); she thought he never ventured this far from his Suffolk parish. Prince Khalid was there to see Frankel race in the flesh for the first time.

The Newbury executive counted in a much bigger than average crowd. You could speculate that it was due to the lovely spring day but really we know the reason.

The good weather was a continuation of a dry few months that had caused Henry some difficulty with Frankel, unable as he was to work him on any of the overly firm grass gallops. So today Frankel, a horse Henry was far from satisfied was fully race-fit, was to be tested on yet another type of unfamiliar going: good to firm. This was to be five races with four different types of ground. The distance, seven furlongs over which he had raced twice before, presented no problem. But the going? There were plenty of questions to answer.

As for Frankel, though he had muscled up and matured, he hadn't grown a considerable amount over the winter, which is fairly common of horses between two and three. However, with Henry's aversion to weighing his horses we can't be empirical about this. But Stephen as the farrier had every reason to note such things, recalling that Frankel saved most of his growing for the transition from three to four years of age, when his shoe size went from seven to eight. But few who crowded around the Newbury paddock thought he looked anything other than magnificent. As he cantered calmly to the post, taking a lead from his stable companion Picture Editor, he was the very vision of the perfect racehorse. Such was his impeccable behaviour some speculated that his wild days were behind him. They would soon be disabused of that notion.

For all Frankel's potential to slay his five rivals – betting-wise he looked an almost certainty at 1–4 on (bet four to win one) – the Greenham Stakes was a more competitive race than the odds might suggest. Collectively the field, all three-year-old colts carrying the same weight, had twenty runs between them, with fourteen wins. Only Frankel was unbeaten but Strong Suit had two wins from four, including a Group 2. Vanguard Dream had been unbeaten at two years with three from three. Shropshire had a 50 per cent strike rate. Excelebration was two from three. The only one you could strike a line through with any certainty was Picture Editor, owned by Prince Khalid, trained by Henry Cecil and purposely entered as a pace-maker for Frankel.

Pacemakers are usually employed to set a fast pace, ensuring a true-run race – this was the first time Frankel had been given the benefit of one. Their use is not universally popular or confined to horse racing; Roger Bannister broke the four-minute mile in 1954 with the benefit of two pacemakers, and they are regularly used in marathons and long-distance Olympic races. In horse racing not every nation approves of their use; some ban them, others do their best to discourage them. But in Britain they have official sanction. They even get a mention in *The Rules of Racing* (Part 4 57.2 if you care to look), the only proviso being that the pacemaker tries its best, running a clean and fair race without manoeuvring for the benefit of its companion. Basically the plan was for Picture Editor to run as fast as he could in the first few furlongs with Frankel content-edly following in his wake, until a spent Picture Editor fell away leaving Frankel a clear path to the finish. Unfortunately it didn't turn out that way – Picture Editor simply was not fast enough.

So we arrive at 16 April and the Greenham Stakes at Newbury.

As Frankel is loaded into stall three of six, the race commentator asks, 'Will this [the race] be a precursor to an extraordinary year for this son of Galileo?' The first half-furlong suggests that question will be answered in the affirmative until, just as everyone is starting to settle down, it begins to unravel. Tom releases Frankel from the stalls level with the others, gently easing him back to tuck into the middle of the pack with Picture Editor setting the pace. But then Shropshire, racing on their left, turns his head almost at right-angles to Frankel and despite the best efforts of jockey Michael Hills to pull him straight, tries to drag himself into the pack, cutting in front of Frankel. At that moment Frankel all but loses it. There is no way he is going to put up with such an interference; he clearly sees it as some sort of affront. So, as if to prove he is not to be messed with, he jinks left, bumps Vanguard Dream on his right in the process, pushes Shropshire out the way, effectively dragging Tom with him as they all but draw level with Picture Editor. At this point Tom starts shouting at Ian Mongan, Picture Editor's jockey, to go faster as he tries to calm Frankel who is simply no longer behaving. Watching on television at home, Shane can see Frankel beating himself up for no good reason; he is trying to do too much too soon.

With two and a half furlongs to go Picture Editor is done – he simply wasn't up to the task. As he falls away he leaves Frankel in front, but not for long as Excelebration comes from behind and takes the lead. For a quarter of a furlong the Frankel dream looks shattered, that mid-race acceleration nowhere to be seen. He is going to be bested by a 25–1 outsider. But Frankel is having none of it. He turns his head. Looks at Excelebration. And digs in. Taking the lead, but only just, Tom urges Frankel with hands and heels while Excelebration's jockey goes for his whip. A furlong from home Frankel is a length ahead; it is not enough. For the first time ever Tom goes for his whip, hitting Frankel twice to keep him straight as they go two, three and finally four lengths clear.

It takes Tom a mighty long time to pull Frankel up; once lit up he simply doesn't want to stop. In the front was his rightful place regardless of leaving the winning post well behind. Enraptured the commentator asks yet another question. 'Oh Frankel, how good might you be?' The 2,000 Guineas in precisely two weeks' time will tell us that.

15

Leading from the front

Two days off was Frankel's reward for his Greenham win; on Tuesday, with Shane and Bullet Train they were back leading the first lot up Warren Hill. Even though he was the hot favourite at 1–2 on for the 2,000 Guineas, he was officially afforded no special treatment at Warren Place. Unofficially, everyone looked out for him; the yard was collectively both excited and nervous amid a whole swirl of conflicting emotions.

For Henry this was the comeback crowning. He stood on the brink of his twenty-fifth Classic success, already the most success-ful Classic trainer of the twentieth century. For Tom it would be his first British Classic, a seminal moment in the career of any up-and-coming jockey. For Sandy, who admits to being nervous every single moment of every single day from Newbury to Newmarket, it would be the culmination of his winter dreams with maybe more to come. But why was the 2,000 Guineas, and winning it, so important? Why had this race been Frankel's target since almost the first day he set foot in Warren Place? It might be plainly obvious to those who live and breathe racing, but to the outside world isn't it just another big race? The simple answer is no.

Firstly, it is one of the five Classic races run each season, aside from the Derby, the most pre-eminent; the racing world will be watching. Win this and everyone will know your name. For the Guineas attracts the cream of a generation; the coming together of the best milers in a single race. It would be tempting to compare the contest to some human sporting endeavour such as the Olympics or World Cup, but there is a critical difference: you get just one shot at the 2,000 Guineas which is confined to colts and fillies of three years of age. At least at the Olympics you get to come back in four years' time. Don't forget multiple gold medallist Usain Bolt's debut Olympics ended in failure, eliminated in the first round of the 200 m in Athens in 2004.

Frankel had no such option for second chances. If he lost there would always be one better and that could never be struck from the record. And that matters in bloodstock. The prize money, all £200,000 of it, looks like a reward in itself but it pales to insignificance compared to the stud value of a Guineas winner who will earn that sort of money in a matter of a few days, for months at a time and for years or decades to come. And that takes no account of the sheer kudos associated with owning, riding, training or having any connection with a Classic winner. It is what racing dreams are made of.

And the Frankel express had become inextricably caught up in events way beyond the world of racing. It was as if God or some higher being had become his PR guru, for on the Friday before the Guineas Saturday, as heir but one to the British throne, Prince William was to marry Kate Middleton. As the nation became enveloped in a wave of national pride, the populace had taken not just the royal couple to their hearts but Frankel. He vied for front-page space. He was the headline writers' dream. Wedding yesterday, coronation today: you get the idea. The race was being written up as a processional. Frankel only had to turn up to be crowned the king. If only. Things were to turn complicated.

Think of Warren Place as a cocoon. For all the huge value of the bloodstock, with all the implications that flow from success or failure, and away from the frenetic excitement of the racecourse, you might be surprised how ordinary, and I say that in a good way, the daily routine is. It is calm. It is ordered. If you dropped by unannounced you'd have no way of distinguishing Frankel from the other 154 horses such is the equal love and care lavished on each. There is the world. And then there is the world of Warren Place. Henry fought a daily battle to keep them separate. A potentially fractious Frankel could as easily lose the race at home as on the racecourse if he sensed the nerves of his human … I was going to say masters but let's settle for companions.

The day starts early high on the Heath, at 4.30 am. Dee, as the head girl for Frankel's section of the yard, was the first of the staff to arrive. She'd head for the Garage before anything else; she couldn't start her day without knowing Frankel had made it through the night. There he would be, head over door, recognising Dee for what she was – purveyor of breakfast. Sometimes he'd still have on his blanket. But more often it would be shed, kicked and scuffed in the corner of his box or other times neatly folded outside thanks to the care of a prior visitor. However ungodly her hour of arrival Dee was rarely alone; most mornings a figure would loom out from the shadows. Occasionally it startled her. But usually the smell of smoke and coffee was prior warning enough: 'Morning Dee', intoned Henry. 'Everything fine?'

Henry set his alarm for 5.20 am every morning, however most mornings he was up at 4 am, patrolling his yard, talking to his horses long before anyone else, with coffee in one hand, fag in the other. Jane had banned him from smoking in the house. Maybe this was the incentive he needed? I asked a few people how many packs of cigarettes Henry smoked a day; we are clearly long past counting the cigarettes themselves. Nobody had a definitive calculation, the general thrust being as many as he could get hold of. Henry smoked all through his cancer, right up to the moment of his death. It was an integral part of his being.

When you saw Henry at the races, in his finest suits, surrounded by the racing press or the glamorous entourages of wealthy owners, it wouldn't be unreasonable to assume he ran his stables like the captain of a mighty ship: an aloof but guiding force. The truth was very different. At 5 am he'd be in the office doing emails and entries. At 6 am in the canteen chatting with Shane and the riders. At 7 am the first lot swung out with Henry in charge. In years gone by he would have ridden with them, but after a nasty fall in the early 2000s and the death of his hack Snowy he gave up the riding. When the lot returned from work they'd all gather together for a pick of grass; forty or fifty horses with their riders, all ruminating in their different ways. Henry would be wandering among them. Chatting. Feeling the horses. Catching their mood. Asking small but important questions. Being among the animals to soak up their nature. Assess how they were after the work. Letting them be what horses naturally are. Part of a herd. Contentedly grazing.

It is impossible to overemphasise how totally immersed Henry was in his horses. All his horses. Unusually for a trainer with such a heavy roster, unless racing or some such impinged, he'd stay for the third lot, treating them exactly the same as the star-studded first. Only then would he head for his own treatment for his cancer in Cambridge, returning in time for evening stables. Then, as the stable hands watered, fed and gave their horses a last pick of grass before settling them down for the night, he would walk, talk and be among them all.

If you are looking for the single key to the success of Frankel it lies in this: Henry's ability to get inside the heads of not only his horses but the people who had charge of them. He bent both to his will. However, determining the outcome of the random draw, the order in which the runners for the 2,000 Guineas were allocated their positions in the starting stalls, was beyond even him.

With thirteen runners, the odds were that the Guineas draw would likely leave Frankel and his pacemaker not far apart. Made as it was two days prior to the race, a bad draw was a complication they could plan for, but of all the complications, as Newbury had shown, a pacemaker who couldn't make the pace was the one to seriously worry about. Step one: we need a faster horse. Called in as pacemaker was Rerouted who had won over six and seven furlongs, another Prince Khalid horse but trained by Barry Hills. Step two: in case the worst happened again, prepare Frankel to be, against everything they had ever trained him to be, out in front alone. So Henry told Shane to have Frankel lead Bullet Train in their work. They didn't have much time.

The few daily canters up Warren Hill were the start to this new look Frankel, culminating in his only full gallop between Newbury and Newmarket when, amid all the usual hoopla, he worked on the watered gallop over on the Racecourse Side that runs parallel to the Guineas course itself. The few doubts from the Greenham Stakes were forgotten; Henry's plan that the Newbury race would bring Frankel to his peak appeared to have worked in spades. Shane said he felt great. Very strong. Frankel was even behaving in front; no chasing down trains. What could possibly go wrong?

The draw. Frankel was drawn one. Rerouted thirteen. Total disaster. On opposite sides of the course, with eleven horses between them, there was little or no chance that as the stalls banged open Rerouted would be able to cut across the other runners to come together with Frankel to give him the lead he required. And anyway, even in the unlikely event that that all happened, it all still assumed Rerouted was fast enough – far from a given. It was time for a new plan.

There was always a chance that Frankel would lose his head, and in consequence the race, long before he even reached the starting stalls. It is common enough. In the paddock, surrounded by the tiered masses, far older and more battle-hardened horses than Frankel have been known to go to pieces. Work themselves, both mentally and physically, into a lather. And it is easy to forget that Frankel, for all his gathering fame, had only five races to his name and it was only just over eight months since he had first set foot on a racecourse. It would never be fair to call him temperamental but he could be difficult. Headstrong. Exuberant. Single minded. If he didn't like something he'd let you know. The confined oval of the Newmarket paddock was no place to find out previously unknown quirks, so Henry had Frankel led around double-handed with Sandy on one side and travelling head lad Mike McGowan on the other.

Whether Frankel was well behaved because of Sandy and Mike or just because that was his mood we'll never know, but the paddock parade worked out just fine. As Sandy led him out onto the course, ready to head down the wide, empty expanse of the Rowley Mile, the worst anyone could say was that Frankel was sweating a little between his legs. Freed of the leading rein and free to run for a moment Frankel hesitated, dragging Tom sideways rather than forward, reluctant to move from a walk to a canter. Maybe it was because there was no horse to lead him, but after some urging from Tom and a good look at the crowd, they ambled quietly down to the start, separate to the other runners. All was calm. All was good.

In the stands Chris Cook, with a plan to watch the watcher, like some amateur gumshoe, tracked Henry, Jane and the family from the paddock to the steps at the front of the stands as they pushed through the crowds to find a vantage point. Henry, ever the contrarian, eschewed the comforts of Prince Khalid's private box and the relative privacy of the trainers stand for a more public view. It was what he always did. It was one of his things. Catching Chris's eye he gave him a little smile before letting the crowds swallow him up, hiding him from sight. He was there to watch, not be watched.

It's 30 April 2011 and the 2,000 Guineas at Newmarket.

As the runners circle behind the starting stalls, Frankel is led forward to be loaded seventh of the thirteen. For a minute or maybe a bit longer he waits patiently as the handlers struggle to load the last, a recalcitrant Loving Spirit. As the jockey tears off the blindfold the starter screams 'Ready?' rather by way of warning than question. A fraction of a second later Frankel blasts out.

It is against all the logic of one-mile racing to lead from the front. Centuries of collective wisdom will tell you to tuck yourself in, track the leaders and when they falter pull out to grab the prize. Win cheekily if you like. No horse, not even Frankel, is capable of galloping flat out for a mile. And not on a course like the Rowley Mile that has a wicked, double-dip uphill finish. And on this particular Guineas day, there is a beastly headwind to reinforce the foolishness of such a plan. But that indeed is the plan that Henry had hatched. Make the running. Ignore the pacemaker.

Within twenty strides Frankel is in the lead. To his enormous credit pacemaker Rerouted is soon in second place, but lacks the pace to stay, let alone lead Frankel. He should feel no great shame. No horse that has ever lived would have matched Frankel on this day. He is, in truth, a little out of control but Tom lets him run, not wanting to break his stride, letting the rhythm of the racing be the calming force. And it works. At the halfway point, as Tom sneaks a backward glance between his legs, they are at least ten lengths clear. It will remain forever one of the most astonishing pieces of racing footage of all time. Frankel, extended with his unique long, low stride, consuming the Newmarket turf against the backdrop of an empty Heath with not another single horse or person in sight as the cameraman pulls back, and back, and back until eventually the other horses come into frame.

The first five furlongs of the Rowley Mile are a gentle downhill; for the last of that five Tom gives Frankel a little breather, eases him back a little, in preparation for the rollercoaster that is the last three furlongs. Up they go. Down they go. And up they go again before the winning line is passed. It is as brutal a finish as you will find on any racecourse, anywhere. If your legs are tired and your lungs are bursting these double-dips will grind you to a halt. The fable of the hare and the tortoise comes to mind.

But the moral of this particular tale is that to win a 2,000 Guineas with Frankel in the field you don't give (or let him take) a fifteen-length lead. The crowd knows it, even if Henry and Jane are shell-shocked by the turn of events. A full two furlongs out the applause has begun. That truly never happens. Ever. He routs the field. Good horses that will go on to do good things are nowhere to be seen. There is 165 yards, so nearly one-tenth of the entire race distance, between the first and the last. In the final furlong when Tom simply pushes Frankel out with hands and heels, the others are flat out competing for the not inconsiderable kudos of being second to Frankel.

Devastating. Crushed. Ruthless. Matchless. Magical. Think of any superlative and it was likely used by someone, sometime that after-noon to describe Frankel's win. It was the greatest winning margin in a 2,000 Guineas for over sixty years. His split times over the second, third, fourth and fifth furlongs were those of a sprinter and he still had the stamina to win. Think Usain Bolt doing a sub-ten-second 100 m then keeping going to win the 800 m as he likes. Graham Dench, who wrote the analysis for the *Racing Post*, calls it jaw dropping – dominating the race both visually and mathematically. But I like Chris Cook best: Frankel stuffs the field.

The only real question left unanswered that afternoon is where to next. Henry knows the answer but he has others to convince.

16

Arise Sir Henry

Frankel's reaction to winning a Classic was suitably uncomplicated. Back at Warren Place, as Sandy led him from the horse lorry to the Garage they passed the feed room. After a day of being calm he was finally excited, dancing and prancing as the smell of oats and molasses drifted his way, prompting an outburst of what Sandy calls 'his shouting', whinnying at the top of his voice until the requisite bucket was delivered to his door. As he bent down to pretty well inhale his meal, getting that inside him was as much worrying as he was going to do that evening. Henry, on the other hand, had a decision to make by the following day which was not his alone to make. Would Frankel run in the Derby? He was entered. He was favourite. And the race was just thirty-five days away.

Henry's doubts about Frankel running in the Derby were well documented; he was still immature. It was too much to ask, too soon. 'He'd probably win,' Henry told Sandy, as they sat together on the grass the Sunday after the Guineas as Frankel had a pick, 'but it would be too hard on him.' Jane is convinced that Henry was never, ever going to run Frankel in the Derby but he had an obligation to consider the option. After all, horses the shadow of Frankel have successfully made the transition from a mile at Newmarket to a mile and a half at Epsom. His father Galileo had won not just the English Derby but the Irish equivalent as well; he had the race distance in his blood. After his Guineas win, Frankel was officially joint-rated the best horse on the planet, unheard of in one so young.

I consider it to Henry's enormous credit that when he put the call in to Prince Khalid later that Sunday his advice was no, let's skip the Derby and head for Royal Ascot. After all, he was a very ill man. The chances of having another Derby prospect were at best slim. Why not have one last throw of the dice? But as Shane said, Frankel meant the world to Henry. Prince Khalid thought the world of Henry. Between them they already had five English Derby victories. They had scaled that particular mountain. They didn't need to potentially sacrifice Frankel in an attempt to win a race that neither they nor Frankel needed to win.

Some say this is a mark against Frankel; the failure to contest the one and a half mile Classic. But in the arena of sporting endeavour you have to pick and choose your niche within your chosen sport. We don't diminish the status of Roger Federer, the winner of more tennis Grand Slams than any other player in history, because the wins are all singles and none doubles. Nobody says Usain Bolt needs to win a marathon. Or Cristiano Ronaldo have a stint in goal. The truth is that Frankel's destiny lay in races elsewhere.

Royal Ascot. The world's greatest pageant of horse racing. Five days in mid-June when the impeccably dressed (people) and the impeccably bred (horses) vie for attention. Most years it is a toss-up as to which of the two will fill the front pages; this year there was no competition. Frankel was the headline act, running once again over one mile in the feature race of the first day, the St James's Palace Stakes. It looked the ultra-competitive race with six Group 1 winners in the field, but Frankel was expected to dispatch them with disdain, putting on a show for Her Majesty the Queen. After all he had his pacemaker Rerouted to try again, with three of the other remaining seven opponents already past conquests. The money spoke of just one horse: Frankel was 1–3 on if any bookmaker would take your bet. The rest were 10–1 or longer. What could possibly go wrong? As it turned out, nearly everything. And the day had started so well.

This was one occasion when Henry passed the winning post ahead of Frankel, riding as he did in a horse-drawn carriage with the Queen and Prince Philip as the royal party, as is tradition, arrived at the course in the Royal procession just ahead of the first race. Henry was accorded this considerable honour by invitation of the Queen who had knighted him Sir Henry Cecil in her Birthday Honours List that had been announced three days earlier, on the second Saturday in June, her official birthday. That same Saturday was also Frankel's second gallop on the Racecourse Side within three days and that was perhaps, just maybe, the harbinger of what was to transpire in the race itself.

You can read a great deal of why and what went wrong in the St James's; there are many opinions. The tactics were wrong. The pacemaker went too fast. The jockey made a bad call. The others were better than they were given credit for. Whatever the reason or reasons, the simple fact is that as the field rounded the final bend and straightened up with three furlongs to go Frankel had once again splayed his field. It was almost time for the applause to begin. But two furlongs and twenty-five seconds later it looked as if he was going to lose. Sandy, watching from the stands, could no longer watch. He sat down. Put his head in his hands, closed his eyes and wished it all over. But why? What had happened?

It wasn't as if Frankel had misbehaved during the preliminaries, at the start or even in the race itself. He broke just fine from the stalls and Tom had him settled at fourth or fifth in the middle of the pack as Rerouted scorched away, doing for once what a pacemaker should do. So for the first third of the race, things unfolded exactly as planned. But then Tom chose to make his move going from fourth to a clear second, before using the bend into the home straight to wind in Rerouted, easily closing the gap, then passing him with that blistering middle-race pace that was becoming Frankel's trademark. It was as spectacularly dominant a piece of Frankelesque as you could ever wish to see. And then it all turned to mush.

When Frankel and Tom were meant to turn the screw to gallop away into the far distance, it simply didn't happen.

Drawing level with the enormous Royal Ascot crowd at the two-furlong pole, Frankel is leading by six lengths as Excelebration, who had run him close in the Greenham Stakes at Newbury to open the season, comes out of the pack. Tom hits Frankel twice as he idles in front, refusing to pick up the pace. But the gap between first and second narrows rather than widens. Nowhere was this written in the script. With a furlong to go, the lead is still three lengths but quite suddenly Frankel is paddling. His legs are moving but the momentum has gone. In the penultimate half furlong, Zoffany passes Excelebration. He is closing on Frankel with every stride. In the stands Henry is agitated, shuffling along the steps in tandem with his horse, his face a picture of both disbelief and concern.

Mike Marshall, for all the awfulness of the St James's Palace Stakes, considers it to be Frankel's finest race, for he simply wasn't right that day. For whatever reason Henry had done something he never did before or since with Frankel in giving him two strong gallops within a week of a race. Maybe he thought it was required, with a gap of six weeks between the Guineas and Royal Ascot? Regardless of the timing it was the nature of the Saturday work on the Racecourse Side watered gallop that Mike recalls; he describes Frankel as 'flat' that morning. Shane remembers it as well, both for the proximity of the two gallops and that on the Saturday Frankel sweated up badly.

Did he have a virus? Was he simply a bit under par? Without the evidence of a definitive blood test we will never know for sure. The word virus itself is used in as maddeningly a non-specific sense with horses as much as it is used with humans. It can cover everything from a very slight temperature on a single day to a condition that closes down a racing stable for weeks or months at an end. By the Tuesday of the race Frankel may well have been, to all intents and purposes, back to his normal self, except when he was asked to dig deep the effects of the previous week lingered, that reservoir of colossal stamina and speed depleted. When Tom reported that he 'idled', maybe it was to be the one and only occasion when he was saying, 'Guys, I just don't have it in me today.'

As the winning post comes and goes, Henry exhales and raises his eyes to heaven. Frankel has won. Just. In the final one hundred yards, when Zoffany was closing him down. Frankel, never one to let another pass him, found enough to retain a three-quarter-length lead. It is to the credit of Tom, who took much flak in the aftermath of the race for going after Rerouted when, in the opinion of some, he should have bided his time, that he kept calm in those final two furlongs. While all the other jockeys were furiously at work he didn't go after Frankel, just letting him keep on striding out as if this was just another day at the races.

As a win it might not have been pretty. It might not have been spectacular. It surely caused plenty of consternation. In the immediate aftermath some bookmakers priced Frankel as second favourite for the upcoming Duel on the Downs, preferring his older rival Canford Cliffs. But as Jane said to Henry, observing his face of thunder as they headed for the winning enclosure, 'He did win you know!'

As Frankel took a victory parade in front of the stands the crowd were with Jane on that. Everyone from the Royal Box to the farthest stands cheered and clapped. The winners enclosure was mobbed. Long after the horses had been led away racegoers remained, debating what they had just seen.

Henry might not have believed much in modern science but the racing authorities do. After the glory and adulation of the Royal Ascot crowd, Sandy had to take Frankel directly to the less-than-glamorous dope box, as it is colloquially known where winners are drug tested by the Jockey Club's Equine Health and Welfare Department by way of a urine test. This, as you might imagine, is not always an instant process, waiting around in a secure stable until your horse is ready to relieve itself, the output captured in a jug fixed to a long broom handle. If the wait becomes interminable a hair or blood sample is the back-up option. As I say, it is not very glamorous but as a method of deterring wrong-doing it seems to work. In a typical year, of the 90,000 runners on British racecourses around 7,000 will be tested with less than 20 coming back positive.

Frankel was a regular visitor; in fact he never missed out and it was all very normal excepting after the St James's Palace Stakes when Stephen Kielt was called to the dope box. His first thought was how extremely tired Frankel looked as he went about what he had been called to do – remove one of Frankel's racing plates. There was no lameness, in fact Frankel was never lame in his entire three seasons of racing which is extremely unusual, but when this particular aluminium plate had become loose nobody knows. It could have been in the race or sometime after. Even though it hadn't caused lameness it would have been an impediment in itself – think of trying to run with the laces of one shoe undone. One way or another, when you stack up the possibilities – over-preparation, virus, tactics, racing plate – Mike Marshall's assessment of the St James's looks to have more than a grain of truth to it. Teddy Grimthorpe considers it his bravest and gutsiest performance. The more the tale unfolds, the more it seems that way.

Whichever way you cut it, Frankel was now seven for seven, having dispatched every challenger of his generation. But he was only halfway done. He now had older horses to defeat. Those considered by some his betters. As for now, the dope box done with, all Frankel wanted was his Garage box, a bucket of feed and a couple of days' rest.

17

Duel on the Downs

The racing tribe decamp from Ascot in June to Goodwood in July, the latter once described by King Edward VII as 'a garden party with racing tacked on'. I'm not sure the current Duke of Richmond, sucessor of the Third Duke who built the course in 1801, would endorse this royal opinion of a five-day meeting that features some of the best races in the annual calendar, but His Majesty, if a little off-beam, was on to something.

Goodwood is often cited as the most beautiful racecourse in the world, which is true. Perched on the top of the South Downs you have a distant view of the English Channel one way and the Sussex Downs to the other. As you look from the stands across and beyond the course all you see is the most gorgeous, unspoilt countryside for miles around; the vivid green of the ancient oak woodland vying for the attention of your eyes with the ripened gold of wheat fields on the cusp of harvest. I'm told that only one house is visible but I'm yet to spot even that. Whether it is the situation or the timing (Goodwood week was moved from its original May slot to July to give the aristocracy one last meet before retiring to their country estates for the summer) there is a definite informality about the Festival as top hats are swapped for panamas, mixing with the holiday crowds who ride up the hill from a not-so-distant Brighton.

Frankel was entered for the feature race of the week, the Group 1 Sussex Stakes. This was very much his coming-of-age moment, for until now he had only been matched against his contemporaries. Flat racing is very structured in this respect. Young horses are not set against older ones because there would be no contest; the gap in physical development is too wide. Similarly, colts and fillies are sometimes kept apart but that is less of an issue. So two-year-olds race two-year-olds. And in the early part of the season three-year-olds race against three-year-olds. But as with people, age and maturity narrows that gap. There comes a time when youth can challenge the accepted order.

In this particular case it was Frankel, the three-year-old, taking on Canford Cliffs, the four-year-old who had won the Sussex Stakes the previous year and was very much in his backyard. Goodwood is not a course that suits all horses. As you might imagine for one carved along the ridge of the downs, the rises, falls and turns reflect the random hand of Mother Nature, and that's before you even take account of the changing cambers. Idiosyncratic some call it. Others consider it an unlucky course. Gamblers often steer clear of the meeting entirely. It is one where the form, the past racing performances of the runners, can be unexpectedly stood on its head. The balloon bursts for horses who have run well all year, or others, having shown nothing at all, win out of the blue. At Goodwood be prepared for sunshine days of short-priced losers and long-priced winners.

As the day of the race approached, Frankel was once again that short-priced favourite, the weight of the money having erased some

Back in the winners' circle at Ascot with Henry, Sandy and Prince Khalid Abdullah. (Healy Racing / Racingfotos.com)

Queen Elizabeth II watched Frankel's ninth win at Ascot and afterward she shares a few words with Henry Cecil. (Hugh Routledge / Shutterstock)

Work rider Shane Fetherstonhaugh takes Frankel through his paces on the gallops at Newmarket. It was on a day very similar to this that the injury scare took place in April 2012. (Alan Crowhurst / Getty Images)

Lord Grimthorpe, Prince Khalid Abdullah's racing manager, walks the course before a race. (Alan Crowhurst / Getty Images)

Here is the winner. Where are the rest? Winning the Queen Anne Stakes at Royal Ascot by 11 lengths. 19 June 2012. (Healy Racing)

Henry congratulates Frankel after winning the Queen Anne Stakes at Royal Ascot. Frankel is now 11 from 11. (Healy Racing / Racingfotos.com)

By Frankel's twelfth race, at 'Glorious Goodwood' on 1 August 2012, he has achieved celebrity status.
(Alan Crowhurst / Getty Images)

Frankel is not only unbeatable but almost unbackable. The betting screen before Frankel wins his second Qipco Sussex Stakes at Goodwood. 1 August 2012.
(Steve Davies / Racingfotos.com)

Mane and tail streaming, Frankel eats up the turf to win his second
Qipco Sussex Stakes at Goodwood. (Matthew Webb / Racingfotos.com)

Frankel wins his thirteenth race the Juddmonte International Stakes
at York on 22 August 2012. (Louise Pollard / Racingfotos.com)

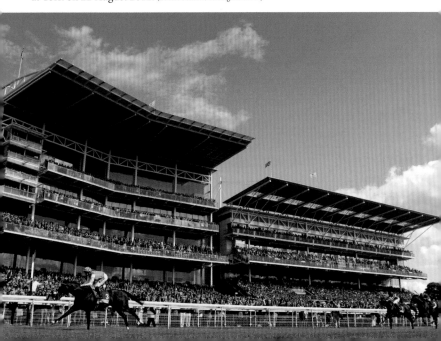

The winners' presentation at the Juddmonte International Stakes after Frankel's thirteenth win at York. From left to right, Lord Grimthorpe, Philip Mitchell, Prince Khalid and Henry. (Frank Sorge / Racingfotos.com)

The team rally behind Frankel on the day of his last race, on 20 October 2012. Sandy still has this jacket. (Action Plus Sports Images / Alamy Stock Photo)

Tom celebrates Frankel's victory. The Qipco Champion Stakes at Ascot racecourse 20 October 2012.

(Tom Dulat / Getty Images)

Frankel and Tom celebrate their final win with Bullet Train and Ian Mongan. (Alan Crowhurst / Getty Images)

Frankel basks in the glow of the spotlight and the adulation of the crowds one last time.

(Alan Crowhurst / Getty Images)

Simon Cooper visiting Frankel at his new home at Banstead Manor in 2018 (with stallion man Rob Bowley, right).

(Photograph by Laura Green / Copyright © Simon Cooper)

of the doubts created by the St James's Palace race. I say some because Canford Cliffs, seeking his sixth consecutive Group 1 win and the champion miler of his year group, was thought by many to be capable of beating Frankel; his trainer Richard Hannon and jockey Richard Hughes were full of hope. The media had dubbed this the Duel on the Downs with the odds as they went down to the post reflecting not only the likelihood of a two-horse contest but the possibility of a Frankel defeat: he was 8–13 and Canford Cliffs 7–4, with the other two runners of no betting consequence. There was also the oddity of big-race specialist Frankie Dettori on the outsider in a Group race. Other than his debut the only time the betting market expressed such doubts about Frankel was when he wrapped up his two-year-old year in the Dewhurst Stakes. Had you ignored the Goodwood hoodoo to bet on Frankel that Sussex day, you would have wagered at the longest odds he would race at ever again. In his final six races the longest price would be 4–11 and the shortest 1–20 (yes, bet twenty to win one in the Sussex Stakes the following year …), an unprecedented average of 1–6. Frankel was certainly exciting but he wasn't going to make you rich.

T E Lawrence, of Lawrence of Arabia fame, once wrote, 'Nine-tenths of tactics are certain, and taught in books: but the irrational tenth is like the kingfisher flashing across the pool, and that is the test of generals.' If that is true, and it probably is, then Tom Queally has another career awaiting him in the military, for after all the opprobrium heaped upon him in the wake of his Royal Ascot ride, the Sussex Stakes was to be sublime.

It is hard to truly appreciate the huge pressure that was building on the whole Warren Place and Juddmonte team; from Prince Khalid at the one extreme to the guy who drove the horse box at the other. Nobody, simply nobody, wanted to be the person who made the mistake or decision, however tiny or apparently insignificant at the time, that was to end Frankel's amazing run. Mike Marshall, Henry's assistant, who took much of the daily burden, admits he couldn't enjoy Frankel as he should have done – the stress that built with each successive victory put an end to that. He thinks, that despite all that Frankel gave Henry in those final years of cancer, he couldn't fully enjoy it either. But however hard it was for them, it was Tom Queally who quite literally held the fate of Frankel, and the burdens that went with it, in his hands.

Tom's association with Henry had come about by chance when he picked up a ride for a Warren Place horse in a minor all-weather race at Lingfield in November 2006, around the time the decision was made to mate Kind with Galileo. It was hardly the stuff of romance, the horse sixth of twelve, but for Tom, brought up in an Irish racing family, Henry Cecil was something of a legend. Bumping into him shortly afterwards in Newmarket, Tom thanked him for the ride, the chance meeting ending in an invitation to become a Warren Place work rider.

For a 22-year-old who already had 170 winners to his name, with stints in the USA and New Zealand, plus having been both the Irish and UK Champion Apprentice, this might not have seemed much of an invite. But Tom saw it for what it was – a foot in the door. That said, it was a door that took a while to lever open while he free-lanced, gaining a reputation as one of the up-and-coming young jockeys. In 2007, he had a single Warren Place winner from fourteen rides, deferring to Ted Durcan who was the principal jockey. In 2008, he rode eighteen winners from ninety rides for Henry, in the same year scoring his maiden century which culminated in the agreement that he would become the Warren Place first jockey the following season. Timing is everything. By the time Frankel was to arrive, Tom would be firmly established, having ended 2009 with a second century, a bunch of Group winners and over £2 million in prize money. He even rode Frankel's future sparring partner Bullet Train in the Derby at Epsom, who, despite starting fifth favourite, tailed off last.

As Tom took a relaxed Frankel down to the start of the Sussex Stakes, the pundits and commentators were still pondering on the Royal Ascot race. Had he won in spite of his jockey? Why had Tom ridden him in such a manner?

Being a jockey is tough. Your frailties and fallibilities are exposed for all to see. When you make a mistake it is writ large; the consequences, at least in horse-racing terms, sometimes life changing. As Tom gave chase to Rerouted it maybe didn't seem such a risk to him. After all, he and Frankel had led pillar to post in the 2,000 Guineas to popular acclaim. His sweeping run around the Ascot bend in the Royal Lodge the previous year had been widely praised as a stroke of genius. But maybe there was something else biting in his head; the memory of a race eight years earlier at Leopardstown in Ireland when, as an unknown nineteen-year-old apprentice to Aidan O'Brien, he claimed his first Group victory.

However it wasn't meant to be that way – he was riding the pacemaker and rank outsider Balestrini. As they streaked away, the plan was being executed to perfection but for one thing – the pair kept on going. And going. And going. They had slipped the field, the closest the odds-on favourite coming to them was five and a half lengths behind at the finish. Who was to say Rerouted, as he pulled further and further ahead, was not about to do the same? Of course to the millions watching, on the track and on television, the implosion of the pacemaker was surely a given. But Tom knew it didn't always work out that way. Perhaps that explains the judgement call that, within a matter of a few dozen strides, on the back of a horse that likes to do nothing better than gallop at full stretch, only he could make.

After all the Royal Ascot port-mortems, the pressure on Tom at Goodwood was immense but he was at least relieved of the pace-maker issue: there was none. Not that that was as helpful as it might seem, for with just four runners the evolution of the race lay entirely with Tom. However, Henry had laid out a definitive plan that revolved around settling Frankel – if there was no pace then settle in front, dictating the speed of the race. Otherwise settle behind, letting Frankel relax. And on the turn for home don't wind up the pace too early. Save it for the last two furlongs. What could be simpler? Well, actually the race itself.

The Duel in the Downs on that 27th of July day was a blockbuster not for the coming together of two great champions but for the utter devastation one wrought upon the other. As the stalls open it is very much a case of 'After you, sir', 'No after you!' as all four jockeys vie to be last; to be sure Dettori and Jarnet on the two outsiders are not going to do Hughes and Queally any favours – if you want to win it you are going to have to do the work yourselves seems to be the general thrust of the conversation. The first furlong from the one-mile start is all downhill: Frankel fights Tom for every yard of it as they drag themselves into the lead, the settling as required by Henry only coming into being as the track starts to rise. Lobbing along as they rise and turn over the next three furlongs it is four in a line; Frankel first, a couple of lengths ahead of Canford Cliffs. We need not worry about the other two.

If you were a student of kinesics clutching a Frankel betting slip, it would have been about the halfway point in the race that you headed for the pay window. Tom's body language tells it all; his trademark action of confidence is a giveaway as he twists his head down and around his legs to sneak a peek at the action behind. Nothing of consequence to see there. He keeps Frankel galloping, just ahead of Canford Cliffs, gently squeezing up the pace until well into the penultimate furlong when, as if finally bored with this game of catch-me-if-you-can, he pulls the trigger ending both the race and Canford Cliffs' career; he was never to race again. In a matter of a few strides Frankel accelerates five lengths clear. It is a devastating annihilation. Tom had never hit him once, even having the time, poise and sheer bravado to swirl his whip like some excited drum majorette in the final fifty yards.

At the pick-up Tom and Frankel sweep past a dancing Sandy. It will take them a little while to return as Frankel could not be stopped, only bringing himself to a halt when the fence at the end of the run-out proves more persuasive than his jockey. Someone in the crowd leads a chorus of 'Three cheers for Henry!' and Goodwood appears as truly glorious as its marketing strapline tells us it is. In the paddock, as Henry shakes Tom's hand, you can see the electric surge of relief that hangs over them. Whatever demons they both carried from Royal Ascot had been blown away across the downs forever.

18

The high-stakes gamble

It was to be nearly another three months before Frankel raced again, the final hurrah to his three-year-old season and maybe his racing career. Henry was keen – Jane says desperate – for him to stay in training as a four-year-old. He felt he'd tamed the beasts inside Frankel who, despite still pulling the arms from the sockets of Shane each morning was, at least relative to all things Frankel, becoming easier to train. Outside his box, where he still remained as belligerent as ever, he was a stronger horse, maturing both in head and body. It would soon be time for those size-eight racing plates.

Henry told anyone who would listen that Frankel would race further and faster at four. The public at large lapped it up. By the end of the year he'd have been unbeaten in all nine of his races. The highest rated horse on the planet. Arguably, even at this moment, the best racehorse of all time. Who could possibly deny the Frankel/Cecil/Queally show another year to take all before them?

But Frankel racing at four was far from being a certainty; it was a huge decision for Prince Khalid on a historic, commercial and emotional level. Having spent a great deal of time with the

Juddmonte people, from the luxury of Banstead Manor to the everyday grittiness of Ferrans during the writing of this book, I've come to understand how intertwined their lives are with those of their horses. The year is measured not by the dates on the calendar but by the equine cycle: the joy of the spring births. The excitement of the races, with all the highs and lows that brings. The covering time. The difficult calls when things don't turn out as they should. The hopes and dreams as the new crop heads off to their respective trainers.

And Frankel represented all that. A culmination and a justification for decades of endeavour. Living proof that one man's dream had been fulfilled. Frankel could be retired at three undefeated. The supreme racehorse. In the absence of defeat there would be no blame. No recriminations for a decision badly made. No shattering of that precious belief in his invincibility. Frankel, the history books would say, was a great horse. No ifs. No buts. He had already dazzled like no other before him. Retiring at three? It was the sensible decision.

But what about the commercial? It is a fact that horse racing requires money. And at this level vast quantities of it. The Juddmonte racing operation, with hundreds of horses and employees spread around the globe, has to translate success on the racecourse into hard cash. And that largely comes not through prize money or the selling of horses but stud fees, the earnings of your home-bred stallions. In some respects being an owner/breeder such as the Prince is a bit akin to being a Hollywood movie mogul; most of your films will lose money. A few will break even or better. But once every few years you need a massive box office smash for it all to make financial sense. And Frankel could well be the equine blockbuster of all time – think of the *Star Wars* franchise with interest on top. Let's put some numbers on that.

There is no reason why Frankel couldn't be at stud for twenty years; his father is getting on that way and his great-grandfather Northern Dancer lived to twenty-nine years old. In that time, allowing for a slowdown in older age, he could conservatively cover 2,500 mares and the value of each covering would be determined, at least in the early years, by his success on the racecourse. If he was retired at three unbeaten, his stud fee would have been in the region of £75,000, so lifetime earnings of £187.5 million. If he races successfully at four you can probably double that to £375 million. But, and it's a huge but, if that four-year-old gamble goes horribly awry, his value would shrink to tens rather than hundreds of millions.

Against this background all sorts of serious discussions were going on, as it was by no means certain that Frankel would be retired to stud in the UK. There was talk of him standing at the Juddmonte stud farm in Kentucky where the US market for milers is much stronger. Philip Mitchell, not wanting to see his protégé leave, cryptically wrote in a report to Prince Khalid, 'Frankel has never flown.' In the end he never had to.

Frankel woke up in the stables across the road from Ascot racecourse; it was the morning of the final race of his three-year-old season, the Queen Elizabeth II Stakes. Sandy, who slept overnight in the stable hands' hostel close by, had been up and down in the night to check him every few hours. Away from Warren Place he and travelling head lad Mike McGowan had been in sole charge of Frankel since they had driven the 100 miles from Newmarket on the Friday afternoon.

All was well early on that beautiful Saturday October morning as Sandy let Frankel guzzle down the bucket of feed which Dee had prepared the day before. Fed and watered the pair headed out for a breath of air, stretching their legs under the reddening trees on the grass behind the stables. After twenty minutes they were done; there was plenty of scope for exercise later in the day, so Sandy sat by Frankel on the ground, as he did every day, as Frankel had a pick of grass. As more stable hands and their horses appeared so did the attention, but it was always discreet. A nod. A wave. An acknowledgement that you been close to this equine superstar. But never that close. After all you didn't want to be the person whose horse kicked Frankel. Did Frankel mind the attention? The looks? Not a bit of it. He is a horse that not only revels in being the centre of attention but enjoys observing the observers. He was going to have plenty of opportunity for more of that later in the afternoon, for this was a big day for not only him but domestic horse racing.

This Ascot race meeting was the inaugural Champions Day, the British response to the increasingly successful Arc de Triomphe Sunday in France and the Breeders' Cup Saturday in the USA. It was a bold move by the racing authorities which Henry endorsed. He could have raced Frankel just about anywhere to close out his three-year-old season but he chose this day. Of course it gave the Champions Day PR people a huge headache. What do we talk about – our race meeting or our racehorse? The fact that six of the world's top nine racehorses would be running that day seemed destined to become something of a footnote. There was one name. There was one race. It was hardly difficult to spin. But it did rely on one outcome.

The race, the Queen Elizabeth II Stakes, had the little look of an old mates club. Frankel had been joined on the journey down from Warren Place by Bullet Train who was, at long last, to be his pacemaker on the racecourse proper. Excelebration was there, a horse who really deserves a little mention of his own for he took on Frankel five times in all. It's a tribute to his trainer Marco Botti who didn't, unlike plenty of others, shirk the challenge, seeing no shame in defeat to such a great horse. Botti clearly understood he had a very good horse of his own in Excelebration, who like Nathaniel simply had the misfortune to be born into the Frankel generation. In any other year he might have been crowned the champion miler. If you exclude his races against Frankel, Excelebration is exceptional: ten races, eight wins, six of which were of Group status with total win prize money of £1.25 million. Dubawi Gold was there as well, his third race of the year against Frankel.

All in all the Queen Elizabeth II was arguably to be one of Frankel's hardest tests to date with three of Europe's best milers competing for glory, plus the winner of the race the previous year. All eight of the runners had won a Group race, a remarkable twenty-four races between them, including ten at the highest level. In theory the Frankel race, which was styled the British Champions Mile, was on the undercard. The Champion Stakes, over a longer distance, was meant to be the feature event but nobody really believed that. Truth be told Frankel probably could have won that as well – he had, or would subsequently, beat half of the runners in that, including the winner. In fact the Frankel name ran like letters in a stick of rock through the careers of twelve of the thirty runners in the top three races that day, all of them combined losing to him on twenty-seven occasions. No wonder the betting market was so lopsided: 4–11 Frankel, 6–1 Excelebration, 7–1 Immortal Verse and the others 14–1 or longer with Bullet Train the rank outsider at a-not-very-generous-all-things-considered 150–1. If you had to pick a hole in Frankel it was his return to Ascot, recalling that close to calamitous St James's Palace Stakes four months earlier. The only consolation was that this race was over the straight mile; no opportunity for on-the-bend displays of bravado this time.

Ascot was jammed to capacity. It was hard to move anywhere – it was easier to just go with the flow of the crowd. More akin to a Black Friday sale, people were camped out by the pre-parade ring well before the first race. There was an audible gasp as Sandy led in Frankel who, as ever, looked both unconcerned and curious. Phones sprang up like daisies in spring, photos by the thousand recording the moment. In the paddock thirty minutes later, saddled and ready to go, it was no different, just multiply the crowd by any factor you like as the bars and restaurants emptied, the racegoers applauding as he arrived. This for a horse that hadn't even run the race. Extraordinary.

Sometimes the power of genius is to make things look easy; by that measure Frankel is on a par with Einstein. There is never a moment in the 1 minute 39.45 seconds (average speed 36.2 mph) of the Queen Elizabeth II Stakes that you ever doubted that Her Majesty would be handing over her trophy to Prince Khalid. True, Bullet Train does draw ten lengths clear of the field and probably twice that ahead of his half-brother who is a bit grumpy about all that, turning his head to one side and racing sideways for the first furlong. But by now us Frankel watchers with eight races under our belts are well used to such behaviour. We'd almost worry if he went completely to sleep.

Just after halfway Tom pulls him around and in front of the others, only Bullet Train somewhere up ahead. But on this occasion there is no urgency; they have played this particular game of cat and mouse too many times for Tom to worry. With two furlongs to go, the three-part-siblings are side-by-side before Frankel, without really any apparent effort, goes two lengths clear. As Bullet Train falls away (he was to finish plumb last) Excelebration, ever game, takes up the cause. However, in a repeat of their opening race of the season at Newbury six months earlier when the winning post came and went, he is again to be four lengths adrift as Frankel powers away trying, ever the contrarian, to run faster fifty yards after the line than before it regardless of anything Tom does.

Beneath the gaze of tens of thousands, who cheer and clap as the winning pair arrive in the unsaddling enclosure, Tom leans forward before dismounting to kiss Frankel on his neck. Not for him the exuberance of a Dettori-like flying dismount. Just a quiet smile and that intimate moment with his horse. Soon enough, there are the grateful handshakes of Henry and the Prince. A trophy from the Queen. Interviews with media from around the globe. But in that moment, despite everything that is swirling about them, it is still just one man and one horse. I suspect he didn't want it to end. Ever. Only Tom knows, and only Tom would ever know, what it was truly like to race ride the greatest racehorse of all time.

As Frankel is officially rated the best racehorse in the world, Henry has his wish – Frankel is to race at four. I would say the decision could not have been more popular but that would be to hide from some of the truth. Of course, it sets the racing public abuzz: their superstar will be returning to the racecourse in both the year of the London Olympics and the Diamond Jubilee of Elizabeth II. We are set for a sort of turbo-charged summer of sporting Cool Britannia.

But the decision comes with huge responsibilities. Sandy's wish that he 'Just wanted to do my job right', feels harder with each passing day. Mike, whose burden as assistant trainer is to become greater still when Henry's cancer takes a turn for the worse, has felt the pressure mounting with each successive win. Shane, the man who has to ride Frankel every day, feels a huge burden of responsibility in case it was his fault if anything went awry.

A long winter stretches ahead but it is to be the following spring when it all goes horribly wrong.

19

Hidden dips

The transition of a racehorse from three- to four-year-old is not as problematic as that from two to three – you don't have that worry about 'training on' in the juvenile sense but sometimes horses, for unfathomable reasons, simply don't improve with age. You can't legislate for that, so for the Warren Place team it was simply a case of closing the gates to settle down for, at best, an uneventful winter.

As with the previous thirty-five winters at Warren Place, the weekly exercise regime was gradually diminished as Henry brought his horses down from peak fitness to an easy plateau. Gone were the Wednesday and Saturday gallops. No more excursions to the Racecourse Side or long round-trips to the Al Bahathri. Come Christmas even Warren Hill disappeared from the roster, after which time all work took place within the confines of the indoor ride.

Aside from that Frankel's routine barely changed. The Garage remained his home, his mate Bullet Train still two doors down. Dee was there each morning soon after 5 am with his early morning feed. Sandy would arrive an hour later. And then Shane an hour after that. After exercise, such as it was, Shane would wash or brush him down, leaving him wearing a light sheet as he gradually cooled down before Dee returned to bandage all four of his legs. Frankel loved to get down in the shavings on the floor of his box rolling, wriggling and writhing as his legs flailed in the air. Then it was breakfast, 15 lb of Canadian corn (three times that of the early morning feed) plus double handfuls of bran and alfalfa chaff sweetened with molasses. Alfalfa is a sort of clover-like hay crop, which is chopped up to mix with the corn, and is rich in calcium, amino acids and all manner of vitamins. In effect it is a health supplement for horses, with some roughage thrown in for good measure.

And that was pretty well it as far as Frankel's day was concerned until Sandy returned at 3.30 pm. It is worth remembering that Sandy didn't just have Frankel to care for; he'd have the two others, Bullet Train and Stipulate, plus helping to cover when someone was off sick or away. But he would always make a beeline for Frankel, attending to his needs ahead of all the others. Whatever Henry might say, however much he might pretend all Warren Place horses were equal, that simply wasn't the case.

I'm not sure it was anything to be ashamed of that Frankel was accorded special treatment – Sandy reckons he received twice the time of the other two combined. He was the only horse, plus a companion he insisted on coming along to keep him company, to have a pick of grass every afternoon. So for forty-five minutes each day they'd be out somewhere at the back of the stables while Henry chatted, stroked and communed with the horse that had given him new purpose. The only time they ever skipped this was when it rained. Not because anyone cared about getting wet but because Henry believed grazing damp grass was bad for a horse.

After that it was back to his box in time for his 5.30 pm feed (much the same as breakfast) before Sandy left him for the night with a heavier rug, plenty of water and a good wedge of hay. There would never be a single strand left by morning; Frankel spent the night scouring all corners for every little last wisp.

You might imagine that Frankel, by now more valuable than most of the pictures hanging in London's National Gallery, would have a crack security team guarding him night and day. Not a bit of it. Henry reasoned that guards would simply signpost ne'er-do-wells in the direction of Frankel. You can see his point. Who would possibly imagine keeping the most sought after horse on the planet in an old garage? Sandy would have been more worried for their own safety, for Frankel, despite his improving demeanour on the gallops and on the racecourse, remained as aggressive as ever within the confines of his box. 'You can't fight with a 550 kilo horse', says Sandy. And he would know.

The only concession to security was a night camera mounted in Frankel's box. However, a camera is only as good as the person watching it, and if you don't have a security guard, who is going to watch your horse? Henry was actually completely against the whole idea until Jane suggested a solution; why not run the feed into their home with monitors in the house, including one in the bedroom? That idea was to become something of a rod for Jane's own back as 'Frankel Live from The Garage' became Henry's major source of tele-visual entertainment.

By general consent Frankel was a bigger, stronger and more mature horse as he turned from three to four. As Shane, who would know better than anyone alive says, he was no longer a tearaway. He still pulled like the proverbial train, but now work mornings were less of a life-and-death tussle. Sure, in the early spring of that four-year-old year, when he was still fresh and carrying a bit of fat, he wasn't averse to rearing up on his hind legs in protest at some apparent slight but he never once deposited Shane on the ground. All was well then, with regular work resuming on 1 February as winter quarters ended with the return of Jane and Henry from their annual holiday.

The progress of Frankel's final season was largely secreted in the head of Henry and the ear of Prince Khalid, but some mileposts were planted for us all to know: an opening race in the Lockinge Stakes at Newbury in May and a closing race in the Champion Stakes at Ascot in October. In between maybe a historic double with a second Sussex Stakes? But that was a mile and Henry definitely wanted to send Frankel into the unknown with a race further than he had ever gone before, probably over a mile and a quarter. When he chatted with Sandy at the afternoon pick, the possible races were a constant source of discussion, each a stepping stone across the pond that was the upcoming season. The route to the other side was never direct, a zig-zag of multiple permutations with Henry always favouring British racing, while foreign raids were rarely spoken of. But racing has many siren calls. How about the Breeders' Cup? The Arc de Triomphe? Much would happen over the coming months, plenty of it unplanned.

The long, straight but undulating London Road that brings you into Newmarket from the west has a sign beside it that warns of hidden dips. It is clearly there for the benefit of car drivers, but in reality it might just as well act as a salutary warning for anyone planning to own a racehorse, even one as good as Frankel. For on the otherwise uneventful morning of Wednesday 11 April, five weeks before Frankel's first race of the year, he struck one of those hidden dips.

It had all been going so well. The Lockinge Stakes for May was firmly in the diary. Frankel's work with Bullet Train had been exemplary, the duo to be inseparable all year on both gallops and racecourse. After another dry spring (the year was to end very differently) Henry was planning to take Frankel to Newbury ten days later for a bit of a weekend away with a gallop on the racing turf. But that was never to happen.

Shane had ridden Frankel in a very normal piece of work over on the Racecourse Side early that morning. It might have been the first or second time that year; nobody can recall exactly. Though they box the horses over at the start of the day, they walk them back. It was a convoluted three-mile amble home, one that suited an ever inquisitive Frankel very well, with plenty to look at as they wended their way through the sand-covered back streets of Newmarket along The Rows, The Watercourse before finally popping out from behind Waitrose to rejoin the familiar Bury Side. It was a while before they finally made it up the hill to Warren Place but that was fine; a very slow walk home was another of Henry's things. He insisted on it.

Back in the Garage box Shane bent down, unwrapping each of Frankel's exercise bandages before sponging down each of his legs in turn. Usually Frankel would stand immobile; it was simply part of his routine. But on that morning, as Shane ran the sponge down the back of his right front leg, he flinched. Shane very gently repeated the action but this time with his hand alone, feeling a tiny bump, not much more than a pinhead, beneath the skin on the tendon behind the cannon bone. Shane called Mike who did and felt the same. When Mike went to find Henry, Shane knew this might be serious.

Initially Henry wasn't too worried. Frankel wasn't lame, so stable vet Charlie Smith gave Frankel a short-acting anti-inflammatory drug with a bandage applied. But by evening stables, though the swelling had reduced it had not resolved, so Ian Wright, one of the world's leading authorities on equine orthopaedics who has been consultant surgeon to Juddmonte for many years, was called in to examine Frankel.

Ian, Charlie, Henry and Dee met in Frankel's box the next morning. The swelling extended from the junction of the middle third of the cannon to the level of the knee. It was centred over and enveloped the flexor tendons. There was no recognisable change in the contour of the superficial digital flexor tendon but, worryingly, there was a palpable increase in fluid in the carpal sheath which encloses the flexor tendons at the back of the knee.

Injuries to the flexor tendons are invariably career threatening and frequently career ending in flat racehorses. Horses' legs are a magnificent design for fast running. The horse's knee is the equivalent of the human wrist and all of the bones from this point down are elongated which create long-lever arms for mechanical advantage. Muscles are situated above the knee so that the forces they create and the energy produced by the horse's weight and speed are borne by tendon and ligaments in the lower limb. This highly efficient but vulnerable system is seen at its best in the galloping thoroughbred. Tendon injuries are rarely life threatening but healing is slow and invariably includes inelastic scar tissue which limits athletic capability. As a rule of thumb, the slower the equine sport, e.g. dressage, the greater the horse's chance of returning to competition. Tendon injury in a fast horse in a fast sport is therefore a major concern. The superficial digital flexor tendon in the cannon region are most commonly affected. This is situated at the back of the leg and should be firm and straight. When injured it becomes thickened and often produces a shallow convex contour to the leg which generations of horsemen have termed a 'bow' or 'bowed tendon'.

How had Frankel struck himself? Did one of his rear-leg hooves strike the back of his front leg? The truth was nobody was quite sure. Shane recalled nothing untoward during the gallop. Nothing on the walk home. Back in his box he wasn't lame, unable or unwilling to stand or move. But something was not right and Ian's examination had proved that. So Charlie performed an ultrasound scan on the tendons in Frankel's box which revealed no evidence of damage in the cannon area. That was good, but more sophisticated equipment was needed to evaluate the carpal sheath, and that required a delay of six days to allow the acute inflammation to reduce. In the meantime it was walking exercise only for Frankel, with Dee and Sandy applying cold water hosing and iced bandages to the leg before and after exercise in order to reduce the inflammation and associated swelling.

It was to be a long week, only to be enlivened by one moment of black humour on the Saturday, Grand National Day, when Clare Balding, fronting the BBC's coverage, announced to a global television audience that Frankel had been retired due to the injury on the gallops. This came as news to everyone associated with Frankel, not least Teddy Grimthorpe who was at the Aintree meeting. Teddy soon put everyone right.

A week after the Racecourse Side gallop on 18 April, Frankel made the short trip across town to Newmarket Equine Hospital, a state-of-the-art facility next door to the July Course and National Stud. It must be said Frankel himself seemed fine. He hadn't exactly loved his week of inactivity but the fuss made of him by Sandy and Dee had massaged his ego. However, the outcome of this examination would determine whether he ever raced again.

In the subdued light of the scanning room, Sandy and Ian watched while an ultrasound scan was performed by imaging consultant Gaynor Minshall who had pioneered examination of the carpal sheath. The area was examined using a number of different ultrasound techniques to evaluate individual structures and adjacent blood vessels. Radiographs were also taken. Like a bad hospital drama, Henry and Teddy waited in the hospital office for what must have seemed an eternal hour. At the conclusion of the scan they convened in Ian's office. Door closed, the good news was given. The scan had shown no evidence of structural damage and Frankel could return to training.

At first glance a ten-day interruption might look to have been fatal to Henry's plan to run Frankel in the Lockinge Stakes on 18 May but it wasn't really. Aside from his belief that you could only bring a horse to its absolute peak twice a season, Henry also liked to get his horses fit then cruise them up to a race. But bearing in mind that it was 100 days between the end of winter quarters and the Lockinge, then the hiatus was just a minor blip.

Henry and Frankel treated it as such. The planned trip to Newbury didn't happen but instead, with ever an eye to the media and keeping the racing game in the headlines, Henry arranged for Frankel to have that run-out on a racecourse, with Tom riding, in front of the gathering crowds on 2,000 Guineas Saturday two weeks before his return to the racecourse proper. As Tom let him go two furlongs out, Frankel did what he always does: powering up towards the finish, looking beyond the winning line. Tom says it is like having an unexpected extra gear that effortlessly engages. When he tells you he has never felt such power in a horse before or since, you can sense he is a little wistful that, for all the privilege of riding Frankel, he'll never be able to experience such a thing in another. So all was good. Frankel was back on track. The injury scare was just that – a scare. Everyone settled back to plotting the route to Frankel's tenth race. But on that road there would turn out to be a number of hidden dips.

On the day of travel, the Friday before Saturday's Lockinge Stakes, Dee and the team pulled the usual wool over Frankel's eyes, leaving the application of his protective bandaging until the very last minute. That bit worked, but for some reason Frankel got on one of his 'heads', lashing out a rear leg that struck the Garage wall and dislodged the aluminium racing plate so that it hung from his foot half on/half off. Normally they would have called over Stephen Kielt, the farrier, but he had already set off for Newbury to await Frankel's arrival. If you are getting the idea that despite Henry's laconic air a military-style operation was gathering around each of Frankel's successive races, you'd be right.

As Stephen turned his car around to return to Warren Place it was urgent that the shoe came straight off; if Frankel put any weight on it the danger was that a dislodged nail might pierce the soft tissue of the hoof ending any chance of his planned return. With a highly agitated horse, who was unwilling to cooperate, it was a really hard thing to do. Not only did Frankel have to be calmed but, between them, Dee and Mike had to grasp his leg, a wicked weapon in itself, with his hoof held bottom side up so that they could use a shoe puller, a sort of very long-handled set of pliers used by farriers, to lever off the shoe, nails and all, in the hope of not causing any injury. Or at the very least hoping not to make anything that may have already happened worse.

When Stephen returned, Dee, Mike and Sandy were standing watch over Frankel who was still in something of a state. Yes, the shoe was off as instructed but he couldn't travel without a replacement. Stephen cleared the box, leaving just him with Sandy and Frankel while he fitted the new racing plate. Hours later than planned the horse box finally pulled out of Warren Place. Frankel had walked without any apparent discomfort from the Garage, up the ramp and into the lorry. But it was only a matter of a few dozen yards, hardly a rigorous examination. It told nothing of what tomorrow might bring. The foot might flare up overnight. It might be perfectly fine. Or worst of all, Frankel might break down in the race itself, limping to an inglorious defeat, his perfect record shattered by his own temper. It was what many had feared for a long time, but perhaps not exactly to a script like this.

Sometimes, in replay, the Frankel races don't look as exciting as they should. Years later we have forgotten the heart-stopping uncertainty of each successive race. The ratcheting up of the tension as the Warren Place team doubled down time and time again to extend his unbeaten run yet further, testing him over distances and in conditions as yet untried. At Newbury on that May Saturday, the public knew of the uncertainty surrounding the interruption caused by the gallops injury scare. In private Tom knew he was riding a horse who might turn out to be lame. Henry knew Frankel was in need of the race, he had said as much in interviews, but a long season beckoned; he couldn't peak him too early. It was a fine balance between having him ready enough to win, but not over-ready. And the Lockinge Stakes had the look of a tough race: another Group 1 over a mile, with opponents itching to bring Frankel down.

Excelebration was back for another go but now under new ownership and with a new trainer, none other than Aidan O'Brien. The Ballydoyle team don't run horses for also-ran money and they were serious – Excelebration had his own pacemaker, Windsor Palace. This is how the theory ran: the closest Frankel had come to defeat was in the ill-starred St James's Palace Stakes at Royal Ascot when the race pace was furious. If there was a chink in Frankel's armour it was to be found by going hard and going fast from the get-go. Of course, Frankel has his own lieutenant in Bullet Train but with another front-running speed merchant Ransom Note included, the pace might not be of the making by the Warren Place pair. Dubawi Gold completed the field of six, ready for his fourth attempt to beat Frankel in what would be his final race.

Whatever had ailed Frankel the day before, it is certainly gone by 3.40 pm on the day of the Lockinge Stakes at Newbury. As he walks, last of the six, calm as you like, into stall five, Tom gives him a reassuring stroke along his mane, though that might be as much for the benefit of jockey as horse. As the stalls open it is Bullet Train who takes the role of pacemaker, his jockey Ian Mongan looking round after half a furlong to see that Frankel has cruised up to occupy second place a couple of lengths behind. And that is pretty much how the race plays out. Frankel is never passed and it is tempting to ask: where are all the pacemakers? As ever Frankel isn't exactly pleased to be directly behind Bullet Train, twisting his head to look around and ahead, but there is none of the fighting-with-Tom of old. Past halfway and the field bunches a bit behind Frankel with Bullet Train still setting the pace ahead.

With two furlongs to go Tom makes his move, pulling out and beside Bullet Train before taking the lead with Excelebration in his slipstream. If the Ballydoyle strike is to come, this is the moment. But it never comes. It never really looks like coming. Excelebration's jockey, Aidan O'Brien's son Joseph, is already hard at work, as are all the other runners, while Tom just eases Frankel further and further into the lead. He can win by pretty well any distance he likes but in the end, five lengths ahead of Excelebration with Dubawi Gold four behind him, is demonstration enough of Frankel's effortless superiority.

And that is the thing about Frankel's races – he sometimes makes it all look too darned easy. Sometimes you have to look back at the horses behind. Understand that as they struggle to even get close to Frankel they are good, and in many cases, great horses themselves. Invincible is the word that comes most easily to the commentators and journalists that day. A sort of happy inevitability. With the Lockinge Stakes won, Frankel has now extended his winning sequence to ten with his fifth Group 1 in succession. Aidan O'Brien, whose powerful Coolmore stable is embarking upon a third season in the shadow of an all-conquering Frankel, mixes sanguinity with fatality. 'He's a great horse', he says in the paddock afterwards. 'Perhaps we should take him on next time with a team of ten and add two fences.'

As Prince Khalid remains in the paddock for a few minutes signing autographs and Sandy leads Frankel away, you sort of wonder whether even that would halt the progress of the Frankel express.

20

Flying the standard

There is a flagpole in the garden of what was then Jane and Henry's home. Today it looks rather forlorn; the white paint is shabby and the lanyard has rotted away to nothing. But when Henry was alive it was a totem to the success of Warren Place, the Burnett family standard (Henry's maternal lineage) raised to celebrate notable victories. As Frankel returned on the evening of his Lockinge win, it was fluttering proud once again, the three holly leaves above the Horn of Leys against the greyish background announcing what the world already knew: Frankel was back.

As he was led into his beloved Garage, Frankel's shining health was so different to that of Henry. One was young. Strong. Healthy. Life in the ascendant. The other was frail. Weakened by illness. The truth was Henry was dying. The stomach cancer he had lived with since 2006 had spread to his lungs. In this, Frankel's final season, Henry would undergo 700 hours of chemotherapy, fitting it around the Warren Place routine, driving himself the fifteen miles to Cambridge Hospital after morning stables. Once there he would urge the nurses to speed up the treatment so he could be back in time for evening stables. Henry didn't really engage with people about what was happening within him; he didn't want to talk about it with anyone, including his GP. As Jane says he loved life. Just wanted to live. Like his protégé he believed in his own invincibility. Determined to be there for his horse. See it out to the very end. Which indeed he did. Henry Cecil died on 11 June 2013, 234 days after the pair stood together on a racecourse for the very last time.

As racegoers will know, Royal Ascot starts with a royal procession; thirty minutes later with Her Majesty and her guests safely ensconced in the semi-circular luxury of the royal box, Frankel had a procession all of his own. Not that his ten opponents meant for it to be that way. It is an oddity of the royal meeting, all five days of it, that they jump straight in with one of the feature races of the week opening the meeting. With an equine megastar entered, most racecourse managements might ponder on the wisdom of such a policy. But Royal Ascot is all about tradition. The Queen Anne Stakes is by tradition the opening race of the royal meeting – the first race of the first day – and a nod to the Queen who founded the track in 1711. Even Frankel was not going to change that. It was set for 2.30 pm; and 2.30 pm it would stay. No time for Henry to arrive in a royal carriage this time. In fact no time for the present-day Queen who ushered her guests up to the royal box while she remained to see Frankel led into the paddock.

Did anyone doubt that Frankel was going to win on this day? Be the curtain raiser of all curtain raisers? If you followed the money, the answer was emphatically no. At 1–10 Frankel was to be one of the shortest-priced winners at Royal Ascot of modern times. But if you were standing by Shane and his then partner but now wife Claire, you'd see two people plagued with doubt; perhaps surprisingly, this was the first time one of Frankel's most constant companions was to be at the races with him. The truth was Shane didn't really want to be there; he was content to shred his nerves each time in front of the television at home, but with an old jockey pal visiting from Dubai the decision was out of his hands.

It was one of those official Frankel mania days. The combination of the world's top-rated horse putting his ten-race unbeaten reputation on the line once again, but this time among the royal pageant, was media manna from heaven. If you hadn't quite got the message, the Ascot Authority were handing out Frankel flags. Anyone with any connection to the horse unwise enough to make it known was scooped up for interview or comment. Shane, it must be said, kept his counsel. He could not believe what was happening around him. The way that Frankel, so much part of his everyday life, was loved and admired by so many. He never realised until this moment that what was so normal for him was so very special to others. Today, several years after that day, he still shakes his head in wonderment and disbelief. 'Bizarre', he says more than once, but I think it's in that sense that he can't believe he'd never truly comprehended how big the Frankel thing had become. And that, on the day, made him very, very nervous. Riding Frankel was definitely easier than watching him.

But Shane need not have worried. This was to be the day when all his work was repaid in the most spectacular fashion. Those thousands of miles in the saddle. The filthy-cold early mornings. A horse that could at one moment be truculent and difficult and in the next powering you away, unlike any horse you had ever ridden. So much so that you screamed at the top of your voice 'Whoa!' both in shock and total exhilaration, returning to the coterie of gallop watchers with a smile so wide it might just bust open your head. And today was to be a day for more screaming as Frankel was to demolish his opponents. Take them apart spectacularly, securing his status for all time.

* * *

For the Queen Anne Stakes, Frankel has earned the right to load whenever he chooses, so he and Tom hang back, circling around behind the starting stalls at the end of the Ascot one-mile straight in front of the royal entrance gates, the recent wheel tracks of the royal carriages still visible in the pliant grass. For some reason Bullet Train is reluctant, pulled from the front and squeezed from the rear by the handlers until he goes into stall six. Frankel ambles in last but one into stall eight. It is a near perfect draw.

Bullet Train might have been reluctant to load but his regular jockey Ian Mongan isn't going to let him race that way, pinging him out as a pacemaker should, glancing to his left after a dozen strides to get a fix on Frankel who breaks well. Joseph O'Brien on Excelebration, back for another try and back again with his own pacemaker Windsor Palace, the latter never getting anywhere near the front, decides to mix it up by challenging Bullet Train for the lead while Frankel settles in third or fourth, front and middle of the following pack. But the Bullet Train/Frankel double act is working in perfect tandem as the elder sibling slowly winds up the pace until they are three furlongs from home.

What happens in the next quarter of a mile is one of the most spine-chilling examples of Frankel's utter brilliance. He edges from the pack, bundles Excelebration aside, draws level with Bullet Train then eviscerates the competition as Tom lets him go using that huge, free-flowing stride to burn up the Ascot turf and have the stop-watchers doubt the validity of their sectional timings. For if you have to ask what sets Frankel apart from mere mortal horses, it is that blistering acceleration which he is able to switch on not only at will but at any moment in a race, with a burst of speed that will last longer, and go on further, than any other horse alive. Or probably any horse that has ever lived. Time and time again he didn't just beat horses, he broke their will. Canford Cliffs, Excelebration and

Nathaniel, to pick just three, stayed with him momentarily before they fell away, the hopelessness of the challenge clear for all to see. As Henry said afterwards, 'He keeps on going when others don't.'

If you want to put some numbers to that, here they are: he beats second-placed Excelebration by eleven lengths, more than twice that of the Lockinge Stakes, a rout in itself. It would have been more but for the fact Tom begins easing Frankel down a hundred yards ahead of the winning post. Frankel hits a top speed 42.53 mph, faster than the sprinters later in the afternoon. He even covers the final furlong faster than them; in human terms that's like Olympic and World Champion Mo Farah running his middle-distance race but still beating Usain Bolt over the final 200 m. In a race of just 97.8 seconds, Frankel is only 0.69 seconds outside the course record on ground that is good to soft; with a firmer surface he would have blown that record apart.

It is no wonder that the crowd don't just cheer Frankel home. They roar. As ever it takes Tom forever to bring Frankel to a halt. That is more than demonstrated at Royal Ascot as Tom uses his tried and tested slowing-down technique of steering Frankel towards the rails. Which is fine until Excelebration draws level, at which point Frankel whips his head around to size up the looming competition but even he eventually understands it is only Joseph O'Brien leaning across to shake Tom's hand in congratulation.

As the victorious pair jog back in front of the stands, Frankel pricks his ears forward in acknowledgement as the waves of cheers and applause sweep over them. In the melee out on the track he had to jink around an over-eager photographer, losing a racing plate in the process. This was picked up by a sharp-eyed punter who, with an even greater eye to its value, auctioned it for charity making £25,000. Up in the stands Shane's pre-race nerves are washed away by the wall of sound. Looking around he feels proud to see the sheer joy, happiness and delight which the horse he rides every day brings to other people. But with that realisation comes the enormity of what he holds between his hands. God forbid that anything should go wrong. The occasional sleepless night has been replaced by almost constant worry and pressure. Shane isn't alone in this. As the wins rack up – Frankel is now eleven from eleven – the fear of failure is beginning to take on a greater consequence for everyone connected with him. No longer is he just rated the best racehorse in the world (that is almost old hat by now) but there are plenty, after this awe-inspiring Royal Ascot race in front of the international racing elite, who are talking of him as being the greatest racehorse of all time. He has three more races to prove it.

21

Always summer

It is only in recent times that pretty well every sport has become data driven. Rugby players have tracking devices in their shirts. Hawkeye technology plots the height, speed, spin and trajectory of every ball struck at every major tennis tournament. In swimming the length of a fingernail is now enough to separate gold from silver. But in that great debate – who is the greatest exponent of any given sport in history – the evidence may only take you so far; for in most cases, it simply isn't there or jaundiced by progress. Thanks to ball and club technology your average golfer today could well outdrive the Major winners of fifty years ago. There are no video replays of the Preston North End 'invincibles' racking up their unbeaten run in the Football League of 1888–89. But horse racing is different.

The data *is* there. Horses have been ranked since almost the very outset of competitive racing; that is, in effect, what handicapping is. Picking the best horse and loading it up with extra weight to create an even contest with less good horses. Races have been timed over the same track, distance and turf for centuries. The 'form', that record of every thoroughbred race ever run, has been meticulously compiled. Even without the aid of a television archive history may be accurately relived.

So, as Henry contemplated Frankel's next races, the rule was being run over his unbeaten sequence of eleven by the national and international ranking experts on a weekly basis. For it is not only the manner and nature of Frankel's victories that matter but those of his rivals. Their races past or future are important – 'franking the form' as they call it. Winning alone is not enough. It is no good being just the best of a poor generation; you have to be the best of a good generation, and that in horse racing, unlike many other sports, is quantifiable.

So Frankel, for his brilliance, still had things to prove if he was to end the season the first ever horse to be top ranked at both two, three and four and be officially rated the greatest racehorse of all time. Chief among those things that Henry had to demonstrate was Frankel's ability to win over a longer distance; all his races to date had been over seven furlongs or a mile. Now there is nothing inherently bad about being a world-beating one-mile specialist, but in the international bloodstock market your kudos is enhanced with versatility. Your genes will be in greater demand from a wider pool of breeders, not to mention the 'greatest of all time' tag hinging on the proof that you are able to win over a variety of distances.

As with most things Henry, the plan was pretty simple: Frankel was to race over what they call an extended mile and a quarter, namely ten and a half furlongs, at York in early August and if successful repeat a similar distance in the Champion Stakes at Ascot to close out the year in October. Whether Frankel would stay that extra distance nobody knew. Would the sprinting lineage of his mother Kind trump the middle-distance stamina of his father Galileo? Henry was confident that the answer to that was no. His riders at home and on the racecourse, Shane and Tom, said the same.

But only the race would truly reveal the depths of Frankel's stamina. And in between there was just the small matter of Frankel's finale over a mile to create the historic double by winning the Sussex Stakes at Goodwood on the first day of August.

It was to be something of a strange contest. A strange day in fact. Surreal in the way that the elements came together to make you ask, did that really happen? It was also a day notable for its absences. Henry finally acceded to the effects of his punishing chemotherapy schedule; too ill to travel to Goodwood he relinquished the care of Frankel, for the one and only time in his fourteen-race career, to Jane and Mike Marshall. And further absent were opponents. Just three, which included Bullet Train, were to line up against Frankel. For his final race at a mile, he had seen off all but one of the serious contenders for his scalp. Farhh, whose withdrawal at the start of Frankel's second race two years before had so annoyed Henry but the following year went on to win the Champion Stakes, was the only one stepping up to the challenge. Even Excelebration had thrown in the towel.

For Frankel the summer living was easy; Henry had brought him up for the Queen Anne Stakes and now he was bringing him down as the Warren Place routine became the comfort blanket protecting them all, horse and people, from the mania. The twice-weekly gallops with Bullet Train and the daily canters up Warren Hill were all Frankel needed to keep him in tune. When it was high summer they chased the dawn across the Heath to beat the heat and saved the evening pick for the cool, but otherwise nothing changed. For all the daily tensions in Dee, Mike, Sandy and Shane, their prized horse, excepting what by now we consider normal for him, was becoming the picture of calm. The elder statesman of Warren Place. The matured athlete. He was the boss. Everyone, equine and human, deferred to him. It was the natural order of things as far as Frankel was concerned. He absolutely loved it, lapping up the attention of photographers and film crews, who arrived almost daily. For at this moment, with impeccable timing, Britain was the world epicentre of all things sporting as the opening of the 2012 London Olympics loomed.

It was a dream-like day up there on the Sussex Downs. The holiday crowd. The summer dresses. A racecourse part removed from the real world. A horse so totally in command of his own destiny. The bookies shouted themselves hoarse trying to find takers at 1–20, his shortest ever starting price, but few stepped forward. Wagering money on Frankel was no longer required. The pleasure of watching him race far exceeded any pecuniary gain. Even the jockeys not riding in the Sussex Stakes, who'd usually hole up in the weighing room between races, came out to see him in the paddock. Now that is true veneration.

The race – we have to call it that – is, as Shane recalls with a palpable sense of relief, the easiest of all Frankel's contests to watch, this time safely back in front of his television at home. It is, for all that will be said afterwards, still a Group 1 event with nearly £300,000 up for grabs. And it is easy to dismiss the risks that are taken each time horse and jockey step out on the turf, however glorious the scene. That day two horses fall and a third has to be put down. But in the Sussex Stakes there is to be no pain or suffering for Frankel, just unconfined delight, as he proves he is able to win any race, any way he likes.

You probably know how it all unfolded without me really having to tell the tale. Frankel is supremely calm both in the paddock and during the pre-race parade in front of the stands. In fact, he is unnervingly calm. Usually Tom keeps him on a tight rein heading to the start, both hands gripping the reins, as he stands perfectly poised and balanced in the stirrups, not moving a muscle for fear of setting Frankel alight. But today Tom sits back in the saddle, letting the reins hang slack in just one hand, while he adjusts his stirrups. Maybe they are both becoming more relaxed? Regardless, this is a race that proves another of Frankel's unique attributes: he can turn on that devastating turn of foot at any point in a race. Early, middle or in this case, late. He can wait or he can go. Whatever you might try, he has it covered. He is the poker player who will read your cards or call your bluff. You choose, but you still lose.

As for the race, Bullet Train sets the pace a length or two ahead. Frankel bobs along in second as easy as you like. As they turn into the straight with three furlongs to run, the order is unchanged as Tom swivels his head to assess what is a non-existent danger behind – Frankie Dettori is already hard at work on Farhh. This is the moment, you think, but Tom keeps absolutely still. Two furlongs out and still nothing, as Frankel draws level with a tiring Bullet Train. Still Tom waits, sneaking a glance at the pair behind with that trademark look between his legs. Then, just to make some sort of point, he pauses for another half furlong until, as casual as you like, he releases an inch of rein. Frankel needs no other invitation. He surges away. In a matter of a few strides the race is over. The competition dismissed. As the winning margin increases you struggle to see Frankel exerting any apparent effort. It is rather like when a rocket separates from its booster in space; you know in your head the gap is widening at warp velocity but it just doesn't look that way.

By the time they reach the winning line Tom and Frankel have slowed to half speed, even having time to do a cheeky pose for the photographers. Farhh and the rest are an irrelevance. Some say the Sussex Stakes was no more than a training gallop. Tom disagrees; it isn't even that strenuous.

* * *

The Juddmonte International Stakes at York was exactly three weeks away; one of the shortest gaps between races for Frankel. A frail Henry, who was now walking with the aid of a stick, didn't have long to bring Frankel back to his peak for his first attempt over the longer distance. But he wasn't overly worried. He had been telling anyone who would listen since Frankel's three-year-old days that he'd easily stay a longer race. In fact it was probably only Henry's natural caution, and the counsel of others, that had held him back. But it was really now or never. Unless Frankel stayed in training at five – fairly unlikely but not impossible – the moment would be past for good.

In between Goodwood and York the summer routine rolled on: Warren Hill canters interspersed with twice-weekly work. Henry picked the last Wednesday before the Wednesday of the race for the defining gallop. Odd to tell but Frankel had never run beyond a mile even in exercise; these nine furlongs along the Cambridge Road over on the Racecourse Side marked his first strides into the unknown, though still a furlong short of what would be expected of him at York. But Shane, like Henry, never doubted Frankel's ability to race further. The daily battles to pull him up long after most normal horses would have packed up and headed for home were evidence enough. As they cruised up the summer gallop, which then turns left parallel to the Cambridge Road itself, Shane felt in his hands and knew in his heart that beneath him was a horse that was ready for that longer race. The demons in the head of the younger Frankel were gone. The only horse that was ever really going to beat Frankel was Frankel himself. That alter ego was long gone.

For all the confidence of the Warren Place team, history didn't bode well for this attempt in the Juddmonte International to extend Frankel's unbeaten sequence to thirteen. Such perfection had been put to the test once before by another racing great, Brigadier Gerard, who had come to York in 1972 for the exact same race with his own unbeaten sequence of thirteen to extend. He failed, beaten by the Derby winner Roberto. For all the rightful adulation Roberto deserved it was a sad, sad day for British racing. Like Frankel, Brigadier Gerard was home bred and home trained, capturing the public imagination before retiring after eighteen races as, with just this one defeat, the highest rated British-trained horse of the twentieth century. But the defeat burst a bubble. Yes, Brigadier Gerard was a great horse but there was, on one given day, one better and that will always be a mark against his name. It still physically hurts to watch that race. Not many wanted 2012 to be a replay of what had gone down forty years before.

But it was always a possibility, for Frankel had to not only stay the distance but win. And win against the crack field that was lining up to challenge him; the racing colossi of the Coolmore and Godolphin stables were not going to let the possibility of a famous victory pass them by. It was almost as if having seen off all the best milers in the world, it was now the turn of the middle-distance horses to take up the cudgels against Frankel. St Nicholas Abbey was the next up from the Aidan O'Brien stable to take up where Excelebration had left off. Not far behind Frankel with four Group 1 wins of his own including a Breeders' Cup, he was entered with not one but two pacemakers, Robin Hood and Windsor Palace, to probe any weaknesses in Frankel's stamina. But then again Frankel had his mate Bullet Train to counter the Ballydoyle moves. Farhh was back for another crack but for the other two who completed the field of nine, Sri Putra who won over the course and distance the previous month and international traveller Planteur, this was to be their Frankel initiation.

You'll often hear people call York the Ascot of the north; that sense of a special occasion gathered around a feast of the very best horse racing in the summer sunshine. In fact, in 2005 it was that very thing as the royal meeting decamped from the south when the Berkshire course was being rebuilt. So the York officials are well versed in the ways of special visitors, but Frankel's arrival as the headline act of their four-day August Yorkshire Ebor Festival took things to a whole new level. A huge, record-breaking crowd was anticipated with every square inch of viewing space in the pink geranium bedecked stands taken. The management were not to be disappointed as the queues formed at the gates long before opening time.

But Frankel himself was well away from the gathering crowds, quietly munching hay in his box in the Bottom Yard of racecourse stables that are across the other side of the racecourse. As ever he'd travelled up the day before with travelling head lad Mike McGowan, farrier Stephen Kielt and, of course, Sandy. All were relaxed just waiting for the call to come to walk the two-thirds of a mile from the stables to the track across the Knavesmire, the public common on which the racecourse is built, fifty minutes ahead of the race itself.

They may have been calm but that was in complete contrast to the occupants of the Cecil Mercedes Benz. Henry was always ultra-organised. He hated being late for anyone or anything. You could say he was obsessive about it. At home he'd be tutting and cajoling others well before the appointed departure time, but for all that they were late on this day, stuck in traffic. Dee was driving instead of Henry who was far too ill; Jane recalls this special York day as the frailest and weakest she ever saw Henry on a racecourse. He may have not been well but it didn't assuage his fury. When they finally reached the course the Owners & Trainers car park was full, the barrier down. He was incandescent. Jane, at Henry's insistence, leapt out, lifted the barrier and they simply dumped the car but their difficulties were far from done.

Now you'd have thought that Henry could walk into any racetrack in Britain, and probably for that matter the world, unchallenged. And not least at York where he'd been one of the leading trainers for four decades. But today, of all days, officialdom barred his entry. If you are a trainer you are issued with a rather lovely metal badge that allows you entry into any UK course, the design and colour of which varies from year to year. Henry had a collection going back many years but for sartorial rather than kleptomaniac reasons. He liked his trainer's badge to match his tie, so he'd regularly wear a badge that was ten or twenty years out of date. The eagle-eyed man on the gate spotted the discrepancy. Henry was not coming in and that was that. Nothing would change his mind despite Henry being plastered all over the *Racing Post* and York race card. Eventually, Clerk of the Course William Derby was summoned and amid much apology the Cecil party was finally admitted.

The man on the gate might have not recognised Henry but the crowd immediately recognised Frankel. In what was fast becoming a rite of passage unique to our racing superhero, the applause broke out even as he cantered down to the start. You sort of dreaded what it might be like with a winning return. Such was the anticipation that Frankel had been accompanied by a four-man security escort on the walk across the Knavesmire from the overnight stables to the pre-parade ring. The townsfolk of York turned out en masse – dog walkers, cyclists and just those out for a breath of air – all out on the public common for a close-up glimpse of a horse of many lifetimes. Comparisons with Halley's Comet 75-year orbit are not really adequate; Hale–Bopp's appearance once every four millennia is closer to the fact.

It is hard to truly appreciate the huge pressure on Tom Queally who throughout Frankel's racing time – remember he was still only in his early twenties and the only jockey to ever ride Frankel – dealt with the pressures and difficulties with great modesty. Perhaps being Frankel's rider wasn't the best thing for his future career, as he hasn't benefited as much reputationally as some argue he should. In a nutshell, his problem was that when Frankel won it was just a 'steering job'; and if he lost, or nearly lost as in the case of the St James's Palace at that first Royal Ascot, all manner of hell would be heaped down upon him. Shane, Henry and all the Warren Place team could only do so much. In the end, on the racecourse where it really matters, it was Tom who had to keep in check those demonic traits in Frankel. In the heat of contest, with no second chances and surrounded by others who are there to beat you, it was solely his actions and decisions that determined the final result. And the simple fact is, he did that right. And he did that right fourteen times. But how much he enjoyed that or took pleasure from it, I don't really know. There is a certain sadness to his remarks after this race. 'He's not even gone yet and I'm missing him. He's been an amazing part of my career and everything I do from now on will be an anti-climax.'

The rest of Tom's life might be anti-climactic but York's Juddmonte International certainly is not. Plenty, including Tom, rate this his best race ever. As Chris Cook of the *Guardian* points out, with hindsight you feel a little silly for ever mentioning with caution that this is to be his first attempt at middle distance. The odds of 1–10 (again) look hilariously generous. But interestingly enough it is Tom's unique perspective from the saddle that drives home what a complete racehorse Frankel has become.

Drawn in stall seven with Bullet Train in six, Tom has his pacemaker where he wants him, protecting them from the others as he keeps Frankel back to come out last of the nine. The track holds no fears for him; York is the flattest and most regular circuit he is ever to race on. The only danger from the track could come in the long, unforgiving straight, the one that had done for Brigadier Gerard. But that is a few furlongs away as Tom slots Frankel in at the back of the field, the pacemakers streaking away at one point at least twenty lengths or more ahead. But Tom is not worried. As he says, some of the other races like the 2,000 Guineas may have looked more spectacular from the stands but for him, looking ahead with the path to victory framed by Frankel's ears, this is the one. He has so much up his sleeve. So much to play with. 'I was showboating,' says Tom, 'playing with them.'

And play with them he does. As they turn into the straight with half a mile to go, Tom has Frankel still third to last as they track across to the stand side running rail. At three furlongs Tom starts breezing up towards the lead. At two and a half, the field is stretched nine in a line across the course but still Tom, as at Goodwood, is perched immobile. Poised for his moment. And it comes a furlong later when, in perfect synchronicity, horse and rider stretch out, spread-eagling the field in a matter of fifty yards. The York crowd roar in appreciation. A wave of adulation breaks across the Knavesmire. The screaming words of the exultant commentary, 'Frankel, the undisputed Champion of the World' are lost to the ever-elevating applause. There is no doubt. This is a destruction of the most emphatic kind. Frankel first. The rest nowhere. Not just on this day but for racing ever more. Frankel was, and is, the greatest. Ever.

The celebrations off the track never really do justice to what has just happened on the track. Of course the media and the public crowd in. Three cheers for Henry. Three cheers for Frankel. The full-throated appreciation adds a sort of poignancy. Everyone knows that the sands of time are running out for both, but in different ways and to different places. Such is the size of the well-wishing crowd that it takes Dee thirty minutes to escort Henry the fifty yards to the lift to

Prince Khalid's box where, after days of worry and little food, Henry wolfs down a grouse, lobster and dessert in rapid succession.

The journey home is a little less fraught than the journey up; it is just Dee and Henry bowling down the A1 as Jane has volunteered to attend the celebration dinner. 'Yak, yak, yak', as Dee describes Henry's incessant chatter about anything but horses, with his shoes off, feet up on the dashboard. They break the journey at a Little Chef. It is hardly the most likely venue to reflect on one of the most momentous days in horse racing, but there, over a cup of tea, they do just that, watching the sunset from the concrete picnic benches as the traffic roars by.

As in the words of Captain Charles Ryder in Evelyn Waugh's *Brideshead Revisited*, 'If it could only be like this always – always summer …'

22

The end of days

Frankel was to end his career as he started it – in the foulest of conditions.

In the aftermath of York there had been all sorts of speculation and discussion as to where Frankel should race next. Henry was, and always had been, set on the Champion Stakes at Ascot in late October, but the thought of the earlier Prix de l'Arc de Triomphe at Longchamp on the first Sunday in the month excited many in the media and elsewhere. However, Prince Khalid was not keen and nor was Henry. As it turned out they were wise; the Arc was won by a rank 33–1 outsider in freakishly heavy going.

A November trip to the Breeders' Cup in Santa Anita, California had more appeal, not least as a tribute to Bobby Frankel at his adopted home track. But the race would have been in an unfamiliar country, with an unfamiliar style of racing and that's with no thought to his first trip on a plane being a twelve-hour transatlantic one. Henry mooted, then discarded, the idea of the Group 1 Prix du Moulin in France as a preparation to fill the gap between York and Ascot, but in the end he decided to leave both his and Frankel's passports in the office drawer. Ultimately, there was little to be gained by taking Frankel on some confected overseas tour to see out the season. He was the champion. It was up to any challengers to come to him.

For all the talk of the Champion Stakes, Frankel's future beyond that was far from settled. Would he race at five? There was endless discussion, for it was easy to argue the pros and cons. The case for retirement at four was that Frankel had done it all. Proved himself to be the complete racehorse. Beaten all there was to beat. Achieved what Prince Khalid wanted for all his horses, to be the best they could possibly be. There was also a certain sense that they had ridden their luck with three essentially trouble-free racing years. That in itself is pretty extraordinary – racehorses are fragile and fickle. Frankel had hardly missed a day's work. Never felt the prick of a needle bar the routine vaccinations. And barring that gallops incident he never troubled Charlie Smith, the Warren Place vet. Going again at five was a big roll of the dice.

But, and there is always a but, racing is all about the gamble. Rolling that dice is exciting. Frankel was not just the complete racehorse but an improving one. Every time something new or extra had been asked of him, he had delivered. He was better at three than two. Better at four than three. What was to say he would not be better at five than four? Henry certainly thought so. His greatest concern was his own illness, not for him but for Frankel: don't let my illness stop you, he told the Prince. Even as late as a week before the Champion Stakes he was on the phone to Prince Khalid outlining his plan for Frankel at five: the King George VI and Queen Elizabeth Stakes at Ascot (Britain's second richest race), the Prix de l'Arc de Triomphe and then the Breeders' Cup.

However, in the end, Henry could only state his case. The decision rested entirely with Prince Khalid, a decision he would make in the moments after the Champion Stakes. As he stepped onto the Ascot escalator to travel down from the stands to the winners enclosure, racing manager Teddy Grimthorpe said, 'You know the question you are going to be asked?' Prince Khalid nodded before giving his three-word reply.

Trials on a racecourse before the start of the race meeting proper are fairly common; it is a good way for a trainer to bring a horse back from a layoff to remind him of the routine. Usually these go off uncommented, the early arriving crowd more concerned with lunch or bagging a good table for the day. But, in the absence of a trip to France, on the last Saturday in September Henry chose to give Newmarket racegoers a treat with a race-that-really-wasn't-a-race as he set up a three-way contest on the Rowley Mile between Bullet Train, Frankel and another Warren Place four-year-old who had been lent for the occasion.

The event was not going to go unnoticed; this might be the last opportunity for Frankel's home crowd to see him on the racetrack. An hour before racing the pre-parade ring was packed, as was the paddock and the stands. It was, as pretty well always, a Frankel tour de force, with him cruising past first Specific Gravity and then Bullet Train in the last couple of furlongs to win amid genuine, if slightly regretful applause, by as far as Tom felt like pushing him. It was, as Henry said, the perfect blowout. Few watching were left in any doubt that Frankel was ready for the Champion Stakes in three weeks' time. If they'd have returned early one morning ten days later, they'd have headed off to the local betting shop to stake every last penny on the basis of the work gallop they saw. Frankel, ridden by Shane, streaked thirty lengths clear of Tom, getting the rear view of Frankel for a change on Midsummer Sun (deputising for Bullet Train) with still a furlong left to go. Everything was set. But for the weather.

It didn't just rain in the run-up to Ascot but it *really* rained. And rained. And rained. Frankel was plenty familiar with wet ground. His first ever race was on soft, and three others on good to soft. But this was something beyond that, officially listed as soft but arguably closer to heavy, especially to a well-built horse like Frankel whose hooves would penetrate deeper than most. Shane describes the conditions as 'horrendous'. Chris Cook 'properly soft'. Mike Marshall 'terrible' as the rain kept coming. Deep down Henry had his own misgivings. He told Shane, 'I have to race him. People have come from around the world to see Frankel.' He knew Frankel's most potent weapons, speed and acceleration, would be blunted by going so very different to that he had encountered at York. And to compound Henry's angst, the French challenger was Cirrus Des Aigles, not only the winner of the Champion Stakes the previous year but rated the second best middle-distance horse in the world at that time. He was ominously a soft-ground specialist.

And he wasn't the only significant challenger. Nathaniel was back in, a rather neat circle of lives, having ploughed his own successful furrow since their debut race together on that rainy August evening two years and two months earlier. With an eleven-race career he hadn't run quite as often as Frankel, but since breaking his maiden at a third try he had raced exclusively in Group company. Only twice was he anything other than first or second, winning three Group races including the prestigious Eclipse Stakes and the King George and Queen Elizabeth II Stakes, amassing prize money of close to £1.5 million in the process. Like Frankel he was something of an Ascot specialist, both racing here for the fifth time, but like Cirrus Des Aigles, Nathaniel liked the soft. When you added it all up this looked, coming at the end of a long season with the ground and opposition as they were, to be Frankel's toughest race. As the stalls sprang open it had all the makings of his worst.

For the first and last time, all the Warren Place team were gathered at a racecourse together: Dee, Mike, Sandy, Shane and Stephen with Henry and his family a little way away. To say everyone was nervous is to incredibly understate the case – this was not just the culmination of weeks but months and years. If this was to be the end, though few would admit it out loud, it was an end to be welcomed. The gnawing nerves. The daily twisting of stomach pits. Sleepless nights. The worry of a tiny detail overlooked. Being aboard the Frankel express was a thrilling ride, but it came with the certain knowledge that any derailment would have consequences and carnage far removed from normal stable life. For all the joy Frankel brought to the outside world, it was hard to enjoy if you were caught in the midst of the maelstrom.

'I told you we shouldn't have come', says Shane turning to his wife Claire as Frankel stumbles out of the starting stalls, for the fourteenth and final time in his race career, ten lengths behind the other five runners. If this was some kind of deliberate plan like that at York, those thoughts are soon disabused as Bullet Train's regular rider Ian Mongan takes a panicky look around, easing back down the field to somehow connect with his running mate. That is hardly the job of a pacemaker. 'This is a disaster', Henry mutters to Jane.

Tom is left with unpleasant choices; shake Frankel up with all the attendant risks that involves or fall yet further behind. The plan to switch him off to settle mid-field was shot to pieces. Two years before, or even a year before, this would have been the disaster Henry predicted, but Tom is still supremely confident. He can now control the will of a mature, head-screwed-on Frankel, as he shakes him up to make up the ground while keeping him settled. In check. Willing to speed up and then slow down to merge into the back of the pack with just one behind. As Bullet Train falls back in search of

Frankel they have a bit of luck as Cirrus Des Aigles and Nathaniel press on in the lead, setting the pace but choosing to race four or five horse-widths off the running rail, keeping out of the ground that had been heavily cut up in the first four races. Why they do this is hard to tell. Surely as mud lovers that is the place to be? Sapping the stamina of Frankel, if he chooses to follow, or forcing him out wide on his own. It is almost certainly a mistake.

As the runners come around the corner of Swinley Bottom, at the furthest point from the stands, some sort of order is restored as Ian Mongan, having located Frankel, kicks on to have Bullet Train mix it up with the leaders. The pace starts to settle as Frankel, now back in the pack, gallops along without any apparent care in the world; ambling, one commentator describes it, more in awe than defamation.

A bell rings as the horses turn into the final straight; it is a uniquely Ascot tradition that tells of just three furlongs to run. It tolls for all but Frankel. He is still only fourth on the wide outside, with Cirrus Des Aigles, Nathaniel and Bullet Train in a line ahead, but it seems just a matter of time even as Cirrus Des Aigles and Nathaniel kick on to stretch the lead as Bullet Train falls away. With two furlongs to go Nathaniel is beaten. If Cirrus Des Aigles is to displace Frankel to become the world's number one horse that moment is close, but, as at Goodwood, Tom pauses. And waits. Until with just a furlong to go he pushes the button, that extra gear the feel of which Shane will take to his grave. Engaged not with a jab but with measured ease, as Frankel first draws level, then pulls away from Cirrus Des Aigles.

It is over long before the winning post. Frankel has made the biggest challenge of his life look easy. Fourteen from fourteen. Racing perfection. The superlatives echo through the tannoy as the crowd bellow. Cheer. And applaud the greatest of the greats. Champion of champions. Tom, who will never sit on Frankel again

– as he says afterwards, he was trying to eke out every last moment in the saddle as the best chapter of his life was closing – parades Frankel all the way down to the furthest point of the stands. In the most touching of moments he comes alongside Bullet Train, and the two jockeys stand up in the saddle to hug each other. It is fitting and it is right.

As he arrives at the ground floor, Prince Khalid, ultimately the architect of the greatest racehorse that has ever lived, has made his decision. 'That is it', he tells Teddy as they make their way to a waiting world.

The story of Frankel the racehorse is over.

Epilogue

In early December I went to see Frankel for the last time in the writing of this book. And I took a carrot.

It's been nearly nine months since we were officially introduced and in that time I have retraced on foot nearly every yard he ran. Seen the things he saw. Went to all the places he ever went. Met most of the people who were part of his daily life. Spent too many of my waking hours trying to divine the secret of his greatness. The impact he had on lives.

His final nineteen days at Warren Place after the Champion Stakes were confusing for Frankel, but mostly hard on the people who loved him. The purpose of a racehorse is to race. The purpose of a racing stable is to prepare for just that. But when Prince Khalid said 'That is it' that purpose ebbed away.

The job of Henry, Sandy, Shane, Mike and Dee was to now decompress Frankel. Bring him down from his racing high. Keep him safe for his next career. Prepare him for a different kind of stable life. Nobody enjoyed those final days. In fact Henry hated them. Shane couldn't wait for him to go. Sandy was more nervous than he had ever been. Mike was counting the days. Dee had to contend with a grumpy Frankel as she slowly reduced the size of his buckets of food.

Calories in. Calories out. Frankel was no longer allowed on Newmarket Heath. The risks and dangers were just too great. Shane ran down the clock with daily trotting around the indoor ride, the old team of Bullet Train and Frankel doing their thing. It is an odd thought but Frankel has never galloped since that last race at Ascot. In fact, he will never be asked to go faster than a trot again. And when Shane dismounted for the last time on the November morning when he departed for Banstead Manor, he became the last person who will ever sit on Frankel's back. That seems sort of right to me.

Frankel appears to like the carrot I have brought him; it was the biggest one I could find rummaging through the greengrocers' selection. At least for a while I'll have his undivided attention. It has been good to catch up.

He's been very relaxed. This is his downtime. The southern hemisphere mares have been and gone; the northern hemisphere contingent will not start to arrive for another two months. We've spent the morning with a photographer taking shots for this book. Frankel is a real pro, though I think deep down he just loves the attention. Does he miss the racecourse? I'm not so sure. For this is his destiny. His duty to the equine herd. To pass on his genes so that one day perhaps, however remote the chances, one better will be born.

As he is led away I feel a little sad; it is sort of over now. I never thought I would define part of my life by a horse. But Frankel, let me tell you this if you understand: I am glad to have known you.

The Newmarket 11

What became of the competition?

6.35 RACE 3   European Breeders' Fund Maiden Stakes (Class 4)   Winner £4,533.20   **RUK**   1m July

£7,000 guaranteed **For** 2yo, which are E.B.F. eligible **Weights** colts and geldings 9st 3lb; fillies 8st 12lb **Entries** 31 pay £35 **Penalty value** 1st £4,533.20 2nd £1,348.90 3rd £674.10 4th £336.70 £10k Racing Post Yearling Bonus Scheme qualifier   ADJUSTED AVERAGE WINNING RPR 97

No	Horse	Details	Jockey	Weight
1 (11)	**BRETON STAR** 10	b c Medicean-Wannabe Grand	Chris Catlin	2 9-3
	D M Simcock J M Cook			
2 (1)	**CASTLEMORRIS KING**	br c And Beyond-Brookshield Baby	Robert L Butler(3)	2 9-3
	M C Chapman C O'Connell			
3 (3)	**COLOUR VISION** (FR) 10	gr c Rainbow Quest-Give Me Five	Adrian Nicholls	2 9-3
	M Johnston Sheikh Hamdan Bin Mohammed Al Maktoum			
4 (4)	225 **DORTMUND** 10 48 BF	b c Dubawi-Zacheta	Antioco Murgia(7) 92	2 9-3
	Mahmood Al Zarooni Godolphin			
5 (12)	**ELRASHEED**	b c Red Ransom-Ayun	Richard Hills	2 9-3
	J L Dunlop Hamdan Al Maktoum			
6 (10)	**FRANKEL**	b c Galileo-Kind	Tom Queally	2 9-3
	H R A Cecil K Abdulla			
7 (2)	**GENIUS BEAST** (USA)	b c Kingmambo-Sharwanda	Ahmed Ajtebi	2 9-3
	Mahmood Al Zarooni Godolphin			
8 (7)	6 **LEMON DROP RED** (USA) 21	b c Lemon Drop Kid-Skipper's Mate	Tom McLaughlin 65	2 9-3
	E A L Dunlop R J Arculli			
9 (5)	37 **MAHER** (USA) 20 BF	b c Medaglia d'Oro-Bourbon Blues	Kieren Fallon 86	2 9-3
	D M Simcock Sultan Ali			
10 (6)	**MAN OF GOD** (IRE) 10	b c Sadler's Wells-Jude	Saleem Golam	2 9-3
	J H M Gosden B E Nielsen			
11 (8)	**NATHANIEL** (IRE)	b c Galileo-Magnificient Style	William Buick	2 9-3
	J H M Gosden Lady Rothschild			
12 (9)	6 **BONITA STAR** 10 15	b f Beat Hollow-Catch	Alan Munro 91	2 8-12
	M R Channon B P York			

2009 (8 ran) **Dashing Doc** (6) D R C Elsworth 2 9-3 11/4F   Philip Robinson RPR76

BETTING FORECAST: 7-4 Frankel, **7-2** Nathaniel, **11-2** Elrasheed, Genius Beast, **13-2** Dortmund, **12** Maher, **16** Colour Vision, Man Of God, **25** Bonita Star, **33** Breton Star, Lemon Drop Red, **66** Castlemorris King.

Keeneland to fenland

*Maher was keen early on ... but he is well up to winning in
maiden company if settling a little better.*

Racing Post

The comments of the *Racing Post* race reporter turned out to be a tad
optimistic; Maher, in common with Dortmund and Elrasheed of the
Newmarket eleven, was never to win a race. In fact, his decline from
the hottest maiden of 2010 to a lowly race at Wolverhampton on a
bitter cold January afternoon the following year was precipitous.

Wolverhampton racecourse is something of a curious thing,
jammed as it is in what is now an industrial/urban landscape. But it
wasn't always this way. Back when the course was built in the 1880s
this would have been open countryside, the perfect location for the
horse-drawn carriages that made their way from a booming
Birmingham a few miles to the south and for the holiday crowds
who arrived on the steam railway that passed close by. Today, it is
rather different.

The giant railway viaduct is still there. The grey brick and giant arches remain things of great Victorian beauty, but the encroaching town less so. Admittedly the drive thru McDonald's is a useful landmark for those arriving for the first time, before turning into the entrance through a modern housing estate that brings you in turn to the track. Or is it a hotel? The first thing that catches your eye is the bright green and white logo of a Holiday Inn. Is this a racecourse with a hotel attached or a hotel with a racecourse attached? I am not sure if it matters if the symbiosis works. Racecourses for the most part walk a perilous financial path, so if this arrangement is of mutual benefit, smoothing the bumps, then it has to be to the good. That said it is still rather odd to collect your race badge from a hotel reception.

As you make your way from the hotel, past the parade ring, through the stands and out to view the track, you'll notice an absence of grass. There simply isn't any. Which is unusual for racecourses who usually pride themselves with immaculately coiffured lawns, the stripes every bit as impressive as those of Wimbledon's Centre Court. And there is a reason for this – Wolverhampton is, in the jargon, an all-weather track where the racing surface looks more akin to a recently ploughed sand beach. In turn everything has been honed down, so that whatever the weather the show will go on.

As Maher, under the gaze of a small Monday late afternoon crowd, cantered to the start of his all-weather career, he might have pondered as to the how and why of his current situation. He was, after all, a long way from home – Kentucky to Wolverhampton and just turned three years old. He could have justifiably thought he was born to more than this. His father Medaglia d'Oro (trained by none other than Bobby Frankel) had been sold to Sheikh Mohammed for reputedly $50 million the year after he sired Maher. His family was on an upward trajectory. At the time of Maher's conception the stud fee for his father was $40,000. Today, it stands at $250,000. At twenty years of age, his father is one of the most successful stallions in the USA and has handsomely repaid the faith of the Sheikh by a factor of two or more even at the conservative end of the calculations. It wasn't unreasonable to expect he had something of his father in him.

Others had clearly thought the same, the name on the buying sheet at the Keeneland sales indicating that to be Rabbah International Ltd, who had paid $70,000 for Maher as a yearling. Rabbah is the named company that oversees the racing and breeding interests of the friends of Sheikh Mohammed, another of those truly global horse-racing operations. On the day Maher was knocked down to them, this company was truly on a roll, buying twenty-one horses for $5 million at the sales. The following month at Tattersalls in England, they bought a further ninety-six. With over 400 horses in training in England, Ireland, France, Germany and the United States that is a mighty operation to feed, which in that year alone won 131 races. If you work on the assumption that the average racing expectancy of a flat racehorse is somewhere between two and three years (our twelve averaged 2.7) then Rabbah needed a new annual crop of a hundred and fifty horses just to stand still to replace those whose racing careers were over. So it was that Maher, as yet unnamed and still just a bay yearling of eighteen months of age, was flown across the Atlantic to an English racing stable in Newmarket to prepare for his two-year-old debut.

If you were looking for a good each-way chance, a 'bit of value' as the pundits like to term it for the Newmarket race, Maher would not have been the daftest choice in the world. Of the line-up he was the second most experienced with two races already under his belt compared to Dortmund's three and the single outings of Lemon Drop Red and Bonita Star. At 8–1 he was fifth in the betting. Ignore his patchy form and well, maybe … as the stalls opened you'd have been more than happy. He came out in the leading pack, up at the front until nearly two furlongs from home. And then he provided what is now a little footnote in horse-racing history.

The notes of the race reader say Maher edged left; that is to say he moved off the straight line, which is a common enough thing for inexperienced or tiring horses towards the end of a race. In doing so he created the opening through which Frankel made his winning move when the finishing post was just 300 yards away. Had he edged right he may well have closed the opening, Frankel becoming the jam in the sandwich between Maher and Nathaniel. Now that is not to say Tom Queally might not have anticipated such an outcome, pulling Frankel around for an alternate clear run. But equally Maher might have hampered Frankel, and momentum lost, Nathaniel would have won. But none of that happened. Maher edged left. Frankel took the gap.

Maher travelled a long way in his three years of racing, through varied owners and trainers, trying his hand over hurdles as well as the flat but never found success. His record reads fifteen runs, zero wins. Total prize money £4,030. However, he did have his moment in the sun and for a few furlongs outpaced the greatest racehorse that has ever lived. It is not much of an epitaph, but it should be to his eternal credit that when the pace became too hot he moved away to the left leaving the path clear for history.

A six-figure loss

Dortmund, second on his first two starts but then beaten too far to be true as favourite at Newcastle 48 days ago, also ran a good race. Markedly stepped up in trip, he saw it out and is certainly capable of winning a maiden.

Racing Post

Of the Newmarket dozen, Dortmund was the first to race and the first to race for the final time – he glowed then fizzled in the space of three months. It was, even by the standards of competitive flat racing, a short career which promised some but delivered less. You probably wouldn't be far off the mark if you concluded that Dortmund's finest hour was in defeat to Frankel. The race reporter that day may have thought him capable of a subsequent win, but he was only to have one further chance to prove it.

Things looked promising for Dortmund early on, sold as he was as a yearling at the Tattersalls Newmarket sales for a more than respectable £100,000. Not the most expensive of that particular

October day, but up there as one to look out for at a later date. With an Irish father and British mother, plus American and French grand-parents, he was a true child of the international bloodstock business, sold as he was by an Arabic bloodstock combine having been raised on a broodmare farm on the edge of the Cotswolds. And then to top it all he was named after Germany's eighth largest city.

Dortmund was a bay, that is to say he had a reddish-brown body colour with a black mane, tail, ear edges, and lower legs. Bay is the most common of all the seven official colour classifications you will see denoted on race cards and stud records, by, in this case, the letter 'b'. In fact of the Newmarket twelve, ten were bays, with the remaining two brown and grey respectively. To a certain extent this is inevitable; the term 'bay' really means brown, the most common colour for a horse, which covers every hue from bright through to dark bay, the latter essentially being black to all but the most expert of eyes.

You might well then ask, why aren't they all simply called brown? Well, a brown horse (br) is distinctly different in that the mane and tail will match the remainder of the body colour – no black tail and so on. Likewise a chestnut horse (ch) with be reddish or ginger with matching mane and tail. Though greys (gr) are often the ones that catch the eye, ranging from bright white to steel grey, with a tendency to become lighter with age, it is the bays and chestnuts that account for over nine-tenths of all thoroughbreds, with 75 per cent and 18 per cent of registrations respectively, that predominate in the sales rings and on the racecourses.

The septet of colour classifications is rounded off in increasing rarity by black (bl), then roan (ro), which are pale with an even mix of white hair to the dominant colour, with the rarest of them all being white (wh). Which one makes for the best racehorse? Well, everyone claims to be colour blind, trotting out the old adage 'a good horse is never a bad colour' and that is not as trite as it sounds

– there is no statistical data to favour one colour over another. That said the racing public have a habit of falling in love with greys while racing professionals avoid the less common colours in the same way that you don't see many pink Ferraris – the unusual scares off buyers.

Horse racing, for all its global reach, is a much interconnected world; in this particular case the missing link between Dortmund and Maher was their simultaneous ownership by Rabbah International who purchased one while selling the other within the space of the month in two different continents.

Having bred Dortmund in the UK, Rabbah sold him at that October yearling sale for a decent sum.

Dortmund arrived on the day of his sale from somewhere a bit different to the lofty studs of Newmarket, Tipperary or Kentucky. He may have been bred by one of the world's leading groups of owners but his home had been somewhere different, a broodmare farm that is one of those bits-beneath-the-bonnet part of the engine that powers horse racing but is little noticed. In fact, if you drove past the entrance to Biddestone Stud you probably would not notice it yourself. There is not much to see from the road; pleasing avenues of lime trees. Oak post and rail fencing, silvering with age. The round-topped dry stone walls tell you this is the bit of Wiltshire that is edging into the Cotswolds. The grass is mown. Everything is tidy. But this is not grand. The stables are steel sheds, with concrete floors and metal stalls.

This is the business end of English breeding where livings are made by looking after horses at either end of their racing careers. If you bought a yearling at auction, it is here you might well send it to be schooled until it was old enough to enter training proper. Alternatively, if you wanted to be an owner/breeder but didn't want to keep the mare yourself, a place like Biddestone will do that for you: take your mare to the stallion, stable her through the pregnancy, ensure a successful birth and then care for both mother and foal until they go their separate ways.

But for all the lack of grandeur you can't help but smile at the scene. This is horseflesh of the most idyllic kind where mothers gather in groups in sunny paddocks, while the foals ebb and flow around the edges, the bravest and most inquisitive breaking a few yards distant in a bid for short-lived independence. But they only go so far. The apron strings are still tightly wound. For all the youthful exuberance they show as they cavort, kick up their hind legs and spin around in playful chases, the foals don't stray far, ready to dash back to the maternal side at the slightest hint of something untoward. The mares, for all their apparent indifference as they idly pick at the grass and gently swish tails to keep annoying flies forever in the air, are no less wary. The eyes and ears are constantly alert, a raised head or short whinny enough to bring the offspring back to their sides.

I think it is fair to say, without wanting to offer any criticism, that Dortmund lived out his racing life in the commoditised compartment of high-end bloodstock. He was bred and raised to a corporate plan, then sold at auction to be bought by the Godolphin operation, one that dwarfs Rabbah by any metric you care to choose, from worldwide reach to sheer number of horses both at stud and in training – we are talking thousands of animals at all stages of life. So, even with his £100,000 price tag, Dortmund wasn't destined for one of the top Godolphin trainers but was set to be trained by Mahmood Al Zarooni in Newmarket, who was in his rookie year as one of Sheikh Mohammed's trainers.

We can't really blame Al Zarooni's newcomer status for Dortmund's lack of success, as he was a winning trainer from the very outset until it all ended badly and abruptly three seasons later with an eight-year ban for administering steroids to his horses. But

Dortmund wasn't to be one of his winners even though, as it turns out, he was from what has become a powerful bloodline. His father Dubawi, though an unremarkable stallion at the time he was born, has gone on to become one of the leading European sires, multiplying the stud fee of £25,000 paid to produce Dortmund by a factor of ten today.

So, even with the advantages of a young trainer and father both in the ascendant, the summation of Dortmund's racing career is that in his five races he managed two seconds and a third. Had those been Group races, or even some of the Classics, you might have cause to cheer, but in racing all success is relative. It is not only where you finish, but who you beat and who you are beaten by. So temper those statistics by saying that they were all, excepting that one famous occasion, modest races against modest opposition. Dortmund's total lifetime earnings of just £3,425 more than hint at that, a sum that probably barely covered jockey fees and travelling expenses.

For all that, Dortmund didn't arrive at the Newmarket August race completely out of it. With two seconds to his name and plenty willing to overlook (unwisely) a poor third race at Newcastle seven weeks previously, he was third in the betting, only Frankel and Nathaniel thought the better of. And for the first five furlongs Dortmund bested them all, leading the field for over half the race, even momentarily repelling the first challengers a furlong and a half from home. But Frankel, Nathaniel and then his stable companion Genius Beast came past to beat him into fourth place by a total of five and three-quarter lengths.

Even had that Newmarket race featured what you'd call a 'normal' field, you'd assume, as did the *Racing Post* reporter, that Dortmund was not without some talent. Knowing what we know now about the runners that evening, you'd be even more certain. But we'd all be wrong. That five-and-a-bit length defeat was as good as it got.

Two weeks later a third in an inconsequential maiden at Beverley closed the book on Dortmund's racing life. Ninety-three days and that was it. He was gelded in the autumn of the following year. It seems all there is to show for his career is a six-figure loss in the accounts of a racing empire.

Last man standing

*Man Of God, who cost 290,000 guineas, was green and
is sure to come on for the experience.*

Racing Post

Yesterday I went to meet God and I was genuinely excited. Of all the horses that ran that day at Newmarket ten years ago, here was the only one still in a racing stable. Man of God is the last man standing.

As his owner Rachel Talbot did the introductions – 'God,' an inevitable nickname I suspect, 'meet Simon' – it had become clear to me in the writing of this book that if you work with horses, conversing with horses is a fact of life. Everyone, virtually without exception, talks to their horses. It is, most obviously, a one-way conversation, but it seems to matter as much to the horses as it does to the people. The question is, why?

Like cats and dogs, they pick up the intonation we inflect in our manner of speech be it encouragement, admonition or whatever and as we, as much as animals, are creatures of habit they also pick up the daily signals. If I appear every morning in God's box clutching a bucket of nuts with the words, 'Morning God, here is your breakfast', it is not going to take him more than a few days to piece it all together. However, it does seem there is more to it than that.

There is this thing called cross-modality, which is the interaction between our five primary senses: sight, hearing, smell, taste and touch. It was once thought that the ability to put together the data received via two or more of the senses to reach a conclusion – cross-modality – was a purely human trait. However, recent research suggests it is not unique to us and exists in horses as well. Essentially what is happening in God's head is that over a period of time he builds a mental picture of each person to match the voice. So, when I first met God leaning over the stable door when Rachel said, 'God, meet Simon', he looked at Rachel, looked momentarily at me and then looked back to Rachel, locking onto her as the auditory and visual clues gave him a match. Of course, if I became a regular part of his life I'd become familiar as well, worthy of a longer glance, but in the end it will always be the person he knows best who he looks the longest at.

There are two additional, and interesting, wrinkles to this theory if you want to try it out for yourself. Firstly, in the research the mares performed the recognition task much better than the males. Why? Well, nobody is exactly sure at this stage but the likely explanation is that as the nurturer the mother has a duty to her foal to determine friend from enemy as quickly as possible. Males, with more aggression plus nobody to care for, have less reason to worry. Secondly, and this applies equally to both sexes, stand on the right of the horse so he or she is looking at you with the right eye. Again, why? In horses the left hemisphere of the brain controls the right side of the body and vice versa, so with the cross-modal bit of the brain controlling the seeing and hearing match in the left, it is the right eye that will be assessing you.

Whether I had stood on the right or left I am not sure God thought much of me or maybe he simply has a nervous manner, as he didn't take easily to the pat of a stranger, raising up his head, raking back his ears and showing the white of his eyes. I like to think he was just having a bad afternoon because Rachel says he has been a whole lot calmer since she's found him a companion in a little Shetland pony called Ossie who lives in the stall opposite, the two always travelling together in the horse box when God has to go to the races. This co-dependency is not as uncommon as you might think.

All horses, and not just thoroughbreds, are herd animals – being solitary is not in their DNA but they like the company of all sorts of creatures, not just other horses. You'll notice stables are rarely an equine monoculture, usually being home to a myriad of farm animals – chickens will peck around the yard, geese gently honk in the fields while haughty cats seek out the warmest and most comfortable lairs. And all the while the horses will hang their heads over the stable door, idly watching these minor daily rituals. It is calming and restful activity.

But actually this companionship, such as with Ossie, Man of God and the general stable menagerie, often goes a whole lot further. The famous Seabiscuit was a nervous wreck of a horse until his trainer Tom Smith found him what was to become a lifelong companion in a pony called Pumpkin, who was joined in time by the stray dog Pocatell, and if that wasn't enough a spider monkey by the name of Jo Jo, who completed this strange quartet. At night Pumpkin would sleep in the next door stall, Pocatell curl up in Seabiscuit's straw and Jo Jo settle in the crook of his neck, long arms and tail wrapped around the horse. If you are remembering the movie *Seabiscuit* you might not recall Jo Jo and you won't – for some reason he was not included in the script.

Of course, don't run away with the idea that Seabiscuit was tolerant to all-comers. Before Smith alighted on the pony he tried him with a goat. Goats are popular companions. Why do they get along? Well, goats like horses are ruminants and herd animals, not to mention they both like much the same plant-based diet making it easy on the owner. But Pops, Seabiscuit's nickname referring to his relative old age as a racer, had clearly not read the manual. Within a short time of introducing the goat into Pops' stall, the stable hands found him walking in circles, clutching the distraught goat in his teeth and shaking her back and forth before throwing the goat out and over the stable door. You have to conclude that Pops was a one-off – the goat was a no, but the spider monkey a yes. Very odd.

By the time Rachel Talbot raised her hand to bid for the eight-year-old Man of God at the Ascot sales, he had experienced, by many measures, the most full and varied life of all Newmarket twelve. He raced on the flat at two and three years, went hurdling in Ireland between four and six before returning to Britain to continue over the hurdles as a seven- and eight-year-old, and then still had the appetite to race at nine in point-to-point. In all, he had a pretty impressive tally of twenty-nine races before Rachel bought him; we will gloss over the number of wins and prize money for the moment.

God had been in the auction ring before. As a yearling he was sold for more than any of the others of the Newmarket group that ever changed hands in the public arena, selling for 290,000 guineas. A 'guinea' is one of those wonderful horse-racing traditions, like furlongs, that cussedly persist in use today as a nod to history. It is a throwback to a time when the guinea, a gold coin, was English legal tender and the preferred currency of the aristocracy, the prime purchasers of horseflesh and also the instigators of the 1,000 and 2,000 Guineas Classic races.

Originally the guinea (named after the African country where most of the gold was mined) was valued at a pound, but when the price of gold rose so did the value of the guinea coin, fixed by the Bank of England from 1717 to 1816 at one pound, one shilling or as we say today, £1.05. But dealing in guineas had a purpose beyond noble habit; it offered a convenient way of getting around the delicate matter of commission, so it became understood that when a horse was sold in guineas the seller took the pound and the auctioneer kept the shilling. Today you will not find many sales where the guinea is the unit of measure; if an animal is knocked down to you in guineas, you know you are either buying horseflesh among the crème de la crème or purchasing a ram. Male sheep are the only other livestock still sold in guineas.

So, converting Man of God's sale price into more contemporary currency, this untried, unraced bay yearling, just seventeen months old, made £304,500. It was far from being the highest price of the year which ran to millions but it might still look like a reckless gamble. It is a bit like Nike signing up a ten-year-old child on the evidence of a few minutes of beach tennis. That said if the child in question was the product of a love tryst between Roger Federer and one of the Williams sisters, you might just see the logic. It is all about the genes.

The briefest glance at Man of God's pedigree gives a clue to his genetic allure; his father was Sadler's Wells, which makes him a paternal relation of Frankel. Sadler's Wells is Frankel's grandfather. Sadler's Wells is also Nathaniel's grandfather. So there, in the two words – Sadler's Wells – you have the primary reason why Man of God made the price he made. Even though three hundred thousand plus looks like a lot of money, the sums do add up. The stud fee for

Sadler's Wells in the last decade of his life was a closely guarded secret. However, we do know that in 2000, the last time the figure was made public, it was 150,000 Irish guineas. It is not unreasonable to assume that a decade later at Man of God's conception, the figure was double that. Effectively you were buying Man of God, a fit and well yearling, for more-or-less the cost of the stud fee, with the added bonus of having avoided all the risks and costs associated with the breeding. You are, to use another analogy, jumping the queue for one of the hottest shows in town but only paying for the ticket at face value.

Had you been the person who bought him you'd have been reasonably happy with an eighth-place finish to that fellow debutant Frankel. A month later you'd have had every reason to break into a wide smile and pat yourself on the back for a canny purchase; you probably received a congratulatory text from your bloodstock agent. Success has many fathers. For on 16 September not only did Pope Benedict XVI arrive in Britain for his first Papal visit, but Man of God provided a bit of divine support, leading nearly all the way to win at Yarmouth in only his second race. As the trainer John Gosden, who also trained Nathaniel, put him away for the winter you'd have been entitled to a few dreams for the three-year-old season to come. Unfortunately, it was to be another six years before Man of God was to win again. Clearly the Pope needed to visit more often.

Whatever the dreams his owner may have had for a feted three-year-old career, it soon proved not to be. After his Yarmouth win, Man of God next raced the following spring, the first of seven races that took him through to October without, as you know, a win. He criss-crossed the country competing in low-value flat races but never was his nose in front. Why? Maybe he simply wasn't good enough, that day of the Pope's visit an ecumenical intervention, his brief moment in the racing sunshine. Or maybe it is something in his head? Rachel tells me that whether he is out following the blood-hounds or hacking along the lanes, God prefers to tuck himself in behind other horses. Maybe the front was a place he never wanted to be. So, in the month he turned four, Man of God was gelded.

Ascot racecourse might be one of the finest tracks in the world, but don't get carried away with the notion that the annual July horse auction held there, without wishing to do it any disservice, is another Keeneland or Newmarket. This is a clearing house. An auction where flat, jump horses, point-to-pointers and breeding stock are offered for sale having exhausted the patience, money or quite possibly both, of their current owners. It was to this that Rachel arrived and at which God got lucky, because Rachel never really intended to buy a horse that day. It was all about just taking a look. In the back of her mind was this vague plan to go point-to-pointing, but it all coalesced before her as Man of God, last lot of the 181 horses to be sold that day, caught her eye. Rachel had just £1,400 to spend; it was all she could afford. But as the hammer fell for precisely that amount, he was hers. That was a long, long way from the three hundred thousand pounds plus he had been sold for seven years previously. But after four owners, three trainers and twenty-nine races in England and Ireland, Man of God was finally at the end of an itinerant life.

Hackwood Park is a large field on the edge of Basingstoke in Hampshire that occasionally hosts a race meeting. If you are used to the more formal surroundings of a proper racecourse, you'll be in for something of a shock; the entrance which brings you in via a wood looks like taking you to a hillbilly logging camp. You'd be well advised to come in a four-wheel drive, or at least with a tow rope in your boot, for paved roads haven't yet arrived here.

If that sounds bad it isn't really. This is a point-to-point meeting, as close as you will ever come today to the meetings our great, great, great grandparents attended two centuries ago. As you break out of the woods a carnival atmosphere greets you; like the travelling fairs of old the races have arrived for just one day. The racetrack is roped off. White marquees dot the centre, with temporary bars, food stands and the paraphernalia required to run what is in truth a strictly organised, but in essence amateur, race meeting.

Cars are backed up to the ropes, the boots open distributing haphazard picnics. Jodhpured jockeys in silks, a stock (a type of formal tie crossed with cravat worn by equestrians) and shiny, black boots wander among the spectators seeking out friends to calm nerves ahead of races to come. Bookmakers, more used to bundles of hundreds, patiently explain for the umpteenth time an each-way bet, happy to take a pound coin simply for the joy of it all.

As the race approaches a huntsman appears on his mount in full pink-coated regalia, sounding his hunting horn to gather the runners – for point-to-points, though regulated by a strict set of rules laid down by the Jockey Club (for instance all horses must be registered thoroughbreds), are run by the local fox hunts, with whom the horses must have been regularly hunted. The name has its origins way back in the mid-eighteenth century when the Irish invented the concept of steeplechasing, horses racing from one steepled church to another taking on whatever ditches, hedges, streams and bucolic obstacles lay in their path. Quite literally racing from point to point.

Of the two that day I suspect it was Rachel who was the most nervous; after all it was her first racecourse ride. As for Man of God the track would have had echoes of some of the rural Irish tracks he had raced on, but the obstacles, well they were different. Up to this moment all his races had been on flat or hurdles, never over fences which are taller and wider and never as far as three miles, the minimum distance for a point-to-point. But the auguries were good: Rachel had schooled him over the autumn and winter in preparation for this spring day. He had never once fallen in any of his eighteen hurdle races and completed all but one even in the boggiest conditions.

For eleven of the fourteen fences all went according to plan. Naturally, Man of God did his favoured thing, tucking in behind the five others. As he adjusted to the big obstacles he began to make headway on the leader, until with just three fences between him and the third win of his career he took the next fence wrong, landed badly and while he didn't fall himself, he ejected Rachel onto the turf. As the race comments record: unseated rider three out. But, and it is a happy but, a few weeks later Rachel achieved her ambition, winning with Man of God who resisted his temptation to always follow others by taking the lead two fences from home, running on well to win the Hunt Members race at their local Whitfield point-to-point by an easy three and a half lengths.

A month on from that day, and after one further but unsuccessful point-to-point, God's racing career was over. Rachel had done what she set out to do. For both her with a young family, and for Man of God at nine years of age, the risks of continuing were just too high. They were both still fit and well with plenty of years ahead to enjoy days of trail hunting after bloodhounds and team chasing over cross-country courses. In his thirty-three races, Man of God may not have scaled the heights his breeding and high yearling price suggested was possible. But of the Newmarket twelve he was the last to set foot on a racecourse long after the others had retired or died. For that at least he deserves a contented retirement.

Man of God is currently living with Ossie and Rachel in Oxfordshire.

The worst Derby
runner ever?

Castlemorris King holds some fancy entries, but his yard is not renowned for its 2 year old winners (last one in 2001) and he was duly outclassed.

Timeform

The Timeform race reporter was certainly correct on two counts: you can't be much more outclassed than to be beaten by Frankel, and equally you can't have a much more classy entry than to the Derby at Epsom, arguably still the greatest and most prestigious horse race on the planet. It is a headline-grabbing event in the life of every owner, trainer and jockey though perhaps not in the way this trio might have intended. Castlemorris King was one of the favourites – to be last.

The *Guardian* said, 'The form book says he could prove to be one of the worst horses ever to line up in the Derby.' The *Daily Mail* was a little less brutal but no more optimistic as to his chances saying, 'A forlorn outsider (500–1) trained beside Tattenham Corner is set to gate crash the Queen's parade at Epsom in a fortnight.' How is it that such an apparent dud could make it into the starting line-up?

Horse racing sometimes gets a bad rap for being elitist and exclusive, so you might have supposed that a race with the status of the Derby has all sorts of conditions of entry to blow out the chaff. But there is none of that. You pay your entry fee and so long as your horse is a registered, entire thoroughbred, he or she is in (the race is open to fillies though the last one to win was in 1916). Of course there is a cost to this, but if you show a little bit of foresight by first entering your horse just short of its second birthday (initial entry fee £560) and then pay the increments at each of the next three declaration stages up to the day of the race, your total bill will be £7,860.*
That in itself is not an insignificant sum but set against prize money to the winner of over £850,000, with even the sixth place picking up £20,000, and there only being somewhere between twelve and twenty runners, the odds are not so bad. That said you have to keep the faith – if you do a last-minute entry you'll be slapped with an £85,000 bill.

Slight (or perhaps more realistically non-existent) Castlemorris King's chances might have been for that first Saturday in June, but he was doing what none of the Newmarket twelve, including Frankel ever did, in contesting the blue riband of all races. The reporters who wrote off his chances were not exactly being unfair. A brief examination of his two-year-old races shows his best finish was fifth – of six, that race and the other three races fairly lowly affairs. Maybe a change of trainer might do the trick? So, in preparation for his three-year-old campaign Castlemorris King moved to a dual Derby-winning stable. However, fifth of thirteen in a £2,000 handicap at Warwick a month prior to the Derby was no indication of

---

* These are the costs for the 2020 Derby.

Classic-winning potential in the eyes of the trainer, so the owner Charles O'Connell moved the horse to new trainer Michael Attwater whose stables are right beside the Epsom track. As Attwater joked at the time, the owner may have shelled out seven thousand pounds in entry fees but he won't have any travel costs to pay.

This particular Derby had a little extra frisson to what might be regarded as a 'normal' Derby as the Queen had a live prospect in a colt called Carlton House who was on a hat-trick of wins, having taken victory the previous month at York in the Dante Stakes, universally regarded as the leading domestic Derby trial. As an owner and breeder for most of her adult life, the Queen has been hugely successful with over 1,600 race wins including four of the Classics but never the Derby. Maybe Carlton House, her tenth runner in the race, was to be the one? The betting public certainly thought so. Her horse was 5–2 favourite.

Not everyone was happy with the inclusion of Castlemorris King and another 'no-hoper', Marhaba Malyoon; there was plenty of press comment suggesting that they diminished the status of the race and could possibly, albeit accidentally, interfere with some of their more fancied rivals. But as the jockey Mark Coumbe said, 'If it's such a problem, they should change the rules.' It is to the credit of the racing authorities that they haven't. Racing is, in the end, all about dreams and they do sometimes come true. Even the Derby has been won not once but on three occasions by 100–1 outsiders, and in 1989 Terimon was runner-up to Nashwan at odds of 500–1. And after all Castlemorris King wasn't so badly bred – like Frankel his grandfather was Sadler's Wells.

When they lined up at 4 pm that afternoon who would have been the more excited and nervous? The Queen with the horse fancied to win or Charles O'Connell fulfilling a lifetime ambition, who by the simple fact of owning a horse in the race, had just that tiny sliver of hope? My guess, for what it is worth, is the Queen. Expectation was high and the auguries good.

As the horses broke from the stalls at the start of the one and a half mile race, sorting themselves into full racing pace, O'Connell maybe had more to cheer about than the Queen as his horse settled into fifth place, while Carlton House, after a slow start, was held up at the back. For a moment put yourself in the shoes of the owner, jockey and trainer, Derby debutants all, as Castlemorris King bowled along, eating up the furlongs of the famous Epsom turf, just a few lengths off the lead and with all the best opponents behind him. Don't you think you'd fleetingly suspend reality? Dream the impossible? The leaders fading, the wide expanse of the finishing straight greeting a surging Castlemorris King, the roar from the stands impelling him ever faster, seeing off each and every challenger to write the racing fairy tale of all fairy tales.

Of course that didn't happen. As they turned for home at Tattenham Corner, a stone's throw from his stable box, Castlemorris King ran out of puff, fading fast to beat just one other, Marhaba Malyoon. As for the Queen it was a little better: Carlton House came with a run and as he took second with just a furlong to go, a crescendo of sound rolled out across the Epson Downs as the crowds rose and cheered in anticipation of a royal victory. But it wasn't to be. In one of the most amazing finishes of recent times, the French challenger Pour Moi came from last to first to snatch victory in the final few strides, relegating Carlton House to third.

Racing is a great leveller: the winning dream had eluded both royalty and commoner in equal measure.

Where do you go after running in the Derby? A good run, if not necessarily a winning one, will open up a plethora of valuable races here and abroad. You might contest the St Leger, the last of the five British Classics, or perhaps the French equine showcase, the Prix de l'Arc de Triomphe at Longchamp, or even cross to America for one of the Breeders' Cup World Championships where a single race has prize money of $6 million. For all those riches it is not unheard of for the Derby winner to never race again, whisked straight off to stud to lock in the value of that gene pool.

Needless to say, none of these were on the cards for Castlemorris King. Life was to be far more mundane; as in common with three of the other Newmarket twelve, Elrasheed, Lemon Drop Red and Maher, his destiny was to run on the all-weather track at Wolverhampton where, instead of competing for £710,000 in front of hundreds of thousands in a race screened around the globe, he was now racing for £2,000 in front of hundreds in a race largely piped into the betting shops.

But, to his credit, he did chalk up a first win, doing the same again the following month in a similar race, the two combined recouping half Charles O'Connell's Derby costs. However, flat racing wasn't really his thing so at the end of his four-year-old racing season Castlemorris King found himself with a new owner, new trainer and gelded, but about to find his métier as he went hurdling.

There was a time when hurdling did not have quite the same prestige as chasing; it was seen as either a convenient home for failed flat racers or a transitory stage as horses graduated to jumping the fences in 'proper' steeplechases. The latter is still true; nearly every steeplechaser will have its first few competitive races over the hurdles. The obstacles themselves are narrow, flexible panels of just 3.5 feet in height, which the horse is able to take in its stride with little loss of momentum, with falls being rare. Fences on the other hand are taller, 4.5 feet or more, wider and often with a ditch on the take-off or landing side all of which requires the timing of both a big stride and jump.

As to the latter, hurdling has very much come into its own in recent decades. Its races, shorter than chases and run at a faster pace, are well suited to the television age and though it doesn't yet quite have a global equivalent of a Grand National a successful hurdler can race frequently, rack up hundreds of thousands of pounds in prize money and become a familiar favourite to the racing public over a top-flight career that may easily last four or five years, far longer than any flat horse.

Castlemorris King didn't quite scale those heights but there is no doubt he was a proficient and successful hurdler. Between the age of five and eight he raced twenty-one times, winning seven of them, which by any standards is an impressive strike rate, for prize money of over £40,000. He'd have probably even shown a small profit for his owners, no mean achievement in itself. In fact all in all, of all the twelve yearlings, this brown colt was the one who proved to be the most adaptable and resilient. At forty-four races he competed more times than any of the others. Only Man of God, who raced at nine, raced longer. And he competed in all five of the professional racing disciplines – flat, all-weather, hurdle, chase and National Hunt flat. His grandfather would have reasons enough to be proud of him. Castlemorris King deserves a long and happy retirement.

Up in the air

*Bonita Star. Has weaker races to contest, and that should
be enough to see her win soon enough, again offering plenty
with the way she travelled.*

Timeform

Bonita Star, the sole filly in the race, had already had three owners
by the time she reached Newmarket. She had been bred at the St
Simon Stud in Newmarket to be sold eight months later at the
Tattersalls Foal Sales for just 2,200 guineas. A year later she changed
hands again for a good profit making 22,000 guineas before heading
off to be trained by Mick Channon in Berkshire.

You might well wonder as to the wisdom of putting a filly
up against a bunch of colts. After all in most areas of human
sporting endeavour women almost always lose out to men in a
battle of the sexes. Not so in horse racing where the females, both
jockeys and horses, are more than able to hold their own in most
instances.

Essentially, as far as the horses are concerned, this is down to physical development. As two-year-olds, fillies are more or less at the same stage as the colts, able to run as fast and as far. That said there is a divergence at three when the colts put on a spurt, but by the autumn of that same year the fillies will have caught up with the sexes in lockstep until the end of their respective careers. If this sounds an over-generalisation, the data is there to prove it. The British Horse Racing Authority ratings put a number to the ability of every horse that runs – zero for a dud, 140 for a champion. Their median rating for colts is 69 and for fillies 64. The stopwatch confirms something similar. The record time at Belmont Park in the USA over one mile and one furlong stands at 1 minute 45.4 seconds by the colt Secretariat and 1 minute 45.8 seconds by the filly Go for Wand. Just by way of comparison the world record for men and women runners over a mile shows a difference of 29 seconds.

All of which might make you ask why two of the British Classic races, the 1,000 Guineas and the Oaks, are set aside for fillies. The answer is that they are run in May and June respectively of that three-year-old year, right at the moment when the difference in the sexes is most apparent. By the time the final Classic, the St Leger, comes around in September the colts and fillies are back racing together on equal terms. Such is the rapid convergence of the sex gap that the Prix de l'Arc de Triomphe, the world's second richest turf race run at Longchamp in early October, open to all horses three or older, has in the past ten runnings (2009–18) been won on three occasions by three-year-old fillies and by fillies generally seven times in that period.

Having finished fifth to Frankel, Bonita Star's owners must have thought her a tough filly, for in the next eight weeks she raced four further times, including a trip to the Curragh in Ireland, winning just the once in a minor maiden at Beverley before being sold back at Newmarket in the October horses-in-training sale for 7,000 guineas less than her last purchase price. But someone must have thought they had a bargain, for they shelled out to buy Bonita Star a one-way plane ticket to California.

Horses fly more than you might imagine: DHL, the freight shipping company, have a division specifically dedicated to this purpose. Irish trainer Aidan O'Brien, in common with other big-time trainers who have water between them and the European racecourses such as Ascot or Longchamp, have taken flying horses to their heart, running a day return service. Air travel for equines has become commonplace; it has truly both Europeanised and internationalised horse racing. Take Royal Ascot week as a case in point for someone like Aidan O'Brien, based in Ballydoyle in southern Ireland, who might easily have a dozen runners on each of the five days.

In the past the horses would be loaded in a transporter and driven the three hours to catch the ferry to mainland Britain. If all goes well, the five-hour sea trip will be calm, but the Irish Sea has a reputation for being anything other than that. Rough seas, with the rolling cargo decks that clang and bang, are hard on horses who have to be largely left alone as the stable hands are not allowed below deck with them barring exceptional circumstances. On the landing side it is another five hours down motorways before bedding down in an unfamiliar racecourse stable box. Put all that together, with the inevitable possibilities of delay, and you are looking at close to 400 miles and 15 hours door-to-door, which is tiring and stressful for both the people and horses. At best it is a day there, a day back, with a day at the races in between. These days it is all over in less than twelve hours.

I mean how cool is it to be a star of Ballydoyle? You wake up on race morning in your own box, smelling the familiar straw, slurping down the Irish water and munching on your regular race-day breakfast. The hustle and bustle is comfortingly familiar. Sure, you'll know something is in the air; the pitch and tension of any racing yard notches up on big race days. A bit later you'll be led into a horse box, whisked to Shannon airport and onto your very own plane that leaves when you are ready to leave. An hour later, you land on the outskirts of London. Another horse box collects you at the doors of the plane. Another short journey. And as the crowds stream through the Ascot turnstiles you'll be stabled and ready to race.

After your race, win or lose, you'll be washed down, bandaged up and there is a good chance that you will be back on the road long before the last race of the day, slipping out of the gates, unseen by crowds facing the other way. Soon you'll be in the air, pulling at a net of hay as the plane eats up the miles. Home beckons and in all probability you'll be hanging out over the door of your stable before the sun sets behind the Tipperary hills. Life can be sweet when you are a four-footed athlete at the top of your game.

You might imagine that horses fly in special cargo planes, with cavernous interiors akin to military aircraft, with rear ramps more used to swallowing up tanks and the hardware of war. But the planes horses travel in are not so different to those we use; think of a regular Boeing 737 that is typically used by Ryanair or British Airways but with the seats and most of the comforts stripped out and you will not be far off the mark. Essentially it is a hollow tube, with a flat floor, big doors in the side and no windows. In fact the fleet scattered around the world dedicated to this trade largely consists of ex-passenger Boeing 737s minus 150 or so seats.

Horses are cargo. Admittedly very special cargo, but it is surprising how routine and frankly ordinary the transporting of what are potentially highly strung and temperamental animals has become. In many respects it is a huge tribute to everyone associated with the thoroughbred that this has become possible. Not only that ability to train them to run fast but also to be able to cope with all sorts of pressures and uncertainties, including travel, be it by land, sea or air. And it works; I've seen more people than horses go to pieces at the prospect of an air flight.

When you see horses airside on their way to the plane you might be amazed to see how unconfined they appear to be, loaded as they are into something that looks not unlike a giant cutlery box, with three aluminium compartments, each just large enough for one horse, open topped, the sides about the height of a stable door, with the horses hanging their heads over the end, as if it was indeed a stable door. As the airport tractor trolleys the triple stall to the plane, it does all look rather incongruous as amid the concrete, airport buildings and fuel trucks, with not a blade of grass or tree in sight, the horse heads happily bob and weave. At the plane the box, horses and all, is slid off the trolley onto a scissor lift, that raises the trio, accompanied by the steady pneumatic whine of the lift mechanism, level with the open cargo doors. In general the horses show absolutely no concern for what is happening around them, however alien the whole process might be. In fact almost the reverse happens; they appear almost fascinated, all the time looking around taking it all in, the three of them like excited friends heading off on a much anticipated holiday.

Inside, with the triple stall (often one of six or seven with a plane taking anything up to twenty horses) fixed to the floor so the horses face to the front of the plane, you'll notice there is not really very much headroom. If the horse raises and stretches its neck it might easily rub against the ceiling, especially the outside pair where the ceiling curves down, so the tallest horse usually takes the middle stall. However, if any of them reared they could certainly claw the roof with their hooves. That being the case you might expect them to have complicated tethers, but they don't have anything particularly out of the ordinary. It's just the usual head collar, the leading rope tied to the end of the stall and a rope collar that hangs loosely around their neck, with two ropes attached that are tied to the corners of the stall to prevent them rearing.

And that's it beside a bit of bedding, water and maybe some food. On board will be the occasional goat acting as an equine travelling companion and the regular stable staff (a few regular seats are left in for them) who are there to fuss and cosset if need be, not to mention sharing in the advantages of private jet travel to the races. But the special treatment doesn't end there; the pilots have a role to play, coaxing the planes into the air with long, slow gentle ascents (airports with extended runways are favoured) minimising that ear-popping sensation that you and I find mildly annoying but horses find upsetting. Turns in the air are wide, avoiding any G-forces that may create a 'floating' sensation that has them scrabbling to find a floor that they haven't in fact left. And when it comes to landing, pilots aren't beyond pulling at the heart strings of air-traffic controllers when a holding pattern becomes unbearably long, peeling out of formation to jump the queue.

So Bonita Star left Britain forever in a certain amount of style, fourteen hours later landing in America's sunshine state. It was to be a successful move. She ran twenty-four times in California between February 2011 and August 2013 and won four races (three claimers and an allowance race), retiring with total earnings, including her $8,000 from the UK, of $152,264.

She is currently a broodmare in California, with three recorded foals between 2015 and 2017, the first of which has already won a race.

A 99 per cent write-down

*Breton Star. Was a big price and always in
rear after a slow start.*

Timeform

It may sound harsh but twelfth of twelve, beaten by thirty-three
lengths (roughly 90 yards) by Frankel was to be about as good as it
got for Breton Star. His British racing earnings were to be a
less-than-impressive £871, the least of all the Newmarket dozen.

Like Frankel, Breton Star was debuting that day, having followed
a familiar route from birth to racecourse: bred in Newmarket and
sold as a yearling at the Tattersalls December sales to an owner who
was to place him with a Newmarket trainer. To say he hadn't travelled far in life would be something of an understatement: that
particular moment was yet to come.

There was nothing in Breton Star's parentage to suggest he
wouldn't be capable of winning a race or two. His father was
Medicean, who sired ten top-tier race winners and was a well

thought of stallion who stood for many years at the Cheveley Park Stud in Newmarket until he retired at twenty. Breton Star's mother was Wannabe Grand, a successful filly who was one of the best juveniles of her generation, who followed up as a three-year-old by being second in the fillies Classic, the 1,000 Guineas. Her father, so Breton Star's grandfather, was Danehill, one of Frankel's great-grandparents, who probably deserves a book in his own right.

If I run off a series of statistics you'll see what I mean. In thirteen years as a stallion, standing in three different countries, Australia, Ireland and Japan, Danehill sired 2,008 runners, 1,545 of those winners (a remarkable success rate of 77 per cent) who between them have amassed £203 million in prize money, some of them becoming global superstars in their own right. He is currently the most successful sire of all time measured by the quality of the races his offspring have won. Even in death Danehill racked up another eye-watering number. At the age of seventeen, with maybe eight to ten years still ahead of him, he died in a freak accident at his home at Coolmore Stud (where Frankel was conceived four years later) in Ireland. Between covering mares he was being led around his paddock by way of distraction and a bit of downtime, when he reared playfully. He was always something of a heavy-topped horse, so as he fell sort of sideways, he put huge strain on one of his hind legs which fractured, the weight and pressure of the collapse causing massive internal injuries. He was dead before he hit the ground. The resultant insurance payout was rumoured to be in the region of £36 million.

How did he achieve all that? Well, aside from being a damn good stallion he pretty well invented the concept of shuttling for high-end sires. As you probably know by now, all northern hemisphere thor-oughbreds, regardless of their actual date of birth, are regarded as being 'born' for horse-racing classification purposes on 1 January of the year of their birth. So, in theory, you could have in a two-year-old race horses ranging in age from two years and a day to two years and 364 days. However, in practice, breeders aware of the risks associated with a poorly timed birth tend to cluster matings in such a way for the births to happen in the prime February–May period. In the southern hemisphere, the same rules apply but to a different date – 1 August. This, as I am sure you have twigged, opens a window of opportunity.

All this brings us back to how Danehill became a shuttler, using international air flights to split his year between the southern and northern hemispheres.

He'd been a reasonably successful racehorse, though had that been the total achievement of his life we probably would not be talking about him today. On retirement his owner/breeder, coincidentally Frankel's Prince Khalid, sold him to an Irish/Australian partnership, who sent him to Australia to start his stallion career in the antipodean spring of 1990 before he came to Coolmore in Ireland in time for the European spring and his northern hemisphere mare selection.

It all sounds so simple in hindsight, but like so many ground-breaking ideas it comes with risks and difficulties. As the stallion owner you have to fill a massive order book of up to 200 mares a year, convincing broodmare owners at different ends of the globe that your sire is the one for them. And then your stallion has to have the constitution for the job in hand. Consider Danehill's year: in August he's relaxing 150 miles north of Sydney in the Hunter Valley, which is as good for horses as it is for wine, ready for the roughly 150 mares that will come his way from around the southern hemisphere, some of whom have to be mated with more than once, between the Australian spring and December. Then it is on that plane for 22 hours (plus stops) to be back to Europe in time for Christmas; here is a horse that largely misses out on summers. His festive gift is two months off stud duties before his European contingent, of a similar size and with similar demands, keeps him occupied from mid-February to mid-July before, you guessed it, getting back on that plane again.

In some ways the bloodstock business is all about raw economics – supply and demand. Based in just one of the hemispheres your stallion has a physical limit to how many mares he can cover in a breeding season, and there are only so many mares suitable for his particular bloodline. But shuttling doubles the supply, doubles the demand and doubles your income. It is a really clever use of a finite resource, and the Coolmore Stud have taken the Danehill model that they pretty well invented and fine-tuned it to perfection, with today nine of their thirteen Irish stallions 'shuttlers'.

So, with all this genetic history behind him, Breton Star must have looked reasonable value at 22,000 guineas. Of course, we know better. It seems a little unfair to recite his racing record but it does illustrate how tough it is to even win a race, let alone scale greater heights, even with the benefit of good parentage and the advantages of a good trainer. At two Breton Star raced three times: last to Frankel, fifth of nine at Yarmouth and twelfth of fourteen at Leicester, the latter two both minor races. Total income £155. At three he raced four times, saving his best performance on British soil to last, second on the all-weather at Lingfield just a few days after Frankel had racked up his seventh consecutive win. Total income £756.

If you add it all up – buying, training, entry fees, vet bills, farrier bills, travel, jockeys and the myriad other items that fill up your monthly account as a racehorse owner – Breton Star must have cost in excess of £75,000. The less than one per cent return was clearly not going to be enough, and two weeks later his owner recouped some of his outlay when Breton Star returned to the Tattersalls

auction ring to be sold for 15,000 guineas. Clearly, someone still
believed in him.

The cruellest cut

*Colour Vision. Far too green on debut, as he intimated on
the way to post, and that's something that could well prove
the case next time, too.*

Timeform

For the horse that came second to last at Newmarket, twenty-nine
lengths behind Frankel, Colour Vision subsequently did well. Of the
twelve he was to be the third highest in terms of prize money
(£352,484), and with six wins including a Group 1 at Royal Ascot,
the fourth most successful by wins. He raced until he was five,
running in twenty-seven races, all on the flat. However, no glittering
stud career awaited him; on 16 November, towards the end of his
two-year-old year along with Lemon Drop Red, he became the first
of the dozen to be gelded.

There is no way of explaining this without offending the squeam-
ish but the process of gelding, or to use the correct medical term –
an orchidectomy – is the surgical term for castration. *Ectomy* in

Greek means remove, *orchid* is a testicle. For tropical plant lovers among you that may be a sentence you will never be able to unread; I, for one, see orchids in a whole new light. But, horticultural niceties aside, and this might seem a strange thing to say, the process of gelding is the lifeblood of horse racing and something that has been a common practice since medieval times.

To start with geldings are not just the exception but rather the norm; our Newmarket eleven (Bonita Star was a filly) pretty well prove this point as in the end all but two including some of those of high birth, were gelded. If you want more empirical data look to Hong Kong, one of the international horse-racing hubs where prize money for a single race runs as high as £2.5 million. In 2014–15 there were 1,029 horses in training; four were female, thirty-two entire (i.e. ungelded) with the remaining 996, so 96 per cent, geldings. However drastic an orchidectomy might appear, the frequency of it indicates there must be good reason. In fact there are five: racing ability, attitude, growth, animal and human welfare and, ironically, improving the gene pool.

The gelding itself is not a difficult or protracted operation. It can be conducted under local anaesthetic with the horse standing or fully sedated lying down. It takes about twenty minutes, fifteen of which are taken up by pre- and post-op procedures. Recovery is quick. After a day of stable rest most horses will be walking then trotting daily (the stretching movement aids the healing process) and back to normal work within two weeks. That is the how. What about the whys?

In the end it is all about testosterone, the male sex hormone that is produced in the testes – remove them and you remove it. But, you might reason, surely sex drive is all mixed up with aggression, the will to win and ultimately, in a horse, the desire to be the head of the herd? In that you'd be absolutely right, but those characteristics are not those that will necessarily make a good racehorse. Separate that thought into body and head and it makes a bit more sense.

Gelding a horse at the correct age will change its bodily appearance as the hormones actually stop the bones growing. Remove that hormonal input at an early enough age and your gelded horse will be taller and have a longer stride than his entire counterpart. He'll also be appreciably less muscled at the front; hormones simulate excess muscle mass and encourage the body to fill out which is why body builders take steroids – testosterone is a steroid. And without all that extra muscle weight above the front legs, geldings are less prone to injury. This makes them easier to train, more reliable on the racecourse and ultimately a more consistent proposition for the betting public.

Assessing what goes on inside the head of any horse is a little more difficult than just taking stock of its physical attributes. But talk to any racing professional who has to deal with the adolescent and maturing ungelded horse and each will have a salutary tale to tell. Without reciting a litany of near misses, some quite horrible injuries and frankly life-threatening incidents, I rely on a pithy summary I came across in a veterinarian publication that read:

'Removal of both testicles usually rids the horse of unwanted stallion-like behaviour, including screaming at and fighting with other horses, attempting to mount other horses, erection, masturbation, and potentially aggressive behaviour towards humans.'*

If you put that sort of behaviour in the context of a busy racing stable, or for that matter any place where there are horses, you can see why geldings are preferred. They are loyal, consistent and focused on the task in hand while the ungelded wastes time and energy

---

* Christina S Cable DVM, Dipl. ACVS, *Castration In The Horse*, 1 April 2001, www.thehorse.com.

thinking about things other than racing. Essentially you end up with a better racehorse.

Knowing all this might make you ask why most horses aren't treated like farm livestock who are usually castrated soon after birth. Well, clearly this would be a terrific gamble for the breed not to mention the owner of a champion horse subsequently denied a lucrative stud career. The racing authorities know this, so it is no coincidence that the conditions of entry to Classic races such as the Derby state 'entire colts and fillies only'. After all, there is not much point creating the supreme equine test if the winner can't pass on the winning genes.

Horses can, in reality, be gelded at any age – from the day of birth right on into their twenties. However, for the racing thoroughbred it will generally be towards the end of the two-year-old season when the question will be first posed to, or by, every owner: should I geld my horse?

In answering that question you could do worse than start with the thoughts of Alfred G Vanderbilt, from the wealthy dynasty of the same surname, who pretty well dedicated his entire life to horse racing and breeding. He was one of the leading American owners during the middle decades of the twentieth century, not to mention being a great innovator pioneering the starting stalls, photo finish and on-track pari-mutuel betting (or totalisator as we know it in the UK) which replaced bookmakers. Vanderbilt truly owned thousands of horses in his time, so when he said, 'If I had gelded every horse in my stable, I would have made only one mistake', he was only half-joking – the one mistake would have been Native Dancer who won two of the three legs of the Triple Crown in 1953 before going on to become a great sire.

The serious point he was trying to make was that the odds of any colt becoming a great stallion are so infinitesimal that the default choice should always be to geld. Of course, it is rarely an easy decision to make. At all levels, racing is something of a gamble, a maze that is negotiated by a series of simple decisions that sometimes, in aggregate, however rarely, lead you to the Holy Grail at the centre and then out again. At two, as your colt starts to show an interest in the fillies, this will be one of those decision moments. You'll weigh up the various factors: does my colt have a superior pedigree? Is he growing into a fine animal who will be able to cope with the rigours of racing at three and four? Does he have the personality to be safely trained if left entire? Does he like his racing or is his mind elsewhere? And of course you'll have the evidence from the racetrack itself.

For Colour Vision and Lemon Drop Red all those questions led to the one answer: geld. So both were emasculated before they turned three and on the evidence it didn't do them any harm. Between them they went on to win nine more races, and of the Newmarket dozen Colour Vision amassed all but £4,338 after being gelded. Dortmund, Maher and Man of God followed suit at the end of their three-year-old racing, Castlemorris at four and Genius Beast at six. Gelding may seem ruthless but it both improves racing and prevents the dilution of the gene pool with sub-standard performers.

All-weather man

*Elrasheed. Could never get on terms starting out, but he
was spared a hard time and is sure to step up with the
experience under his belt.*

Timeform

If we were to agree with the Timeform analysis, we'd have to say that
Elrasheed did step up but not by much. The most valuable race he
ever contested was one of the two he won, an £8,000 handicap in
France as a four-year-old. But before he departed to the continent he
took the journey to the Midlands, as did five of the Newmarket
dozen at one time or another, to race on the all-weather at
Wolverhampton and sign off on his English racing career.

All-weather tracks often get a bad rap – they do not have the
kudos or prestige of their turf cousins – but rather than trying to
justify this relatively new-fangled surface (the first arrived in the UK
in 1989) let's ask what is wrong with turf. Well, in most respects
nothing. It looks beautiful and is what wild horses would naturally

gallop on. But turf is incredibly hard to maintain. Every turf track has a team who look after the grass. It has to be mown. Fed. Rolled. Watered in summer. Drained in winter. Protected from the elements. And then come race day it is pounded by hundreds of horses who cut tens of thousands of divots. For the big-time tracks like Cheltenham or Ascot all this is taken care of by a dedicated team. Money and manpower, if not exactly limitless, are available. Frost forecast for tonight ahead of tomorrow's meeting? Let's deploy the protective sheeting around the entire two-mile circumference of the course. The value of the meeting far outweighs the cost of precautionary measures. But for a tiny track putting on a run-of-the-mill midweek fixture out in the sticks in the depths of winter, the numbers will never really stack up. For racing as a whole, though, the calculation is very different.

Before the arrival of all-weather tracks the sport was always at the mercy of the elements, with racing shutting down for days or weeks at a time. The dry spells of summer were relatively easy to navigate; most tracks are able to afford a good watering system to keep the turf if not in prime at least in racing condition. But winter was a whole different affair. An otherwise perfect racing surface could be rendered unraceable by an overnight frost freezing the unprotected turf and making it too hard and dangerous to race on. Extended bouts of heavy rain would make it too soft, just a few horses turning turf to quagmire in only a few strides. Snow looks pretty but has the same outcome. Cancellation.

The drive for something different came largely from the betting industry. Horse racing, before the advent of high-stake fruit machines and internet betting, was the backbone of the high-street shops. No horse racing, combined with expensive real estate and staff costs, was an expensive hole to fill. In fact you never filled it. Betting is largely a discretionary activity. If your customers didn't bet, they can easily find another outlet for their cash; it is no coincidence that the best place for a betting shop is near a pub. Once a fixture has gone, the potential revenue has largely gone forever. Now owners of betting shops are sometimes called turf accountants for a good reason – they can do the maths. Soon after the legalisation of high-street gambling in 1961 they worked out that they needed a regular staple of betting fodder; so they encouraged, then eventually paid, greyhound tracks to race on days and times to suit the off-course gambling market. The dog stadia, eager to oblige, tore up the turf for sand at the prospect of a steady income stream.

The same could not be said of horse racing who didn't see the same need which, to an extent, is fine. After all, that was the choice of the ruling bodies and there is plenty to say in support of upholding tradition. But there is a huge ecosystem that surrounds horse racing both on and off the course. No racing, no pay. At some point something had to give. Too many livelihoods were at stake for the sake of tradition.

All-weather is something of a catch-all phrase covering a multiplicity of racing surfaces, but essentially there are two groups: dirt as largely used in the USA or synthetic surfaces (there are many types) as used here and in other countries. They all have their supporters and detractors. Dirt, as the name suggests, is fine earth mixed with sand on a base of compacted limestone for drainage, the 'cushion' of dirt varying in depth and hardness from course to course. It is, of all the surfaces, the fastest, encouraging pillar to post racing where the horses run the entire race at full speed. Gamblers tend to like dirt as the surface is consistent over weeks and months, providing lines of form that allow precise comparison of the racing records of horses that have raced in different races on different occasions. However, like turf, dirt is natural so needs constant attention, though the care is, admittedly, mostly administered by tractor machinery that ploughs, harrows and rolls the surface between races. In dry weather it needs to be watered to avoid the dust storm that would otherwise envelop the field, and in wet weather the horses and jockeys come home splattered head to toe in mud.

The ingredients of a synthetic track, as the name suggests, are far from organic; they include rubber, carpet fibres, recycled jelly cable and silica sand which is all then coated with microcrystalline waxes, by-products of oil refining, to aid drainage and provide cushioning. The finished product is laid in a deep layer over a membrane base. Track owners like this surface because, once installed, it requires little maintenance and virtually guarantees a working race surface whatever the weather. However, and this is where it gets a little complicated, there are more subtle forces at work.

Horses often show a preference for a particular kind of track, be it turf, dirt or synthetic. To a certain extent this may simply be because any given horse may have trained and raced all its life on one particular surface. However, in the international arena where horses criss-cross the globe to seek out big prizes and show their prowess to owners who may one day bid on their progeny, any new surface they may encounter is a consideration. Some horses who love dirt simply hate turf and vice versa; you can work out for yourself the many other permutations. But you can take it as a general rule of thumb that dirt horses will adapt better to synthetic than turf, and turf horses will adapt better to synthetic than dirt. There are of course plenty of exceptions, but if you are the racecourse executive who wants to elevate his track to the world stage with a high-stakes race for horses that fly in from the five continents, then an artificial surface has to be your choice; in that the billion-dollar desert track of Dubai and the more modest urban Wolverhampton share something in common.

Elrasheed's October run around Wolverhampton was to be his first taste of a synthetic surface, but not his last. All his subsequent races in France, of which he won only one, were either on fibresand or polytrack, with trainer Fabrice Vermeulen at Deauville or Chantilly.

Pinhooked

Lemon Drop Red. Stepped up a little [compared to previous race], though not to the extent he could be fancied to win a similar event near to hand, even if coming on again.

Timeform

Like so many prime American thoroughbreds, Lemon Drop Red was born in Kentucky, USA: the bluegrass state, so called for the wild meadows that shimmer in summer as the native grass grows to full height with blue, blowsy flowering seed heads. Not that you will often see the grass growing tall on the immaculately kept stud farms; grazing mothers and foals plus a buzzing army of weed-whacking Mexicans see to that. For here you are among the worldwide hub of horse breeding where long avenues of gloss-white painted rails lead to the barns that seem to have appeared in a dream. White clapboard sides. Roof shingles, the wood perfectly silvered with age. Gothic turrets of lead or copper designed to let in light and provide natural air conditioning. Huge chandeliers hang in the grandest barns above the heads of horses who pay little heed to their perfect lodgings. On warm nights the huge doors at either end are rolled open, the gentle through-breeze enough to calm the most agitated mare. From a distance the whole scene sparkles as the dim lights sway with the wind.

This is the most rarefied of upbringings but a place to which few of the offspring will ever return. You are bred with an eye to success, but without achieving that you will find no stall reserved with your name hanging from the rope chain. To come back you have to leave, and for most the point of departure is the Keeneland yearling sales held, naturally enough, in Kentucky. They take place each year in September, when the foals of Frankel's generation are around eighteen months old. If you have any doubt as to the supremacy of this auction in the world of horse breeding, just roll the statistics over your tongue. The sales last a full twelve days; 2,500 yearlings will be sold, and $300 million will be spent. And $300 million will be earned. For Keeneland is both the start and end of dreams.

Anyone and everyone who is, was or aspires to be something in the bloodstock world arrives in time to catch the autumn hues as either a buyer, seller or some kind of interested intermediary. For the sellers it is the end of the line. The plotting and planning of the past two or three years will come down to less than those few minutes between the horse entering the sale ring and the gavel of the auction-eer declaring the consignment sold; or worse, not.

The sellers are for the most part the people who bred the year-lings; the breeders who sat down and said 'I am going to mate this sire with that mare' and then went out to make it happen. Again those same people will likely own the mare. So, unless they also own the father-to-be, they will go out into the market to hire the stallion of their choice for effectively as long as it takes him to mount their mare and complete the impregnation. And in this business the lady nearly always has to visit the man.

This is a big generalisation but in broad terms breeders fall into three categories. At the apex are the global operations run by the wealthy, be they individuals, families or close-knit groups. The next layer are the commercial operations which are run as, or like, corporations. At the base are the mom-and-pop breeders, where the term family includes the horses. At Keeneland, or any of the other major auctions around the world, you won't see the global operators sweating nails. Their annual profit and loss account, such as it is, doesn't depend on the outcome of the bids. They plan to keep the best of their crop to race themselves, and maybe even breed with, at a later date. If they are sellers it is usually in terms of stock clearance.

For the family breeder Keeneland is a chance to hit the big time. The once-in-a-lifetime chance to cash in with a yearling that achieves a multi-million dollar price tag. And it does happen. In fact it happens pretty well every year, not perhaps in terms of millions but in terms of life-changing amounts of money. That is the dream. You arrive at the sales with hope and a horse – you leave with a trailer full of cash. Of course, you might be tempted to ask: haven't they sold the goose that lays the golden eggs? Well maybe, but success in the sale ring does not equate to success on the racetrack. And after all, these are breeders not racehorse owners. But don't forget they usually still own the biggest factor in the equation – the mare. If she has produced one stellar yearling maybe she'll produce a second?

So did Lemon Drop Red change the life of breeder Nancy Leonard? The answer is probably not, but at $135,000 the hammer price probably represented a good profit; the sire Lemon Drop Kid had a $25,000 stud fee but the dam Skipper's Mate, with this her first foal at auction and race record of a single unsuccessful run, would not have been overly valuable. However, she clearly caught the eye of pinhooker Paddy Twomey.

Pinhooking is a word used around the world by the bloodstock industry but it actually has its origins in the tobacco fields of Kentucky. Speculators used to buy up the juvenile crop while still growing in the field, identifying their plants at the subsequent auction by hooking a note with a pin to the bales. Today the *Collins English Dictionary* defines a pinhooker as 'someone who trades in young racehorses for profit'. In this case it didn't go too well for Paddy Twomey who shipped the yearling Lemon Drop Red across the Atlantic to sell as a two-year-old prospect in the Tattersalls spring sales in Newmarket.

There are at any one time probably ten to fifteen full-time pinhookers; Paddy is now a trainer in Ireland but he is regarded as one of the most successful. The idea is to see potential in a yearling, hoping he or she will improve physically in the next six months and then find the most appropriate market to sell into. For instance, horses with a particular turf pedigree might do better in Europe than in the predominantly dirt racing USA. It is largely a numbers game. You need to buy a bunch of horses on this basis, accepting that on some you will lose, some break even but hopefully you'll make out on one or two with what they call a 'big lick' to show a healthy profit. There is also the added allure of currency arbitrage; pinhookers watch the $/£ rate as much as they do their horses.

Paddy's Lemon Drop Red made 80,000 guineas at the spring sales, almost exactly the same in pound terms (the rate was $1.6/£ in 2009) to the $135,000 he had paid. If you factor in all the costs (the plane fare alone is £8,000–£10,000) then this particular pinhook lost around £15,000 for Paddy. Unless of course he made out on the currency – the pound had gone down to $1.5 by the spring. However, he didn't lose out as badly as the person who bought Lemon Drop

Red; that person offloaded the colt eighteen months later for 28,000 guineas. A loss, with training fees and other expenses, not far off £100,000.

For really Lemon Drop Red's racing career, without being too harsh, was one of managed decline. But I don't want to be too unfair. He won four races: one over hurdles, two on the flat and another on the all-weather, with total lifetime earnings of £16,721. Winning a race for a thoroughbred, any thoroughbred, is an achievement in itself – only around one in twenty will ever win a race. Four wins actually puts Lemon Drop Red in a pretty elite group. His final race was in the summer of 2014 in a £3,119 handicap hurdle at Worcester, not long after Frankel's first foal had made £1.15 million at auction. Lemon Drop Red finished seventh out of ten.

Scandal

*Genius Beast. A February foal out of the top-class Shawanda,
impressed as really good mover on his way to post. He won't
meet rivals like the first two every day and is likely to make his
mark in maiden company before progressing.*

Racing Post

As the two-year-old season closed for the Newmarket twelve I
suspect, Frankel aside, Genius Beast would have been the horse you
would have picked out as the best-of-the rest for success at three. In
his next race, he did unfortunately meet more good rivals, beaten
into third again this time by the Abdullah/Cecil/Queally Picture
Editor with Nathaniel second. However, he closed out the season
with a win at Haydock over a mile with the post-race reports mark-
ing him down as a good middle-distance prospect, with maybe
Classic potential as his mother Shawanda had won the Oaks. He was
also being trained by one of the rising stars of racing, the Godolphin
trainer Mahmood Al Zarooni who was to shine briefly before

becoming enveloped in one of the greatest doping scandals to ever hit horse racing.

Godolphin is the world powerhouse of horse racing, the brainchild of His Highness Sheikh Mohammed, the ruler of Dubai. By just about every metric you might choose it is the largest breeding, racing and buying operation that stretches around the globe. There is a certain irony that it takes its name from one of those three foundation stallions, the Godolphin Arabian. Dubai today has the most magnificent racecourse at Meydan with, at close to a mile, the longest grandstand in the world that seats 60,000 and hosts the annual $35 million Dubai World Cup that rivals the Breeders' Cup.

Like Prince Khalid, Sheikh Mohammed's first introduction to horse racing was in England when he went to Newmarket to see Royal Palace win the 2,000 Guineas in 1967. Similarly to Prince Khalid the evolution took a little while, ten years in fact, when he had his first British winner at Brighton in 1977. However, since then the expansion has been stratospheric with horse farms and training establishments in Australia, Dubai, France, Ireland, Japan, the United Kingdom and the United States. In 2018 Godolphin notched up their 5,000th winner worldwide.

It would be fair to say that the Arab interest in English horse racing was not welcomed by everyone in the early days, even though an informal delegation from the Jockey Club in the 1970s had done the rounds of the newly emerging Middle Eastern nations to encourage that very thing. It worked. The old order was replaced by a new one, with many of the establishment owner-breeders unable to compete financially or logistically. Within a decade racing became truly international, the injection of wealth driving innovation in training, veterinary care, horse breeding, horse welfare and ultimately the racecourses themselves. For someone like myself who saw the parlous state of British horse racing in the 1980s, the transformation is close to miraculous and welcome.

Genius Beast was a foal from the Darley Stud, Darley being the thoroughbred stallion division of Godolphin, who owned his Oaks-winning mother. Like Frankel he was racing for the first time on that wet Newmarket evening, and like Frankel he ended the year on a high. Of the twelve he was rated the second highest by the *Racing Post* at 94, with Nathaniel third at 91. Frankel was 126. He announced himself as a Classic prospect early in his three-year-old season when he won a Group 3 Classic Trial at Sandown in April, briefly becoming ante-post favourite for the Derby as he was lined up for a similar trial in France, but despite starting favourite he only finished third. The Derby was forgotten as he went, like Frankel, to Royal Ascot and then York, running in different races but without success. Genius Beast did finally have his crack at a Classic in the St Leger at Doncaster in September, his final race on British soil seeing him tailed off eighth of nine. It was, as often it is in racing, a disappointing end; a horse that for a brief while had promised so much. Which in a way is a similar story to that of his trainer.

The training career of Mahmood Al Zarooni was not much longer than that of Genius Beast. Like his patron Sheikh Mohammed he was Dubaian by birth, becoming one His Highness' two principal trainers at Moulton Paddocks just outside Newmarket in 2010. Backed by the almost infinite resources of Godolphin he became, within the space of a year, one of the most high-profile trainers in Europe, sending out major-race winners in Dubai, France, Great Britain and South Africa including his first British Classic the 1,000 Guineas in May 2011. However, two years later the headlines were of a whole different hue as the Godolphin doping scandal broke.

Horse racing, in common with many sports, has struggled to keep ahead of the dopers, people who use illicit substances, usually drugs, to alter the performance of a horse to make it go faster, slower or perhaps recover from injury or illness. The main deterrent is race-course testing where a random selection of runners, including winners and placed horses, are tested at each race meeting, but that is backed up by what they call in athletics out-of-competition test-ing. It was the latter that ended the training career of Al Zarooni. On 9 April a team from the British Horseracing Authority, who police the doping rules, arrived at his Newmarket stables to test forty-five horses. On 22 April, of the tested horses eleven were reported posi-tive for anabolic steroids, outlawed drugs which make muscles grow faster but with harmful side-effects. Justice was swift. Three days after the results were made public, Al Zarooni was banned from racing for eight years having admitted to another four horses. All fifteen horses were barred from the racecourse for six months.

Genius Beast was not one of that group; he had not run as a four-year-old and did not at five, leaving Britain for Dubai after the doping scandal to race at Meydan at six where his single recorded race was twelfth of fourteen. He died aged eight.

Shadow man

Nathaniel. If it hadn't been for Frankel, he'd have been a five-length Newmarket maiden winner and grabbing the headlines himself. He is undoubtedly a smart prospect and, on breeding, looks sure to improve as he matures from this very pleasing debut.

Racing Post

It is not always the very act of being born that marks your destiny but the time into which you were born; peers can so easily deflect the trajectory to greatness. Andy Murray had the misfortune to be born into the age of Roger Federer. Who recalls the wit and intellect of Neville Chamberlain? He is forever eclipsed by Winston Churchill. When the history of the internet is written, will the readers ever believe that Yahoo was once more mighty than Google?

So it was that Nathaniel had the misfortune to be a member of the Frankel generation. They were only to meet twice on the racecourse, by some bizarre quirk of fate, when they both raced together for the first and last time, some twenty-six months apart. But their careers were destined to be intertwined by the fates of racing in numerous other ways.

Like Frankel, Nathaniel is a member of the racing aristocracy by virtue of ownership and birth; his owner/breeder is Lady Rothschild, married to Jacob Rothschild of the eponymous banking dynasty. More importantly his father is Galileo. Now you might think that makes Frankel and Nathaniel half-brothers but not so in horse racing; to be defined as such you have to share a mother. Why so? Well, in most given years a stallion will sire dozens or even hundreds of foals, culminating in hundreds if not possibly thousands of thoroughbred offspring – the term half-brother becomes too general to be of use. But regardless of the terminology they are close, and when Nathaniel left Ireland (he is classified as an Irish horse by virtue of his birth country) to be trained by John Gosden at Clarehaven Stables in Newmarket, just three-quarters of a mile from Frankel at Henry Cecil's Warren Place yard, they were closer still.

Like the great trainer Frankel had in Cecil, Nathaniel was no less served with Gosden. In fact, the two trainers had a connection going back many years, Gosden being an assistant trainer to one of the all-time greats Sir Noel Murless at Warren Place. Gosden's route to the top was a little more circuitous to Henry's. Having left Cambridge with a degree in Economics, he headed for Ireland to be an assistant trainer to Sir Vincent O'Brien. After that came his time with Murless before he headed to California to take his third assistant position with Tommy Doyle.

To the uninitiated these moves might seem a little sideways, but unless you are born into a great fortune, or happen to have great fortune, the path to becoming a fully-fledged trainer, let alone a successful one, is tricky to say the least. As the opening line in an article on how to become a racehorse trainer in *Horse & Hound* pithily stated: find a yard, get some horses and make them win. But even before that you need to learn how to be a trainer and, perhaps as importantly, make connections.

Becoming an assistant does both very well. Most assistants currently in the job will tell you the guv'nor is unreasonable, the hours are criminal and the pay is terrible. Meet them again in twenty years' time when they are standing in a winners enclosure and they'll tell you it was the best job they ever had: 'I wouldn't be here without it.' For as an assistant you are the trainer's right-hand person. Everything that goes on in the yard you'll have some involvement with: horses, staff, veterinary care, race entries, press enquiries, fretful owners, farriers … It is really a very long list, all of which at some point will fall to you, for when the boss is away you'll be in charge. And when you deputise at the races you'll be the one glad-handing the owners, saddling the horses and briefing the jockeys. It is hands-on in every sense of the words, but these are skills that are only learned by living the life.

But if you have ambition you will likely not want to be an assistant all your life, so in the words of *Horse & Hound* you find a yard. In Gosden's case, unable to fill a racetrack barn in California, he applied for stalls for each of his three horses as he started out with his American training licence in 1979. And how did he, or any embryonic trainer for that matter, get those first few horses? Inevitably, it is all about the connections you make as an assistant. Maybe someone has spotted potential in you? Perhaps you leave your boss with his or her blessing plus a couple of horses to get you started. There is always churn in the racing world: horses are sold, trainers retire or go bust, owners get disillusioned. If you are alert to the possibilities and willing to hustle, horses may come your way. Then all you have to do is make them win. Now that might just be the really hard bit, but as a way of lighting up the sky for a newly minted trainer absolutely nothing, but nothing, beats having winners. Or even better, a game-changing horse.

In Gosden's case it was the latter in a colt called Bates Motel, but it easily might never have been, for what the books rarely tell is that you need a good slice of luck. For Gosden that luck came by way of the fact that Bates Motel should never have raced in the United States. Born in Kentucky, the yearling was shipped to the UK to be sold at the Newmarket auctions, but failed to make his $80,000 reserve. The owners, for reasons I do not know, were happy to pay the return fare, so he ended up in California with the unknown, and largely untried, Gosden. It was a long way from the original plan, but those are the quirks of fate by which whole lives evolve.

Bates Motel, named after the ill-starred lodgings in Alfred Hitchcock's film *Psycho*, didn't run at two, and was a minor winner at three but at four he set the West Coast alight winning three major races including the 1983 Santa Anita handicap, California's richest and most important race for older horses. He retired at the end of the season having amassed close to $1 million in prize money for the young English trainer. That is the sort of horse you need to make your name, and Gosden capitalised on his early success with a winner at the inaugural Breeders' Cup the following year and many more major successes until he returned to England in 1989 where the winning vein continues to flow with over 3,000 winners to date.

So it was that Nathaniel and Frankel lined up at their local track with the ten others for the European Breeders' Fund Maiden Stakes in the gathering gloom of that wet, Newmarket evening, in a race designed for the best of precocious young talent. The European Breeders' Fund has been around since 1983, a name you'll often see on race cards, a major sponsor designed to promote the European breeding industry that is largely funded by stallion owners who pay annual dues based on the income from their stud horses, the progeny of which are qualified to run in races supported by the Fund. It might look an innocuous title but in over three decades has put €100 million into racing, covers 45 European countries and supports over 250 races each year. As for being a maiden, it is a race where the criterion for entry is that no horse has yet won a race, so it's a chance for equally inexperienced horses to race together. Like this race, maidens are mostly for two-year-olds and where the majority of horses start their racing careers. The term 'stakes' indicates that part of the prize money has been put up by the owners, usually in the form of entry fees, and suggests a race may attract a high-class entry. In that aim this race certainly succeeded.

As they readied themselves down at the start, the betting market placed Nathaniel in what was to be his racing destiny: second fiddle to Frankel. He went off second favourite at 3–1 with Frankel 7–4. But as they came out the stalls, and as the race unfolded he did, for six and a half of the seven furlongs, best Frankel. Approaching two furlongs from the finish, it was Nathaniel who emerged from a line of seven to take the lead. This was his race to win.

I've watched the replay of this race more times than I care to tell and every time, just for a few seconds, I have this surreal feeling that history is not about to be made. Frankel was not going to pull out of from Nathaniel's slipstream. Maher is not going to edge to the left to give him a clear run. Nathaniel is going to keep on, repel the challenge and take the plaudits in the following day's newspapers. The start of a snowballing dream will belong to the Rothschilds not to Prince Khalid.

As the two horses drew away from the rest of the field a hundred yards from home, Nathaniel had the lead, with commentator Derek Thompson winding up the pitch. Nathaniel's jockey William Buick was 'pumping away' as Thompson asks, 'What has he [Frankel] got left? There is not a lot left. Or is there?' In real time, in the heat of the contest, that was a prescient bit of race reading. For it mustn't ever be forgotten that in defeat by just half a length, Nathaniel ran Frankel closer than any other horse would do in any of his subsequent races. They left the third-place horse Genius Beast for dead, five lengths back, and he was no mean slouch himself, at one point regarded as a Derby prospect the following year. As the *Racing Post* man said, if it wasn't for Frankel, the headlines would have belonged to Nathaniel.

At Newmarket, where the stables share the same public gallops, they would have worked out on the same days, on the same surfaces, often at the same time. As the Frankel legend grew, so did the anticipation for another bout with Nathaniel, but like boxers who have gone one round with many more to come, each was wary of stepping within arm's length. The right punch at the wrong moment could too easily end it all. Gosden announced he thought it might be 'fun' to take on the Cecil horse again, but as the months then a year and more passed by, the stakes became increasingly high. The cost of losing was higher than the gain of winning. Did Cecil deliberately route Frankel to avoid Nathaniel, or was the avoidance of Gosden's making? It was probably a bit of both, but there is no mistaking the parallels of the two horses as they established themselves as the leading thoroughbreds of their generation.

Nathaniel was, at least relative to Frankel, a slow starter. He didn't win as a two-year-old (you know part of the reason for that) but at three he blossomed, winning the King Edward VII Stakes at Royal Ascot, and returning to the same course the following month to win one of Europe's most prestigious and valuable races, the King George VI & Queen Elizabeth Stakes, as his father had ten years previously. At the end of the year, Nathaniel was rated the seventh best racehorse in the world in the World Thoroughbred Racehorse Rankings. No prizes for guessing who was number one. The following year he kept his place in the rankings, becoming something of a soft-ground specialist which was the reason he was to be such a threat when he and Frankel were to meet again for the final time in the final race of their careers.

Nathaniel was a really good racehorse, of that there is no doubt. His lifetime Timeform rating of 131 puts him, with slight under-statement according to the Timeform classification, as an 'above average Group 1 winner'. Frankel, on the other hand, is at 147 an 'outstanding' horse with the highest rating ever. On such numbers much depends. Today, Nathaniel's stud fee is £25,000. Frankel's is £175,000.

Nathaniel is standing at Newsells Park Stud in Hertfordshire. To date, his most successful offspring is the filly Enable, dual winner of the Prix de l'Arc de Triomphe, owned by Prince Khalid.

Acknowledgements

At a talk for *The Otters' Tale* a member of the audience asked whether I had found writing it, my second book, difficult. Apparently second books are the most hard. Being the smartarse I am, I replied, 'I'll tell you when I have written the third.' Now I've completed this, my third book, I slightly rue my glib reply, for the answer is emphatically no – it is the third that is the hardest. And I truly could not have completed *Frankel* without the unstinting help, assistance, encouragement and support of a great many people.

Front and centre has to be my cousin and childhood fly-fishing buddy Lincoln Collins who left England to pursue a career in bloodstock in his early twenties, carving out the successful Kern Thoroughbred operation based in Kentucky, USA. From the very outset Lincoln embraced my project, opened his contacts book to me and smoothed the passage to the doors of Juddmonte. Lincoln, thank you from the bottom of my heart.

Juddmonte Farms is the owner of Frankel, the private racing and breeding operation of Prince Khalid bin Abdullah headquartered in Newmarket, England. Basically, I just turned up on their steps one day to ask if I might write a book about their most famous son. I have no idea why they said yes but they did, and from that moment on I was allowed the access which has made so much of what you have read possible. Douglas Erskine Crum, Teddy Grimthorpe, Simon Mockridge, Mike Saunders, Ed and Victoria Murrell, Shane Horan, Rob Bowley, plus Barry Mahon, John Glennon and Rory Mahon in Ireland, thank you all. Plus the now retired Philip Mitchell.

Naturally, the story of Frankel could never be complete without reference to his father Galileo who stands at Coolmore Stud in Ireland who were very kind with their time and help to me. Special thanks to Tim Corballis, James Mockridge and Aisling Duignan.

The writing wasn't made easy by the fact that the cast that made up Warren Place has been blown to the four winds, but they all remain a tight bunch of friends who bounced me from one to another to pick up the threads. Jane Cecil, Dee Deacon, Shane and Claire Fetherstonhaugh, Sandeep (Sandy) Gauravaram, Stephen Kielt and Mike Marshall all helped in so many different ways. And thank you also to Julie Cecil for letting me reach back into the life and times before Frankel.

And more variously, in no set order, thanks to Chris Cook at the *Guardian*. Bruce Millington and Graham Dench formerly of the *Racing Post*. Simon Claisse, Clerk of the Course, along with the stewards and staff at Cheltenham. Anthea Morshead, Assistant Clerk of the Course and the York Race Committee. Edmond Mahony and Jimmy George at Tattersalls. Roger, Clare, Harry and Tom Charlton at Beckhampton Stables. Lucy Greayer at LG Bloodstock. Matt Bassett for the number crunching. Georgina Bell and Luke Lillingston. Ian Wright MA VetMB DEO DipECVS Hon FRCVS of the Newmarket Equine Hospital who supplied the complete story of the scan and aftercare on pages 230–32. Rachel Talbot, owner of Man of God. Nick Craven at Weatherbys. Barry Rabbetts, Group

Head of Media at the Jockey Club. Joe Rendell at the British Horseracing Authority. Ashley Morton-Hunte, Corporate and Racing Communications Manager at Ascot Racecourse.

Finally, I'd like to thank all of you out there who I met along the way, not just in person but on social media and the many channels through which we talk these days. Your kindness, help, encouragement and insights made this book possible.

The Frankel File

Race record

Date	Race name	Distance	Course	Class	Prize money
13 August 2010	EBF Maiden Stakes	1 mile	Newmarket	4	£4,533.20
10 September 2010	Frank Whittle Stakes	7 furlongs	Doncaster	2	£10,904.2
25 September 2010	Royal Lodge Stakes	1 mile	Ascot	1 (G2)	£70,962.5
16 October 2010	Dewhurst Stakes	7 furlongs	Newmarket	1 (G1)	£180,074.
16 April 2011	Greenham Stakes	7 furlongs	Newbury	1 (G3)	£28,385.0
30 April 2011	2,000 Guineas	1 mile	Newmarket	1 (G1)	£198,695.
14 June 2011	St James's Palace Stakes	1 mile	Ascot	1 (G1)	£141,925.
27 July 2011	Sussex Stakes	1 mile	Goodwood	1 (G1)	£170,130.
15 October 2011	Queen Elizabeth II Stakes	1 mile	Ascot	1 (G1)	£567,100.

dds	Runners	Place	Margin (lengths)	Runner-up	Time	Going	Jockey
-4F	12	1	½	Nathaniel	1:43.69	Soft	Tom Queally
-2F	3	1	13	Rainbow Springs	1:24.83	Good	Tom Queally
-10F	5	1	10	Klammer	1:41.73	Good to soft	Tom Queally
-6F	6	1	2¼	Roderic O'Connor	1:25.73	Good to soft	Tom Queally
-4F	6	1	4	Excelebration	1:24.60	Good to firm	Tom Queally
-2F	13	1	6	Dubawi Gold	1:37.30	Good to firm	Tom Queally
-10F	9	1	¾	Zoffany	1:39.24	Good	Tom Queally
-13F	4	1	5	Canford Cliffs	1:37.47	Good	Tom Queally
-11F	8	1	4	Excelebration	1:39.45	Good	Tom Queally

Date	Race name	Distance	Course	Class	Prize money
19 May 2012	Lockinge Stakes	1 mile	Newbury	1 (G1)	£99,942.5
19 June 2012	Queen Anne Stakes	1 mile	Ascot	1 (G1)	£198,485.
1 August 2012	Sussex Stakes	1 mile	Goodwood	1 (G1)	£179,487.
22 August 2012	International Stakes	1 mile 2½ furlongs	York	1 (G1)	£411,147.
20 October 2012	Champion Stakes	1 mile 2 furlongs	Ascot	1 (G1)	£737,230.

Odds	Runners	Place	Margin (lengths)	Runner-up	Time	Going	Jockey
2–7F	6	1	5	Excelebration	1:38.14	Good	Tom Queally
1–10F	11	1	11	Excelebration	1:37.85	Good to soft	Tom Queally
1–20F	4	1	6	Farhh	1:37.56	Good	Tom Queally
1–10F	9	1	7	Farhh	2:06.59	Good to firm	Tom Queally
2–11F	6	1	1¾	Cirrus Des Aigles	2:10.22	Soft	Tom Queally

Pedigree

		NORTHERN DANCER (CAN)
	SADLER'S WELLS (USA)	
GALILEO (IRE) (b. 1998)		FAIRY BRIDGE (USA)
	URBAN SEA (USA)	MISWAKI (USA)
		ALLEGRETTA (GB)
FRANKEL (GB) (b. 2008)		DANZIG (USA)
	DANEHILL (USA)	
		RAZYANA (USA)
KIND (IRE) (b. 2001)		RAINBOW QUEST (USA)
	RAINBOW LAKE (GB)	
		ROCKFEST (USA)

Timeline

2007

5 March – Kind covered by Galileo at Coolmore Stud, Co. Tipperary, Ireland

16 April – Kind confirmed in foal to Galileo

19 April – Departs to Banstead Manor Stud, Suffolk, England

2008

11 February – Frankel born Banstead Manor Stud

7 March – Arrives at Coolmore with Kind

12 May – Frankel/Kind move to New Abbey Stud, Co. Kildare, Ireland

25 June – Frankel/Kind return to Banstead Manor Stud

17 July – Frankel weaned

17 September – Returns to New Abbey Stud alone

2009

21 April – Frankel moves to Ferrans, Co. Meath, Ireland

9 September – Breaking-in commences

5 October – Frankel ridden daily

December – Decision made to race in UK and be trained by Henry Cecil

2010

14 January – Departs Ferrans

15 January – Arrives at Warren Place, Newmarket, England

28 May – Name registered with Weatherbys, Wellingborough

13 August – First race, Newmarket

19 September – Second race, Doncaster

25 September – Third race, Ascot

16 October – Fourth race, Newmarket

2011

16 April – Fifth race, Newbury

26 April – Sadler's Wells (grandfather) dies, Co. Tipperary, Ireland

30 April – Sixth race 2,000 Guineas, Newmarket (Twenty-fifth Classic for Henry Cecil)

14 June – Seventh race, Ascot

27 July – Eighth race, Goodwood

15 October – Ninth race, Ascot

2012

11 April – Injury scare on gallops, Newmarket

18 April – Hospital ultrasound, Newmarket

19 May – Tenth race, Newbury

19 June – Eleventh race, Ascot

1 August – Twelfth race, Goodwood

22 August – Thirteenth race, York

20 October – Fourteenth (and last) race, Ascot

8 November – Returns to Banstead Manor Stud, Newmarket

Awards

2010

Cartier Champion Two-Year-Old Colt
Racehorse Owners Association Outstanding Two-Year-Old
World Thoroughbred Rankings Joint Champion Two-Year-Old in
   Europe
Timeform Best Two-Year-Old Colt

2011

Cartier Horse of the Year
Cartier Champion Three-Year-Old Colt
Horserace Writers and Photographers Association President's
   Award
Racehorse Owners Association Horse of the Year
Racehorse Owners Association Outstanding Three-Year-Old
Timeform Best Three-Year-Old Colt
Timeform Best Miler
World Thoroughbred Rankings Champion Three-Year-Old in
   World

2012

Cartier Champion Older Horse

Cartier Horse of the Year

Daily Telegraph Award of Merit for 'Team Frankel'

QIPCO British Champions Horse of the Series

Racehorse Owners Association Miler of the Year

Racehorse Owners Association Middle Distance Horse of the Year

Timeform Best Older Horse

Timeform Best Middle Distance Horse

World Thoroughbred Rankings World Champion

Frankel by numbers

0

Defeats

1

Number of jockeys that rode him in a race

10

Group 1 wins

14

Races

23

Individual Group 1 winners beaten by Frankel

14.19

Miles raced (113.5 furlongs)

43

Top recorded speed mph

65

Height in inches (16.1 hands/5 ft 5 in)

76.25

Aggregate winning distance in lengths

88

Horses beaten by Frankel

123

Weight at birth in pounds

147

Top Timeform rating of all time

799

Duration of racing career in days

838

Number of days spent unnamed

1,212

Average racing weight in pounds (estimate)

9164.14

Amount won (in £) if £100 staked on his first race and left to roll
up

211,418

£ earned per raced mile

2,998,302

Career earnings (in £)

18,446,744,073,709,551,616–1

Chances of another Frankel

Bibliography

Bellingham, David, *Gold from the Sand* (Raceform, 2005)

Binns, Matthew and Morris, Tony, *Thoroughbred Breeding* (J A Allen, 2010)

Fitzgeorge-Parker, Tim, *Training the Racehorse* (J A Allen, 1993)

Fox, Kate, *The Racing Tribe* (Metro, 1999)

James, Jeremy, *The Byerley Turk* (Stackpole Books, 2005)

MacGregor, Arthur, *Animal Encounters* (Reaction Books, 2012)

Pennington, Andrew (ed.), *Frankel: The Wonder Horse* (Racing Post, 2012)

Rossdale, Peter, *The Horse from Conception to Maturity* (J A Allen, 2002)

Scott, Brough, *Henry Cecil: Trainer of Genius* (Racing Post, 2012)

Stewart, Lt Col P D, *Training the Racehorse* (Stanley Paul, 1952)

Suffolk, Earl of, *The Badminton Library Racing* (Longmans, 1885)

Index